HOSPITABLE ENGLAND IN THE SEVENTIES

HOSPITABLE ENGLAND IN THE SEVENTIES

The Diary of a Young American 1875-1876

BY
RICHARD HENRY DANA

With Illustrations

WILDSIDE PRESS

www.wildsidepress.com

COPYRIGHT, 1921, BY RICHARD H. DANA

ALL RIGHTS RESERVED

TO
MY MANY FRIENDS
IN ENGLAND

CONTENTS

I. First Days in London — 1

II. Second Week in London — 28

III. The Last of my First London Season — 48

IV. Althorp House: Earl Spencer's via Warwick and Birmingham — 63

V. Lord Young's via York and Edinburgh — 82

VI. Rossie Priory: Lord Kinnaird's — 88

VII. Inverary Castle: The Duke of Argyll's (Princess Louise) via the Trossachs — 100

VIII. Lord Coleridge's — 121

IX. Lord Tenterden's — 135

X. Hursley Park: Sir William Heathcote's and General Review — 146

XI. Paris Salons, and English Embassy — 153

XII. French Assembly and Last Days in Paris — 185

XIII. Athens by way of the Mediterranean — British Ambassador — The Royal Ball and Scaling the Acropolis — 199

XIV. Egypt — The English Embassy — General-in-Chief — Egyptian Injustice — 222

CONTENTS

XV. ROME (VIA NAPLES) — AMERICAN AND ENGLISH AMBASSADORS	237
XVI. ENGLAND AGAIN VIA TURIN AND PARIS	247
XVII. OXFORD AND CAMBRIDGE	257
XVIII. FIRST OF LONDON REVISITED	294
XIX. LAST OF LONDON REVISITED	326
EPILOGUE	362
INDEX	369

ILLUSTRATIONS

THE YOUNG AMERICAN	*Photogravure frontispiece*
LORD FREDERICK CAVENDISH	12
From an engraving	
LORD TENTERDEN	18
SIR WILLIAM VERNON HARCOURT	30
EARL RUSSELL (FORMERLY LORD JOHN RUSSELL)	34
From a drawing by G. F. Watts	
COUNTESS RUSSELL	38
ALTHORP HOUSE: EARL SPENCER'S	70
From a sketch by the author	
EDINBURGH	82
From a sketch by the author	
ROSSIE PRIORY: LORD KINNAIRD'S	88
INVERARY CASTLE, SEAT OF THE DUKE OF ARGYLL	102
From an old engraving	
PRINCESS LOUISE	106
THE DUKE OF ARGYLL	110
From an engraving	
THE ARMORY, OR FRONT HALL, INVERARY CASTLE	120
LORD COLERIDGE AT 56	124
From a crayon by Lady Coleridge, 1878. Reproduced from a photogravure in Ernest Hartley Coleridge's *Life and Correspondence of John Duke Coleridge* (New York: D. Appleton & Co.)	
SIR JOHN TAYLOR COLERIDGE	132
From a painting by Mrs. Carpenter in the Hall of Eton College. Reproduced from *Life and Correspondence of John Duke Coleridge*	

CASTLE OF ROCKS, LYNTON	136
KEBLE'S CHURCH AND VICARAGE AT HURSLEY	148
QUEEN OLGA OF GREECE AND PRINCESS MARIE	216
DEAN STANLEY	316
RT.-HON. SIR ROBERT PHILLIMORE From a painting	326
RT.-HON. WILLIAM E. GLADSTONE	340

HOSPITABLE ENGLAND IN THE SEVENTIES

NOTE

IF this account of friendly kindness by eminent persons in Great Britain to a young man from America should help to bring those two countries into closer union and confidence, and at the same time entertain the reader, this book will have accomplished the purposes for which it is published.

HOSPITABLE ENGLAND IN THE SEVENTIES

..

CHAPTER I
FIRST DAYS IN LONDON

London, Wednesday, July 14, 1875
RAIN!

Arranged letters of introduction and soon became as familiar with the immediate vicinity as if I had been here for weeks.

Thursday, July 15
RAIN again. A quick response to my letters began this afternoon.

As I found it would take me ten hours or more to deliver all my letters of introduction, I had given the more distant ones to be carried by messenger with my calling cards and had delivered only the nearer ones personally. It is customary in England to leave a letter of introduction and one's card with an address on it, without asking to see the person to whom one is introduced. This allows him to read the letter more at leisure and arrange for some future meeting, and, especially in the crowded life of London, works far better and more satisfactorily than trying to see strangers at the first call.

Lodgings I had secured at Mrs. Brooks's, 115 Jermyn Street, where my parents had been before. When I got back to my room late in the afternoon, I found two notes awaiting me: one from Sir Robert Phillimore, my father's friend, and the other from Robert Ferguson, Esq., M.P., Professor Longfellow's, both for engagements the next day, and on that next day, by the morning's post, came another invitation from Sir John Kennaway, Bart., for that same evening. It was quite thrilling to get three such rapid responses to the letters I had only delivered in the late forenoon and early afternoon.

I had come abroad from Boston in July, 1875, after graduation at Harvard and at the end of my first year in the Law School, for a fifteen-months' trip, with a very little baggage containing a few old clothes and some twenty or more letters of introduction, nearly all from my father. Three were from Henry W. Longfellow and one from James Russell Lowell. All these were to Englishmen, excepting two of Longfellow's to members of the Academy in Paris and two from my father to other distinguished Frenchmen.

Purchases and rush orders for articles all the way from toothbrush at Prout's, whose name had so often been in my mouth, to silk hat in St. James's Street, and dress suit at Boutroy's, Sackville Street, had occupied much of the few previous days; but the invitations, coming so surprisingly soon, got ahead of my race for clothing, and at first I had to wear some of my old things.

(I wrote journal letters almost daily to my father. These he preserved for me and they form the basis for the above entries and all that follow.)

Before delivering my letters I called at the bank, and out came one of the directors, the Honorable Arthur Kinnaird, brother of the present Lord Kinnaird and his heir presumptive. He introduced himself as one of my father's friends and admirers. He was very obliging and offered to do much for me — all the more nice as I had no letter of introduction to him. He simply saw my name on the letter of credit. He is a banker, tall and dark, with a keen eye and pleasant, business-like, friendly smile. This continuous rain would be dismal indeed for one who had less to do than I or who was less delighted with being in dear old England.

Friday, July 16
MORE rain!
> "But when we crossed the Lombard Plain
> Remember what a plague of rain."

Lunched with Mr. Robert Ferguson at the dignified and handsome Devonshire Club, St. James's Street. He made arrangements to take me to the House of Commons on Tuesday, the 20th. He is a member of Parliament from Carlisle. We had a most excellent lunch and interesting conversation. He is a diffident man, rarely makes a speech in Parliament, I was told; stutters a good deal, and fills gaps in his conversation with "hems" and "hums" uttered through closed lips. He is extremely well informed, has written a book on "Surnames as a Science," and has led in many good works and municipal improvements in his city, and yet is modest and friendly withal. He is said to be a useful member on committees and is valued for his sound judgment. He is a moderate Liberal and supporter of Gladstone. He talked of his visit in Cambridge, U.S.A., in the sixties and of meeting my sister Henrietta as a child and all the Longfellow family.

In the afternoon went to the Royal Art Exhibition. I was not a little disappointed in it.

At eight o'clock dined with the Right Honorable Sir Robert Phillimore and his two daughters. He is a judge of the High Court of Admiralty and author of a voluminous and thorough work on international law, "Memoirs of George Lord Lyttelton," "Thoughts on the Law of Divorce," etc. He was a member of Parliament for several years and held many important positions, such as that of the Chancellor of the Diocese of Oxford. He is sixty-five years of age, with a square face, pleasing mouth, and gray hair. Lady Phillimore was out of town. Sir Robert was most kind and cordial. The talk ran on art, London life, Boston, and my father, for whom and whose writings, both on law and travel, he expressed admiration.

One of his daughters was doing bookbinding, much in vogue in London society. She remarked that, as it rained on St. Swithun's day, the 15th, it would be a wet season, according to an old superstition. About ten o'clock they took me to a little party at Lady Frederick Cavendish's on Carlton House Terrace at her request. Lord Frederick Cavendish is a younger son of the present Duke of Devonshire and brother of Lord Hartington. (Lord Frederick was afterwards assassinated at Phœnix Park in 1882.) I had a letter to him from my father, who had entertained him and Lord Hartington in the United States in the sixties.

Lord Frederick is short and frail, modest and unassuming. He says important and interesting things in such a quiet way. At first sight he would not impress one as having the ability he undoubtedly possesses. He has sandy hair and blue eyes, or blue-gray eyes. He has no children.

The great Gladstone was expected, but did not come. Among the guests — about ten or more — were Lord Colin Campbell, youngest son of the Duke of Argyll, two sisters of Lady Frederick, and the Honorable

Alfred Lyttelton, Lady Frederick's brother, son of Lord Lyttelton. (If this was Alfred, as I think it was, and not one of his elder brothers, it was he who in 1885 married the charming Laura Tennant, so highly praised by Mrs. Humphry Ward in her "Recollections," and who has won high honors at the Bar and in Parliament.)

Colin told me that his father, the Duke of Argyll, was off yachting, which of course I was sorry to learn as I had a letter to him also.

An American who goes out a good deal in London informed me that it was *de rigueur* to wear patent leather shoes and gold shirt studs. I had not been in the habit of wearing patent leathers at home. My new orders for shoes and clothing had not been filled, so I went this evening in my plain but well-blacked shoes and old dress suit. I found when I got there that Colin Campbell and Lord Frederick Cavendish both had the same footwear and both wore plain mother-of-pearl shirt studs like mine. Tea was served about 10.30. Sir Robert insisted upon driving me home, which was very kind of him, though, to be sure, it was not far out of his way.

I also had, as already stated, an invitation to dine with Sir John Kennaway for this same evening, but had to decline with regret quite sincere, as the Kennaways are noted for their dinners and company.

Saturday, July 17

WENT to the National Gallery in the afternoon and dined at Mrs. Robert Mackintosh's at seven o'clock in the evening. She was Miss Mary Appleton, of Boston, and sister of the late Mrs. Henry W. Longfellow. There were present Mrs. Mackintosh, her brother "Uncle Tom" Appleton, who was very kind to me and was as usual remarkably bright, witty, and entertaining; also Miss Eva Mackintosh and one or two friends. I did not think they half appreciated Tom Appleton, the "prince of prattlers." He showed me a number of his paintings made on the Upper Nile, in Palestine, and in Lower Egypt.

In the morning went over Lincoln's Inn and all the courts with Mr. Rawlins, a young barrister and friend of Tom Hughes, author of "Tom Brown at Rugby," to whom Professor James Russell Lowell had given me a letter. I could not have had a better cicerone. Here was where Pendennis and Warrington did almost everything else but study for the law, and in how many other books do we not read of Lincoln's Inn or Lincoln's Inn Fields!

Sunday, July 18

EXPECTED from Sir Robert Phillimore a card of admission to the Temple, but as it did not come stayed at home all the morning.

Lunched at Spencer House, where were Lord and Lady Spencer, Lord Charles Bruce, who was very jolly and kind to me, and Lady Spencer's sister, Lady Clifden, with two of her children. Earl Spencer is tall, with slightly freckled face, sandy reddish hair, and a very long and full beard of the same color — so large as to remind me of the limerick:

> "There was an old man with a beard,
> Who said, 'It is just as I feared!—
> Two owls and a hen,
> Four larks and a wren,
> Have all built their nests in my beard.'"

He has kind, keen, blue eyes in marked contrast with the color of his skin and hair. He is not "old," however, being just forty, and is still reported to be one of the best horsemen at fox-hunting in England. I saw him in the park riding. He stoops a good deal when in the saddle, and rides with what we should think very short stirrups and knees a good deal bent. He was Lord Lieutenant of Ireland from 1868 to 1874, and during the lunch he and Lady Spencer told us something of their Irish experiences, of horrible shootings by the Land Leaguers from behind fences, their having to lead their conventional society life notwithstanding their fears of assassination, of the warm-hearted qualities of the Irish and the mixture in their lives of gayety and gravity. (Later he was again Lord Lieutenant of Ireland from 1882 to 1885, Lord Lieutenant of the Council and First Lord of the Admiralty under Gladstone, 1892 to 1895, and a Home Ruler. In 1893 in the Home Rule debate in the House of Lords, I was present and heard Lord Londonderry make an uncalled-for and very nasty statement that Spencer, who is one of the most honorable and high-minded of men, supported Home Rule solely for the purpose of getting the salary of a cabinet officer. Spencer did not deign to reply.)

Lady Spencer is indeed handsome, as she is reputed to be, and, in fact, is the most beautiful woman I have yet seen in England. She is the same age as her husband and still has a graceful though not slender figure (as judged from more modern ideas), and has a perfectly bewitching smile, and when her face is at rest, a turn of the lips that foreruns another smile. Her sister, Lady Clifden, is also unusually handsome, is more calm and statuesque, is a brunette, with black eyes, while Lady Spencer has brown hair and blue eyes. Stately Lady Spencer was the third daughter of Frederick Charles William Seymour, Esquire, and granddaughter of the first Marquis of Bristol. She and her two sisters were said to be the handsomest young women of their time in England.

She was surprised that I had been in London only five days and said she would have taken me for an Englishman from my voice, and I took it that she meant to be complimentary. I found that many of the English whom I have met so far talk, in the main, like Boston and Cambridge friends except for the hesitation which some *men* have.

My father told me, in meeting distinguished Englishmen, to treat them in the same way that I would treat Mr. Lowell, Mr. Longfellow, Dr. Holmes, Agassiz, and others, with the courtesy due from a younger man to an elder, to use titles as little as possible, and to be perfectly natural and at my ease and neither forthputting nor, on the other hand, to take the lower seat, because in English society the Bible parable will not hold. They are not likely to say, "Friend, go up higher." I find this advice works perfectly and all is natural and easy, delightful and intimate.

Spencer House is beautifully situated on St. James's Place, looking out on Green Park and opposite Bridgewater House, the Earl of Ellesmere's.

Of course there was the lofty "Jeames" in full togs at the door and a dignified footman in handsome livery between the front door and the reception-room, and others to wait on table. What struck me most in the details was the absence of napkins at lunch, though it was what we should call a heavy lunch, with soup, chicken and game, vegetables, fruit, wines, etc. It seemed strange that they should be so slow in changing their old customs, for, of course, a napkin is as necessary at a heavy lunch of this sort as at a dinner. When Mr.

Mackintosh, son of Sir James Mackintosh, who married Miss Mary Appleton, the same Mrs. Mackintosh with whom I dined a few days ago, came to Boston, at his first lunch at Mr. Nathan Appleton's, his father-in-law, it was said that he threw his napkin on the floor. Appleton, supposing there was a defect in the napkin, had another one brought. This he threw on the floor also, and upon being asked if there was anything the matter with his napkin, said, "We never use napkins at lunch in England."

Another difference was this. It has always been a question whether it is proper to take a chicken bone, for example, in one's hand. In America we were generally taught not to do so, but I find these nice ladies do, in a delicate and fine manner, after the larger part of the meat had been cut off — but not with the little finger curled as I have seen some would-be fastidious women do while holding a teacup or a bit of toast. I do not see why the English custom is not right. The meat next to the bone is the sweetest and the custom seems rational, though I should think it would still further necessitate the use of napkins. (On later visits in England I found napkins in use at lunch. At a lunch in April, 1913, with the Duke of Argyll and Princess Louise, at Kensington Palace, the napkins were very large ones, larger than we usually have at dinners.)

Another small matter that differed from our American custom was the place of the clean knives and forks at the plates. We usually place the fork at the left and the knife at right angles to it at the top. Here they put the knife on the right side of the plate, parallel to the fork (as we have since come to do in the "States"), and when I inadvertently changed it to the American way, out of habit, one of the waiters immediately took the knife and put it back. He was not going to tolerate any such outlandish custom in a great English house.

There was much instructive and entertaining talk about politics, some questions about America's recovery after the war, President Grant and his cabinet, the condition of the negroes in the Southern States, and the feeling between England and America, but mostly was it about persons and affairs English. Spencer had been to the United States in the early days of the Civil War and been entertained by my father. He said the Duke of Argyll, Sir George Lewis, and Lord Stanley, for example, sided with the North, but most of the ruling class were on the side of the South. Disraeli was scrupulously neutral, while Lord John Russell said "the North was striving for empire and the South for independence." Lord Coleridge was at first for the South and later changed for the North, while Gladstone, much as he opposed slavery, was rather Southern in his feelings. The women seem well informed and interested in public matters in comparison to the American women, which is quite natural, as their husbands, brothers, fathers, and sons are many of them members and usually leading members of the House of Commons, if not of the House of Lords. Speaking of Disraeli they call him "Dizzy."

Spencer unfortunately has no son. Though he has been married since 1848 his heir is his half brother. Spencer could hardly be more friendly and made several plans to help me see people and places, and asked me to come again soon and talked of inviting me to his country seat after Parliament adjourns.

Lunch over, I went to Westminster Abbey. I was a little late for the service and had to stand at a distance. Dean Stanley preached, but from my remote position

I could not hear all he said. The music and the associations with the place brought tears to my eyes time and time again. I did not stay to look at the abbey on account of the crowd.

Took afternoon tea with Mr. Henry Tuke Parker, formerly of Boston, and his wife and daughter and went with them to evening church. On Sunday he, like some other people in England (very much as we do at home), had dinner in the middle of the day and only an evening tea or supper so that the servants might go out early. Good singing and an earnest sermon. At supper were also the clergyman and young Dr. Henry P. Quincy, of Boston (who afterwards married in 1877 Miss Mary Adams, daughter of Charles Francis Adams, our former Minister to England).

Monday, July 19

CALLED on Lord Frederick Cavendish at four o'clock in the afternoon according to previous arrangement, and walked with him from his house on Carlton House Terrace to the Parliament buildings. Speaking of the beauty among English women, Lady Frederick, while not as beautiful as Lady Spencer, has fine dark eyes, brilliant coloring, dark hair, and graceful, dignified, and rather slender figure, and regular features lighting up with a friendly smile. She is the second daughter of Lord Lyttelton and maid of honor to the Queen. Lord Frederick was Lord of the Treasury during Gladstone's last administration, was previously his secretary, and now sits on the Opposition bench. He secured me a seat in what is called the Speaker's Gallery. He gave me the orders of the day and a copy of the Agricultural Holdings Bill, with all the proposed amendments. I heard a somewhat interesting but not great debate. There were some rather stupid and long-spun arguments as to the value of certain kinds of fertilizer, etc. It seemed to me that it would have been far better to have got this at committee hearings from experts than to have the time taken up in debate by the private views, on such matters, of the individual members who have had no scientific or chemical training, as is almost invariably the case with educated Englishmen of the upper or reigning class.

The "slaughter of the innocents," or throwing down the less important bills, was to have taken place, but "Dizzy" had not made up his mind what ones to save and what ones to kill. The Opposition think it is full time to know. In reply to this Disraeli made an amusing speech in which he entertained the House and said nothing.

Whalley, the violent anti-Catholic member, soon got up with his anti-Jesuit bill, and before long was called to order in what I was told was the usual way in his case. He is the successor of Mr. Spooner, who, during my father's visit to England in 1856, made just such attacks. Whalley managed to get in quite a little speech, in which he accused the Government of shutting its eyes to the awful danger from the encroachments of the papal party in England. Disraeli answered this by saying that the Government was aware of the great dangers that exist from this source, but the most dangerous persons of all, whom he suspects may be secret emissaries from Rome, are those who, under the pretense of violent Protestantism, make such exaggerated and obviously erroneous statements as to leave an impression on the public mind that after all there is no danger whatsoever. This brought about a laugh at Whalley's expense and some applause, which, by the custom of

LORD FREDERICK CAVENDISH
1866

the House of Commons, consists largely in calling out, "Hear, hear."

Lord Frederick Cavendish, Liberal, and Sir John Kennaway, Tory, sat with me from time to time, told me who the different people were, and explained the proceedings. I heard questions put to the Ministry and answered. One was as to the necessity of passports on the Continent; which to me was quite a practical matter as I was going there soon. The Ministry declared that passports were not necessary, but might be useful for purposes of identification. The answers, as in this case, are sometimes made by the parliamentary undersecretaries. Disraeli is particularly fond of bringing his young protégés forward.

A motion was made to adjourn followed by a general discussion. We allow no debate on motion to adjourn, while in the English Parliament it is customary to tolerate, until objection is made, the most general discussion covering a very broad field on all sorts of matters.

Left the House at six-fifteen and went to dine with Rawlins at the Savile Club, of which I am made an honorary member. This is one of the smaller clubs composed of active young barristers, doctors, etc., much less formal and less expensive than the larger clubs. (This is mentioned in Sir Harry Johnston's "Gay Dombeys" as still existing in 1919.) They had a common dinner at a long table (very much as at the Century Club in New York) and it was the custom there (as in the Century) for members or guests to speak to one another without introduction. The club is select, yet they are sociable and the conversation is bright and entertaining. Spiritualism and investigation into manifestations were discussed at length. They have a committee looking into these matters called the "Committee on Psychic Research," and which uses the aid of noted prestidigitators. Had a long talk with the chairman of this committee, who thought that most, if not all, of the phenomena they have investigated either showed fraud, as was usually the case, or were based on mere coincidences, or could be explained on natural grounds, and that all hearsay evidence was apt to be exaggerated from the prevalent love of the marvelous, and on investigation at original sources the facts were almost always found to be much less remarkable than the current account of them.

Rawlins has a younger brother at Eton and a cousin at Cambridge. He gave me a letter to the former and also to a master at Eton, and advised me to go there on Thursday, which is the great Eton day.

At nine-thirty I went back to the House of Commons and stayed on till it was about to adjourn.

As I sat through the debates I heard, so softly as to be a vibration rather than a sound, the Westminster chimes warning us of the passing quarter hours, and when I went outside I heard above me from the belfry, more clearly, the four peals for the quarters and the solemn, low boom of one for the hour.

I am naturally deeply interested in the effect of having the members of the cabinet in the House, taking part in debate, subject to question, and being responsible for the course of legislation. While it leads to publicity, it also leads to a great deal of tilting and what seems to be waste of time; but, on the other hand, it prevents too hasty legislation and keeps the Government on its good behavior. The Opposition does not hesitate openly to prevent or delay the passage of confessedly good bills merely to injure the work of the party in power. The only check to this abuse is, I am told, public opinion.

There is no regular method of stopping indefinite debate prolonged forever. Of course the English "previous question" is not like ours. Ours is used for the purpose of bringing the issue to a vote without further debate; while in England it merely postpones consideration for the day and until the subject may be again introduced; or, in other words, the object of the motion in America is to hasten final action, and in English practice to get rid of a subject for the time being.

This evening I saw the House go into Committee of the Whole. The Speaker left his chair, the chairman of the committee took his place, and the huge mace was put under the table with great formality.[1]

Without any prompting from my friends, I could easily recognize some of the leading members from the pictures in "Punch" — Disraeli, Gladstone, the Marquis of Hartington, Sir William Vernon Harcourt, etc. Disraeli, who is now Prime Minister, wore a fancy waistcoat, large rings, a striking fob or elaborate watch-chain of some kind, and had the black curls on his forehead and the sphinx-like expression in his face for which he is so noted. Occasional smiles passed over his countenance and the expression changed, yet I felt that he was never revealing his inner thoughts. Gladstone struck one as more sincere. I think his worst enemies — for he has some enemies — at least give him credit for persuading himself to believe what he says. Many of his political opponents think him inconsistent and subtle-minded. The critics whom I mention, who are Tories, are few and their criticisms moderate. Generally, I found almost unbounded admiration for "the grand old man," as he is often called. (In 1893 his inability to have carried out all his Midlothian campaign promises, after his bitter attacks on Disraeli, his espousing Irish Home Rule, his "vacillating and inconsistent policy" in Egypt and the Soudan, resulting in the death of General Gordon, and the suspicion that he favored disestablishment of the English Church, had very much changed matters. I was then present at the debates on his Irish Home Rule Bill in the House of Lords and listened to many bitter personal attacks upon him. These I heard echoed in private conversation with Unionists. Very few people I met in 1893, outside the Home Rulers, believed in him, and many seemed to vie among themselves in denouncing him in terms so bitter as to be absurd. For "subtlety" of mind in 1875, "sophistry" was substituted in 1893. They would n't believe that Gladstone had ordinary veracity. It was commonly repeated that a high ecclesiastic had said he "would n't trust him with a penny round the corner." They accused him of being unbalanced through egotism and as acting only from the motive of keeping himself in power.)

(One feature of Gladstone's debates had been especially irritating to his opponents. He always assumed that he was morally right, or, as President Lowell once summed it up, Gladstone had the good fortune which followed him through life, that whenever he changed his views the Almighty changed his at the same time. In "A Modern Symposium," by G. Lowes Dickinson, is an account of a conversation between a character, evidently intended for Gladstone, ending with an assurance that what he had just said was in accordance with the principles of the Almighty, and a character representing Disraeli who replied in substance: I do not pretend to have that intimate knowledge of the mind of

THE AGRICULTURAL HOLDINGS BILL

the Almighty which my predecessor has just claimed. Tennyson says, "Fame is but half disfame." With Gladstone in 1893 you might well say three quarters. Later, after the heat over the Home Rule Bill of 1893 cooled off, and still more after his death, the perspective changed, and once again his great qualities stood out in their rightful proportions.)

Tuesday, July 20
WENT with Mr. Ferguson to the House of Commons, which met early, that is, at two o'clock instead of the usual hour of four in the afternoon. The House was in Committee of the Whole on the Agricultural Holdings Bill. The main feature of this bill was to allow farm tenants the value of improvements they may make. Then came up the distinctions between substantial permanent improvements, such as the erection of new buildings or thorough tile draining of wet lands, and the using of fertilizers whose benefits might merely outlast a lease by a year or so. There was no good debate and none at all on the general objects of the bill itself. I think these were generally agreed to. The discussion was again on fertilizers and their relative durability.

As the proceedings were dull and most of the important members out of the House, Mr. Ferguson and I left and went to the house of a friend of his, a Dr. Jones, in Green Street, Park Square, for afternoon tea at five o'clock. It was a pleasant and agreeable family gathering. Two of the daughters sang some duets quite well, though they were a little frightened. They made me sing some college and negro songs, which were new to them and which they seemed to like.

I had to decline an invitation for this evening to dine

with Lord Selborne, formerly Sir Roundell Palmer and chief counsel for Great Britain in the Alabama Claims Arbitration at Geneva, for which service, though he did not win his case, he won his new title. I had previously accepted an invitation to dine with Lord Tenterden at the Garrick Club. Tenterden is the permanent head of the Foreign Office, the man who is said to have saved the Treaty of Washington by his tact and ability, thus securing the arbitration of the Alabama Claims contained in that treaty, the first great arbitration of the kind and which averted possible war between Great Britain and the United States. Tenterden is about five feet eight, broad-shouldered, very dark, prominent eyes, swarthy complexion, has a large beard, and a truly winning smile. He has a vast fund of information not only in history and diplomacy, but on many unexpected matters, which is always at command.

At the Tenterden dinner we had an Italian, the counselor, I believe he was, for Count Sclopis, when a member of the Geneva Arbitration Court. Among the guests was a rich American, a recent graduate of Yale College, with a two-hundred-ton yacht, and a few others, but from the English habit of not introducing and from Lord Tenterden's being so entertaining up to the moment I left him, I did not get the names of them all. The American was rather formal and stiff. The Englishmen were bright and well-informed, gentlemanly and charming, men whom I may never meet again, like ships we pass in the night whose lights we see, but whose names we do not read. Lord Tenterden asked me to visit him in his cottage in the north of Devonshire on the seacoast at the end of August, and I accepted.

The Garrick Club is interesting in itself. They have there some celebrated pictures and large portraits, and

LORD TENTERDEN

a host of small ones of actors, actresses, and playwrights, and old handbills about the walls. I saw there a bust of Shakespeare supposed to have been made some thirty years after his death, and which was lately excavated in digging in the Inner Temple. It used to stand on one side of the proscenium of the theatre with a corresponding bust of Ben Jonson on the other. This rather seems as if those in authority who knew Shakespeare personally thought him to be the author of his plays and capable of writing them.

Found a letter from Smalley written at Margate with a message from Tom Hughes — "Tom Brown's School Days" — that he is unable to write, adding that he hopes to be in London again in a week or so and to see me. Smalley thought this was too hopeful a view of Hughes's health, as he had just had inflammatory rheumatism followed by a sharp attack of hereditary gout. Hughes has been in Parliament and is much interested in the working classes and Christian sociology. I should like so much to see him. (He did not get back to London during the season and I never had the good fortune to meet him, but treasure this friendly message.)

Wednesday, July 21
MADE several calls, among others on Sir Robert Phillimore, Sir John Kennaway, Lord Selborne, Mrs. Mackintosh, Mrs. Parker, Lady Frederick Cavendish, and Mrs. Smalley. The Smalleys had invited me to dinner, but unfortunately on a day when I had another engagement. Dined at Sir John Kennaway's. Kennaway is a Baronet from Ottery St. Mary, Devonshire, and a strong Tory. He visited the United States, both South and North, just after the Civil War, was entertained by my father, and on his return wrote a book called "On

Sherman's Track," a vivid and true account of what he saw and heard. There were present Lady Kennaway; her brother, Mr. Arbuthnot, a delightful man; and a number of others. Next to me at table sat an English lady who was pleasant, smiling, and talked agreeably until Sir John told her that I was from America. Suddenly she turned her back on me as much as to say, "Is it possible that I have been talking with one from that nasty place?" The English use "nasty" for almost everything disagreeable. She actually made up a face and ejected some apparently unpleasant remark which I did n't quite catch. I was determined, if possible, to change her disagreeable impression by being really, though not *over*, polite, and yet sincere, and I flatter myself that I had reasonably fair success, for later in the evening she spoke to me with something like a smile. She is the only lady I have met who has shown such unfortunate impressions of "Yankees," though there is still no little trace of the feeling that existed against the North during the Civil War, and we must remember too that some of these people have lost heavily in Confederate bonds.

Opposite me was a sister of Lady Frederick Cavendish, the wife of Dr. Talbot, warden of Keble College, Oxford, and we had a little talk across the table, which, however, is not a common custom, I am told, in England. After the ladies went out, I took part in a most engrossing conversation with several members of Parliament and eminent barristers, one Mr. Westlake, who had corresponded with my father, the names of the others unknown, as usual not being introduced. There were about six or seven of them and almost all Tories, and therefore opponents of Gladstone and supporters of Disraeli.

Later in the evening I went to Mr. Gladstone's by special invitation from his wife for a little family party. It is not at all uncommon in London to invite people to come in after dinner. With us it seems to be considered that if we cannot ask a person to dine, we had better not ask him to come in afterwards for fear it would look as if we were giving him a sort of second place; but that is not at all the way here, for sometimes those who are invited to come later are more distinguished than those at the dinner. Society is so large that one cannot ask everybody. These after-dinner assemblies, beginning about ten o'clock, are informal and delightful.

I may say as to the dinners, you are usually asked for eight or even as late as half-past, and you are always expected to be punctually late to the extent of exactly a quarter of an hour; that is, if you are asked to dine at eight, it means that you are expected at the door at quarter-past, and if for half-past eight, at a quarter to nine. The usual breakfast hour for professional men is nine o'clock, lunch at two, tea at five, and dinner at eight or half-past. For those of leisure the only difference is in the breakfast hour, which is a little later, say nine-thirty or ten.

To come back to Mr. Gladstone's. He is living at 23 Carlton House Terrace. It is a dull period in parliamentary affairs. Gladstone's party, the Liberals, had been defeated a little over a year ago and he himself had nominally retired from politics. The only measure of importance in Disraeli's new government was the ecclesiastical bill to restrain ritualistic practice among the High Church party, which was passed in the spring at the instance of the Archbishop of Canterbury. This brought Gladstone, who was one of the Oxford Tractarians and a High Churchman, out from his retirement, and the Marquis of Hartington, who had been the titular leader of the Liberals, gave way to Gladstone in important debates.

To-day the engagement of Gladstone's elder son, William H., is announced, and all the family are full of the subject and talk of little else than wedding presents, arrangements, etc. The fiancée is the Honorable Gertrude Stuart, daughter of Lord Blantyre. It is a pity that this should come just now, for it gives me less opportunity to see Mr. Gladstone at his best, as he goes into this matter with his usual energy and thoroughness, and it is hard to get him to say more than a few words on any other subject.

He asked me about the number of inches of rainfall in Boston, which I gave him. I remarked that this was greater than the rainfall in London, though London has a reputation of being a wetter place than our eastern American cities, and as I had recently read the statistics in the English Guide Book, I mentioned the number of inches of rainfall in London and thought I had recollected rightly. I was right in the general fact that London had less precipitation than Boston, but did n't put the London water-fall quite low enough, by an inch or so, and Mr. Gladstone corrected me, and when I looked it up again, I found he was right, illustrating how retentive is his memory even in small details.

Gladstone asked me about the general impression of the Reverend Henry Ward Beecher case, in America. The case referred to was a *cause scandaleuse*, linking his name with that of a Mrs. Tilton. I told him what I believed the feeling to be among sober, well-educated Americans, and he felt badly, though it was just what he feared, as he said, and yet he hoped it was not so. I told him that the evidence was such as to injure

Beecher's character for discretion in such matters very much, although there was not enough evidence to convict him of anything further or even to lead a fair-minded man to believe that Beecher was surely guilty. He certainly set a bad example to society and was inconsiderate of the husband.

On the voyage over I had read Gladstone's recent pamphlet on "The Vatican Decrees and Civil Allegiance," Cardinal Manning's Reply to it, and Gladstone's Rejoinder. I spoke to him of these, and how I had studied them, and of his point that the decree of infallibility tends to make "a [Roman] Catholic first and an Englishman afterwards." Gladstone, whose whole time for months had been taken up with the preparation, especially of his rejoinder, evidently did not care to go into a discussion of the subject on this family occasion further than to remark something about Manning's "evasions" and "subtleties," and to speak of the difficulties of distinguishing in practice between matters of faith and morals on the one hand and duty to a country on the other; and he also referred to Manning's point that the infallibility of any papal decree was not settled to be such until passed on by the Schola Theologorum. This Gladstone suggested left the matter in doubt, in some cases for a generation, and meanwhile a faithful Catholic might have to take all papal utterances as infallible till declared otherwise, as his conscientious duty and only safe course.

Gladstone also said a word about the restraints on ritual in the Disraeli law as being a form of persecution in matters of conscience and unwise as a method of avoiding extremes.

Mrs. Gladstone follows with the most intense interest everything that her husband says and evidently worships him. If a wife "makes or mars a husband's career," she certainly gives him inspiration. (Years afterwards Lord George Hamilton, in his "Parliamentary Reminiscences," though a bitter opponent of Gladstone, pays her this high tribute: "No Prime Minister ever had a more devoted, and in my judgment, a more capable helpmate. She never showed in the most difficult and awkward positions either want of dignity or resource, and her inherent kindness of heart and good nature were universally admitted by all who knew her.")

Gladstone, I am informed, asks many questions on any subject in which he thinks his interlocutor is informed. Like Sir Robert Peel, he extracts from a specialist the essence of his knowledge in short time. He has no pride in the matter, for though he has such an enormous amount of accurate information himself, he is quite ready to admit his ignorance of any fact he does not know. Fact, I say, for some assert that, at his present age, he is not easily receptive to new theories contrary to his established opinions.

Gladstone's voice is clear, distinct, resonant, flexible, and has a large range. It is not the ministerial, empty-barrel, deep kind, like that of our General Banks, "*Vox et præterea nihil*," but more like that of Wendell Phillips, combining both cultivation and naturalness. It is free from affectation. There is no stammering or lisping or mouthing. There is a directness of emphasis, if that is the right phrase to use. I mean such a controlling desire to convince as carries the emphasis naturally to just the right word. In talking he uses almost no gesture. There was a conversational charm, a copiousness of words and ideas, no tautology and much courtesy, and yet an eagerness of spirit withal. It was very inspiring to meet so great a man, and also discouraging, for there is evidently a power of brain which cannot be acquired by any amount of self-cultivation or study.

Gladstone is tall, with spare figure, somewhat hollow cheeks with high cheek-bones, and slightly Roman nose, deep-set, eagle eyes of dark color that seem to pierce through you, broad forehead, and long hair, thin at the top, almost bald, a firm-set mouth and strong chin. His complexion is rather pale for an Englishman. He is now sixty-six years of age. He wears his clothes loose, with no attempt at elegance, and has the high, long-pointed collars, so much caricatured in "Punch."

I notice that the majority of the people I have met so far drop their "g's" in the present participle. It is "huntin'," "ridin'," etc. They pronounce "interesting" in three syllables. We naturally slur the second, but they omit it altogether. We pronounce "extraordinary" ĕks-trôr'di-nȧ-rў, while here many of them drop the third syllable, making it ĕks-tror'na-rў. It was noticeable that Mr. and Mrs. Gladstone both pronounced these words as we do in America.

A few days ago I called with John F. Andrew, son of our Massachusetts war governor, the late John A. Andrew, on Mr. and Mrs. Gordon Duff. They had been our fellow-passengers on the *Parthia* sailing from Boston July 3d, and to me they were the most exciting persons aboard. They were a handsome, young Scottish couple on their wedding tour.

> "Or when the moon was overhead,
> Came two young lovers lately wed."

She was a Tennant and probably an elder sister of the famously charming Mrs. Alfred Lyttelton. They asked me to visit them if I should be in their part of Scotland, rather better put than the Irishman's invitation: "If you are within ten miles of my place, I hope you will stop there." We found them at her father's and had a pleasant call and chat about our voyage, the fellow-passengers, etc., of the Reverend Samuel F. Smith, the author of our national hymn "America," and his original poem for our 4th of July celebration entitled "Miss America's Tea Party," in which Boston citizens disguised as Indians made tea in Boston Harbor for the teapot over one hundred years ago; and of the mock trial, the singing, and also the serenade on leaving Boston intended for an Irish priest on our vessel, thrilling us with "Home, Sweet Home," "The Wearing of the Green," "The Harp that Once Through Tara's Hall," and "Auld Lang Syne." The call was a little hectic, however, as they were all to leave their London lodgings in a few hours for the North, and the room had portmanteaus and luggage about and there were servants coming and going in preparation.

Our steamer, the *Parthia*, was small — only 3167 tons[1] — and as customary, even the F.F.B.'s and the English passengers wore rough clothes and flannel shirts, and no one dressed for evening dinner. The boat had auxiliary sails, so in a shift of wind at night I would hear the thud of coils thrown on deck, the rattle of blocks, the lively cries of "Yeo hie, yeo ho!" as the sailors pulled at the sheets, and the boatswain's order, "Make fast! belay!" Every hour during the passage the log was thrown over, just as on shipboard in my

[1] The first Cunard steamer to cross the ocean, the *Britannia*, sailing from Liverpool to Boston in 1840, was 1154 tons. The *Scythia*, the largest of their boats in 1875, was 4557. Our boat used forty-five tons of coal a day. The *Olympic*, the largest Cunard steamship in 1920, is 46,359 tons register and burns a thousand tons or more of coal daily. The *Leviathan* is 54,282 tons gross.

father's day when he sailed round Cape Horn. We recalled how on arriving at Liverpool, when the passengers were all on deck, dressed for going ashore, the Cunard Company took the opportunity to blow out the smokestacks, showering us with cinders, and how, when we protested, the officials replied: "The Cunard Line never lost a passenger." Then, too, what smells we had during the voyage; a mixed odor of bilge water, pickles, oil, brass polish, and general sourness, and how we were waked up in the small hours of the night, before reaching Liverpool, by groans, shrieks, and loud brays suggesting the killing of the donkey engine.

CHAPTER II

SECOND WEEK IN LONDON

Thursday, July 22

STROLLING down the Haymarket in the morning I met Lord and Lady Frederick Cavendish walking up. Lady Frederick and I both smiled, for it was the fourth time we had met in different places during the last eighteen hours, which is, of course, remarkable in such a huge city as London.

In the afternoon I went down to the House of Commons at Sir William Vernon Harcourt's invitation. I sent in my card to him and was shown into the inner lobby, which I had hardly entered when out rushed a member in a state of wild excitement, throwing his arms about and shaking his fists and making short ejaculations such as, "I will expose the villains, all of them!" I heard the word "cheats" and I think "liars." The man's excitement was great and he spoke hurriedly and disconnectedly. For my part I was astonished at the scene. I knew nothing whatsoever of the situation or what he was talking about. The general impression on me was that I never had seen an educated man so thoroughly given up to the passion of the moment. At the French Assembly, or even at Washington, I should not have been so much surprised, but it was very strange to see all this in the decorous House of Commons. I was told that it was Mr. Plimsoll. Good blind Fawcett, the political economist, and other members tried to calm Plimsoll, but all to no purpose. He would not be led away nor even allow a hand to be put on him. The lobby was soon cleared of strangers by the officers of the House, so I did not see how they managed to get the honorable member calmed and away. Soon I learned that the Government had announced the "slaughter of the innocents," and the Merchants' Shipping Bill, which was Plimsoll's pet measure, and which the Government had practically promised him would be carried out at this session, had been included in the slaughter. This bill provided for the ship load-mark and for giving sailors a right to claim from public authorities a survey of the vessel and its food so as to prevent their being sent to the bottom in unseaworthy vessels for the sake of the insurance which the owners might get, or be forced to rely on insufficient, old, or musty food.

To understand the need of the Plimsoll bill one should know that seamen, once having signed a contract, called the "shipping articles," for their services on a voyage, can be forced by the courts to go on that voyage in the vessel for which they have signed. In no other civil occupation can a contract be thus enforced. A coachman who does not keep his contract for service, though theoretically liable in money for damages, cannot by law be compelled to work against his will. In practice sailors sign shipping articles without examining the vessel on which they are to sail, usually having no opportunity to do so, or to know about its supply of food, which is often put on board the last day before sailing.

One should also know that in marine insurance "valued" policies are common. That is, a sum is agreed upon to be paid in case of total loss of ship and cargo without regard to the actual value of the same. On the other hand, in fire insurance on buildings or on their contents, the opposite is true. If a house is insured for $15,000, for example, and the value is only $10,000, under the ordinary policies of insurance, in case of total loss by fire not more than $10,000 can be recovered.

These valued policies on ships and cargoes give additional incentive to sending unseaworthy vessels, called "coffin ships," on voyages in the hope of getting insurance greater than the actual loss sustained, and thus are risked the lives of the sailors.

I am told that while Plimsoll got his sympathy for the under dog from his own early struggles with poverty, that sympathy was specially directed to the case of sailors in the first instance from reading my father's "Two Years Before the Mast." (I regret not having arranged to meet him, but the season was short and people were only too hospitable to me, so I had to leave undone many things that I should have done. Later Plimsoll visited the United States in an effort to eliminate from our histories and school textbooks, the bitter denunciations against Great Britain in connection with the Revolutionary War and the War of 1812.) To come back to the "episode": it turned out that, in the House, Plimsoll had denounced Disraeli in the most violent terms as not being a man of his word and "a liar," and when called to order by the Speaker, would not retract. Some of his friends at the time went so far as to say that he had lost his mind from brooding over his bill. The tragedy of Ajax naturally occurred to me, where the old hero became demented while brooding over the loss of the armor of Achilles.

Soon after Sir William came out and took me into the House, but it was evidently in a very unnatural state. The "Hears" were weak or forced. There was no disturbance, yet no one was listened to, and the speakers spoke as one might speak after a deafening clap of thunder. All were evidently under great nervous ten-

SIR WILLIAM VERNON HARCOURT

sion. (This was before the times of Parnell's leadership of the Irish Home Rule group, when the House became accustomed to violent scenes.) This tension continued for some time, and even Disraeli failed to "amuse" the House. But not long after Mr. Gladstone got up and made a short but earnest speech against the Government's arranging their plans and debating measures in caucus instead of publicly in the House and then not telling the House the results of their deliberations. After this the members settled down to their usual state of mind. The "Hears" were loud and natural, and I think I am not mistaken in saying that it was because they recognized an old leader in whom they had confidence and he, though in the minority, alone set them right. It had a magic effect like the sudden appearance of Sheridan at the Battle of Winchester in the Civil War.

Sir William took me into the Members' Dining-Room. It was against the rule to take strangers there. They had to go to the Strangers' Room. It was just like Sir William to ignore such rules. He goes to the heart of matters and prefers not to be bound by formalities. Besides, he is large and physically powerful, a prominent member in line for being Prime Minister some day, and has such a "blinking smile" as to intimidate any too officious waiter. Sir William belongs to one of the oldest families in Great Britain. He gained first-class honors at Cambridge and has been Solicitor-General (later, 1880, he was Secretary of State for the Home Department and Chancellor of the Exchequer, 1885-86, and again, 1892-95).

At the dinner Sir William spoke of his desire to see entail abolished in England. I told him that in America, where we have no entail, it was not at all uncommon for people to want it reëstablished in order to hold the old family heirlooms together and to keep up large houses.

He had discovered a flaw in the bill under discussion, still the Agricultural Holdings Bill, in that there was nothing to prevent collusion between the tenant for life and the lessee to charge the estate with more than the real value of improvements. That defect he had remedied, but it had led him to say that the defect was just what he wished to see exist, for it would furnish a means of killing an entail. This Agricultural Holdings Bill receives the support of the tenants as they think it will benefit them, while the landlords are mollified by explaining in turn to them that there is nothing to prevent writing clauses into a lease which would deprive the tenant of any of the advantages of the bill, because the bill is permissive and not mandatory, and the landlords feel that in the present demand for real estate they can get the tenants to accept such clauses.

I have not so far mentioned that in the House of Commons the members wear their tall silk hats except when addressing the House. You sometimes see these hats pulled over their eyes, and whether they are sleeping or pondering over debate is a matter only of conjecture. They do not wear gloves as they did when my great-uncle, Edmund Dana, was present about 1801.

Friday, July 23

LUNCHED at Spencer House again, where were Lord and Lady Spencer and Lord Charles Bruce, M.P., son of the Marquis of Ailesbury. Lord Charles had married a sister of Lady Spencer. After lunch Spencer, his brother-in-law and I drove to Wimbledon to see the military camp, target-shooting, and manœuvres. On the way

RIFLE CONTESTS AT WIMBLEDON

we met, driving in her landau, and had a bow from the handsome and stately Princess Alexandra of Wales. Spencer told me she was somewhat deaf. We witnessed the 1000- and 1100-yard rifle contests, and saw three of the American team which had just won the International Rifle Match.

We watched the cavalry shooting, which was done in squads of four. These squads had to mount, gallop off, jump two hurdles, dismount, fire five shots apiece at 200 yards distance, mount, ride farther on, and dismount again for 400-yard shots. I saw two pretty bad spills, but no one seriously injured. I was introduced to several distinguished persons, some of them of title, but with my bad memory for names and meeting so many persons unexpectedly at once, I do not recall the names as I am writing this journal later in the evening.

I saw there a wonderful "bull's-eye" made by Queen Victoria at 1000 yards, and asked how it was possible for her to shoot so well, having my suspicions, however, which were verified when Spencer explained to me that the rifle was set in a vice, the wind tested, the rifle fired several times until it was exactly adjusted, and then a silken cord was tied at one end to the trigger and the other end the Queen pulled.

Spencer gave an illustration of his dignity and tact. He was either the head or one of the head directors of the Wimbledon Encampment. We were standing inside the lines and a captain came up and ordered us back. Instead of ignominiously retiring, on the one hand, or asserting his authority, on the other, he talked to this captain about some of the arrangements so that it began to dawn on the captain's mind that he was talking with one of the chief directors, and then Spencer graciously said, "Perhaps it is better for us to retire within the lines and set a good example to the others." And with composure and calm we walked slowly back.

We drove through Richmond Park to Pembroke Lodge, the suburban home of Earl Russell, formerly and better known to us as Lord John Russell. Spencer had written to have them ask me to dinner (this was before the days of telephones). I accepted, but he himself could not stay on account of other engagements. After the ladies had left the table I got up and sat next to Lord Russell. He was in his eighty-third year. At first he seemed somewhat absent and ignored my presence, but soon he fell to talking and I enjoyed him immensely. We had several people beside the family, two young members of Parliament among them.

Lord John Russell, born in 1792, was prominent in politics as far back as the reign of George IV, was paymaster of the forces in the beginning of the reign of William IV, during which reign he was also Secretary of State for the Home Department, so his memory of big events goes back to those days and the earliest Victorian era. His voice is high-pitched and querulous, and he has the same spare figure, small stature, large head and eyes that we were all so familiar with in the London "Punches." He talked much, easily, and in detail about things that were known to me only in outline, and the topics changed so rapidly that I was unable to make a good report of all he said. I wished I had had a stenographer behind the door to take it all down. They invited me to come Sunday afternoon and spend the night.

I returned to London with the two young members of Parliament, who took me with them into the House of Commons, and I saw the procedure of "complaints on motion to go into committee on supplies." The House

LORD RUSSELL
(FORMERLY LORD JOHN RUSSELL)
FROM A DRAWING BY G. F. WATTS

of Commons, having the sole power over supplies, takes the opportunity, whenever a motion is made to bring up a question of supplies, to slander the Government in every way. The complaints were very general and on all sorts of matters. It is customary to give the broadest license at these times, not keeping the members in the slightest degree to the motion or to any of the items of the contemplated appropriations. One of these members of Parliament who took me in was a young Irishman, and knowing that I wanted to see all the procedure in the House and noticing that there was no quorum present, said: "If you have never seen it before, I will call the Speaker's attention to the lack of quorum and have a counting out." This he did for my special benefit. When the counting began there were only thirty-eight, but one zealous member dragged in three of his friends so as to bring the number above the necessary forty and business continued.

Saturday, July 24
DINED at Mr. Smalley's. The company consisted of Mr. and Mrs. Smalley, Mr. Robinson, and Sir William Frederick and Lady Pollock. Sir William Frederick Pollock is a baronet. George W. Smalley has been for many years the London editorial correspondent of the New York "Tribune." He is now in the prime of life, forty-two years of age. Sir Frederick Pollock is the son of the celebrated Sir J. Frederick Pollock, Bart., chief baron of the Court of Exchequer, who rendered the decisions in the case of the Laird rams so hostile to the cause of the North in the Civil War. The present Sir Frederick who succeeded his father five years ago, seems to have no hostility towards America, but rather a friendly feeling. He is a Queen's remembrancer, has

translated Dante's "Divina Commedia," and has recently been made one of the judges of the Court of Admiralty. He was very kind, and not only offered to show me the courts, but also invited me to dinner five days hence.

Smalley asked me many questions about affairs at home, but I believed he was far better informed than I on the present state of politics in America. We talked about the disappointment in the character and ability of Grant's cabinet, all except Fish, the Secretary of State, who was both able and high-minded; and on the unsettled conditions in the South.

Sir Frederick Pollock begins his sentences at very high pitch with a sort of squeak or whine and gradually comes down lower and lower; but when he is thoroughly interested in his subject and gets well going, he gives up this descent from high to low and goes on in a delightful, rich, and natural voice.

Sunday, July 25

WENT to the Inner Temple in the morning on a pass from Sir Robert Phillimore. Dr. Vaughan preached the best sermon I ever heard. Considering the great reputation of the Temple choir, sometimes thought to be the best in Great Britain, I was a little disappointed. The anthem was a long duet for baritone and tenor.

Lunched with Mr. Ferguson at the Devonshire Club and went with him for coffee to the Reform Club. In the latter it is against the rule to have strangers in any part of the club but a small waiting-room and we were sitting in the large reading-room. The waiter would bring but one cup of coffee, which Mr. Ferguson insisted upon my taking while he smoked. Most of the great London clubs are what we should consider very unsociable. Those clubs which allow visitors only admit them into the Strangers' Room, which is unusually small, unless the strangers are armed with a special invitation from the governing committee, which I had not then received.

Sir John Kennaway one day took me all over Carlton Club, the great Tory institution, but said it was against the rule for him to do so, and he did not like to have me stay long in any of the rooms, and in the end I had to sit on a bench in the hall, doing nothing, while he was attending to some committee matter.

Later on this Sunday afternoon I went again to Pembroke Lodge, Richmond, Earl Russell's, and was most kindly received. A dinner of all the family excepting the eldest son, Lord Amberley, who is away and is in mourning for his wife who died a year ago. (He died the very next year.) The other guests were Admiral Elliot, who is Lady Russell's brother, his wife, Lady Harriet Emily, and their son. (This Honorable Sir Charles Gilbert Elliot in 1881 was made admiral of the combined British fleet.) Lady Harriet is a daughter of the Earl of Ravensworth. After the ladies had left the dining-room, Earl Russell called me to sit down by his side. This especially pleased me, for I was afraid I had been a little too forward, for so young a man, in sitting by him last Friday night without an invitation to do so. We talked much about the present, past, and future of England and America. Russell said he thought George Washington was "the greatest man of the age." He asked me who I thought would be the next President of the United States. I said, "Not Grant." We agreed in hoping it might be Charles Francis Adams, but did not think it likely. I said it was not likely unless the Republican Party would nominate him to secure some of the independent Democrats and those who were inclined to Democracy on account of their opposition to the machine methods of the Republican Party, and possibly to gain some of the Border State votes. Russell said he saw Senator John Sherman and liked him, and should think that he would make a good President.

In the evening Lady Harriet Elliot and I sang some hymns, and our voices went very well together, I singing a sort of alto-bass. Lady Russell showed me her book with many valuable autograph letters, pointing out one from Herbert Spencer which was extremely faulty, notwithstanding his essay on the "Philosophy of Style," as I think it is called. There was one from Queen Victoria in her own hand and of her own composition, which was very interesting, but full of mistakes. One sentence began in the third person and went on in the second, for example, and the spelling was atrocious.

Lady Russell, who has been lady-in-waiting on the Queen and very familiar with her, told me that in private the royal family always speak in the German language.

Monday, July 26

PEMBROKE LODGE, Richmond. Breakfasted at nine o'clock. Took a short walk about the grounds before breakfast and wished at the Wishing Tree (a wish which has since come true) and was greeted by Lady Russell from her window on my return to the house. At breakfast were Lady Russell and her brother, the Admiral and his son, a boy of eight or nine, Lady Agatha Russell, and Rollo, youngest son of Earl Russell. The breakfast, as usual in England, was very informal, and after the servants had once placed the food on the sideboard they

COUNTESS RUSSELL
(FORMERLY LADY JOHN RUSSELL)
1884

disappeared and we helped ourselves and changed our own plates. The gentlemen sometimes waited on the ladies. I took pleasure in doing so whenever I could, but frequently the ladies got ahead of me in walking quickly to the sideboard and serving themselves.

After breakfast I began a pencil and chalk sketch of the beautiful view in front of the house, and was interrupted by Lady Russell, who kindly took me to drive with Lady Agatha and herself round Richmond Park. This was a beautiful drive, the air being clear and bracing like ours at home and not as sultry and damp as usual in England at this time, and I felt so joyous and happy among these good, sympathetic, warm-hearted people in such weather, with the soft green grass, gorgeous flowers, and superb view. I saw great numbers of quite tame deer, which the Duke of Cambridge hunts with his hounds about twice a year. Came back at eleven, finished the sketch, and made one of the house itself.

We lunched at two. The party was the same as at breakfast with the addition of Lady Harriet Emily Elliot, the wife of the admiral, who is Lady Russell's brother, Lord Russell himself, who had not been with us at breakfast, and a young man from Wimbledon. We three young men played lawn tennis, the first time I ever took part in this game. I held up my side in doubles and singles, too, pretty well considering that the others had played tennis a good deal. (In those days the net was six inches higher than at present and the service was underhand so that the play was not then as swift as it is now. This made it an easier game for a beginner to learn.)

Walked and talked and sat out of doors with Lady Russell and her daughter, Lady Agatha. Lady Russell makes a most admirable hostess; she keeps the conversation going without interfering, guiding it by responsive comment or question and only leading when it becomes necessary. She is most attentive to her husband and his wants. He, of course, is now old and feeble, and while able to walk, goes about a good deal in a rolling chair. Lady Russell, while not handsome, has a most sympathetic and intellectual expression of face. Her maiden name was Lady Frances Anna Maria Elliot, and she is the daughter of the second Earl of Minto. She was born in 1815 and married in 1841. She is the mother of Lord Amberley and all the other children of the Earl. Lord John's first wife was widow of Lord Ribblesdale, and she died without leaving children in 1838. (Lady Russell's letters, published after her death, show a wonderful interest in all public affairs, knowledge of persons and character, a deep love for her friends, and keen sympathy for all in need of it.) Lady Russell invited me to come again on Friday next to dine and spend the night and stay till Monday morning if possible. On leaving was driven to the station in a pony carriage and got to my rooms in time to prepare for a dinner at Lord Frederick Cavendish's at exactly seven o'clock. I met there Lord and Lady Edward Cavendish (whose son is now the Duke of Devonshire), Mr. and Mrs. Gladstone, and Lady Lyttelton, stepmother of Lady Frederick, Lady Frederick being the daughter of Lord Lyttelton by his first wife, who was a sister of Mrs. Gladstone, so that Lady Frederick is Mrs. Gladstone's niece. We had a rather hurried dinner and went to the theatre at eight.

Almost the whole talk at the dinner was about the wedding presents for Gladstone's eldest son, who, as I have already stated, was lately engaged and is soon to be married.

All of us but Lord Frederick and Mrs. Gladstone went to the Prince of Wales Theatre and saw the play of "Money," by Lord Lytton. Going to the theatre Mr. Gladstone rode on the outside of the carriage to direct the driver. George Honey took the part of Mr. Graves, Miss Marie Wilton that of Lady Franklin, capitally done, and Ellen Terry that of Clara Douglas, and acted, of course, charmingly. Between the parts I went to see Earl Spencer and his beautiful wife, whom I had noticed in another part of the theatre. Spencer gave up his seat to me and went to speak with our party, and in this way we sat for one scene and then changed back again just as the curtain rose for the scene following.

On the way home Gladstone insisted on walking for exercise, and had I known at the time that the ladies had a manservant with them (for they had to take a cab) I should have walked with Gladstone myself, but thought it was my duty to escort the ladies. We had late evening tea at Lady Frederick's, Mr. Gladstone joining us soon after our arrival. The talk was of the stage as a profession and whether it is one an educated person of good family should follow or not, on which there was a division of opinion. Gladstone, during the tea and also in some of the intervals during the play, was immensely absorbed in the topic of the various actors, how they did their parts, of the play itself, and how it might have been improved by one alteration or another.

He was surprised to hear that in Massachusetts we had a large surplus of women and that women's work as seamstress and the like was badly paid. He said in Wales there were no murders, that the Welsh people were very kindly, fond of music, and sang much in choruses. The party broke up at twelve. They took me into the family as if I were a relative or at least a friend of long standing.

Tuesday, July 27
TOOK a long walk in the morning for exercise, of which I have had only too little in this London social life, and dined with Dr. Charles H. Williams, Harvard '71, and his classmate, Horace D. Chapin, both of Boston. They took me to the Holborn Restaurant and to their rooms afterwards. They gave some amusing anecdotes of their travels and spoke of the low standards of the Germans, especially the Austrians — for they had been long in Vienna — in regard to women and how much higher were the ideals of American young men, at least of those we knew. Charles Williams goes to the hospital in London every day and says the nursing and general care of patients is not as good here as in the Massachusetts General Hospital in Boston.

This was the first evening I had not been invited to dine with English friends and for some single evenings I have had two and in one case even three invitations.

Wednesday, July 28
CALLED on Lord Tenterden at the Foreign Office in the morning, but found he was out and had to satisfy myself with leaving a card. After lunch I called on the following: Mr. and Mrs. Gladstone, who were both out, and Lord and Lady Frederick Cavendish. Lady Frederick was in and I found a Miss Smith calling. I made a rather short but very agreeable visit. The fire was low and Lady Frederick called for a servant to replenish it; but as it happened, the servant whose duty it was to look after the fires was away, and though there were several other servants at hand in the house, both foot-

men and maids, she said she could not ask them to do this simple task; so I did it for her — a very small matter, indeed, but illustrating how amusingly and fantastically the work among the really admirable and civil domestics in Great Britain is divided.

I next called on Mr. Robert Ferguson, who said he would give me a letter to his brother-in-law in Birmingham. Next I called at Spencer House, where I found Lady Spencer and her brother-in-law, Lord Charles Bruce. Spencer himself had just gone out driving. We spoke of the play the night before and the injustice that is done noblemen in such comedies, as a bit of mere claptrap and play to the galleries, or "groundlings" as they used to say in Shakespeare's days, and of the real worth and value of many noblemen in English life, politics, and constructive legislation. Called at Sir Robert Phillimore's, where all were out. Next at Dr. Jones's, where they made me sing a negro melody. At Sir John Kennaway's I found Lady Kennaway in. She was very cordial and sang me a Scottish song, "The Auld Home," and hoped I could arrange my time so as to visit them in their Devonshire home (a really magnificent castle) at Ottery St. Mary. The Smalleys were out of town, and here ended my calls for the afternoon.

During the day Lord Russell's servant appeared with my overcoat, and it turned out that I had taken "My Lord's" by mistake and had been wearing it all day. It was rather strange that it fitted me at all, for he is so much smaller than I. It must be very loose for him. I felt it was no little honor to have worn the coat of such a man. It might have been an omen that by chance the mantle of the greatest of surviving statesmen of his day should have fallen on me, like that of Elijah on Elisha, only in this case the mantle had to be returned, which I feared was an omen the other way.

Dined in the evening at the Devonshire Club with Sir William Vernon Harcourt. He got up this dinner expressly for me and I sat at his right. There were altogether fourteen gentlemen beside myself, and among them Lord Young, Lord Advocate of Scotland; Mr. Mayne, the author of "Ancient Law"; Lord Dalkeith, eldest son and heir of the Duke of Buccleugh, who sat on Sir William's left; young Lord George Hamilton, member of Parliament and under-secretary for India, son of the Duke of Abercorn and a Tory, and on the opposite side in politics from Sir William (afterwards First Lord of the Admiralty, Secretary of State for India, and author of "Parliamentary Reminiscences, 1916"); Millais, the artist; and others, all fourteen being distinguished. Millais is very handsome except for a defect in one eyelid, and is brilliant. He talked too much and too loud. His voice seemed charging up and down the table like a troop of cavalry. He told many anecdotes of Lord Byron, which he had picked up, and some of them were rather "spicy." The talk drifted on to the Constitution of the United States, about which they asked me some questions. I explained that the Federation under which we carried on the Revolutionary War was a combination of States. It worked through a Continental Congress, but provided no executive and no federal courts, while the Constitution, adopted in 1788, after the Federation had proved such a failure, was not an agreement between States, but of the "people" of the whole country, beginning, "We, the people of the United States, in order to form a more perfect union . . . do ordain and establish this Constitution."

SECESSION AND THE CONSTITUTION

The Constitution provides a Supreme Court for the whole nation with power to decide state legislation unconstitutional, thereby nullifying state acts contrary to its provisions; also to decide questions between States, and with power through the President of the United States, the United States marshals, and a federal army, to enforce its decrees. Under the Federation, secession was probably legal, but under the Constitution it is hard to see how it is possible constitutionally and legally for a State to secede. The question of the right of secession, however, is to be clearly distinguished from a moral right to organize a revolution, but the Southern States did not claim that they were revolting; they claimed the right of secession as constitutional. This seemed new to them all excepting Sir William, who has been in the United States, knows more of our system, and, under the title of "Historicus," wrote some famous articles in the London "Times" in the early part of the Civil War, in opposition to the recognition by Great Britain of the Southern States as belligerents.

During the coffee and smoking, after we left the table, three of the company who were members of Parliament — one of them a government whip — took me aside and urged me to stay on in England, give up my own country, and run for Parliament. They were sure they could secure me a seat. They said persons of education were not appreciated in American politics, instancing the cases of my father, Charles Francis Adams, and others, and set forth what a fine career it was for a man in the English Parliament. Notwithstanding this very flattering suggestion, perhaps slightly colored by the delicious dinner and varied wines, I told them that I loved my own country, and in so far as it was defective I hoped to help in setting it right, at least to do my little part, and that especially, as in such matters as abolishing the spoils system and establishing civil service reform, I felt there was much work that could be done outside of legislative positions.

After smoking and talking in the Devonshire Club, some of us adjourned to the Cosmopolitan Club, where public and literary leaders gather late Wednesday and Saturday nights and where a lot of present politics and old political scandals were discussed. I met and shook hands with Anthony Trollope, the author. He spoke very pleasantly of my father and mother, whom he had met on the Continent lately, and of the many good talks they had had together. Lord Young, Lord Advocate of Scotland, was most kind to me, and insisted upon it that I must not fail to look him up when I go to Edinburgh. He tells many funny stories, and by way of an exception which proves the rule, though a Scotchman, has a keen sense of humor and wit of his own, and is quick to catch the points in stories told by others.

Harcourt invited me to the House of Commons to hear the Plimsoll settlement or apology or whatever it might turn out to be, which is to take place to-morrow. The general opinion in the club seemed to be that Plimsoll intended to create a sensation and even contemplated being put into confinement. He certainly did succeed in creating a great deal more sympathy from his disorderly conduct than he could have aroused in any other way. It was, however, clearly not all of it acting; he was really very much excited. The truth probably lies between the two extremes. He was doubtless greatly worked up, took advantage of his opportunity, and let his passion have pretty full sway. Disraeli intimated, but avoided directly asserting it, that he allowed all this scene to come off so as to secure the public backing outside necessary to enable him to pass the bill inside the House of Commons. Many doubted the truth of this intimation and believed it to be but an adroit way of turning an actual blunder to his own benefit. I believed it was nothing but a bit of "Dizzy's" humor. (The main part of Plimsoll's bill passed this session and was perfected the next, in 1876.)

CHAPTER III

THE LAST OF MY FIRST LONDON SEASON

Thursday, July 29

WENT to Westminster Abbey and spent two hours there about noon. After lunch went to the House of Commons by Sir William Vernon Harcourt's invitation, to hear Plimsoll's apology. Sir William came out and took me into the inner lobby, but there we found every place occupied. The Speaker of the House of Commons said he would put me into the Diplomatic Gallery, but even that was full; so as I should have to wait until a vacancy appeared somewhere, which might not occur until the interesting part of the session was over, I, after an hour's waiting, sent in my card asking Sir William not to trouble himself any more, and then took a ride up the river in a steamer as far as Chelsea and got back in time to dress for dinner at Sir William Frederick Pollock's.

There were present Sir William Frederick and Lady Pollock, both very cordial and agreeable, Lady Pollock with a literary reputation, also his son Frederick Pollock (later Sir Frederick Pollock, Bart., in his turn, the celebrated legal authority, lecturer, etc.). Everywhere I go my father's name is a remarkably good introduction. I had no letter to the Pollocks. I had met him at Smalley's. Sir William said that he found in his work as Judge of the Admiralty Courts my father's "Seaman's Manual" was perfectly invaluable, and he kept it by him in and out of court. It is the standard authority, he said, and of course he had read "Two Years Before the Mast." The evening passed very pleasantly. The Plimsoll matter turned out very quietly, "a tame affair" as they called it, ending in an apology for misconduct, but adherence to all the facts as he had stated them, so I did not lose very much after all in not being present.

Friday, July 30
I CALLED on the Honorable Arthur Kinnaird at the bank. He was apparently busy, so I only thanked him for his kindness and delivered a letter of introduction to him which I had just received from Lord Kinnaird, although this letter was unnecessary. Edmund Dana, the only brother of Judge Francis Dana, my great-grandfather, went to England, became a clergyman of the Established Church there and married a daughter of the then Lord Kinnaird, so the family have always taken us as in a way connected with them.

Afterwards I looked at some fine old carved furniture which I stumbled upon by accident in a quaint shop. It had been bought at various auctions or private sales from some of the best families and was wonderfully cheap.

This morning I received a short note from Mr. Gladstone, so that I am a proud possessor of an autograph letter of his addressed to me.

Afterwards left London at the end of the day for Richmond, and when I arrived at Pembroke Lodge I found the Countess on the bowling green with some callers, among whom was Lord Colin Campbell, the youngest son of the Duke of Argyll, whom I had met at Lord Frederick Cavendish's. Rollo and Colin played several games of tennis while we watched them, drank tea, and afterwards walked to see the views. I stood on the mound from which Henry VIII's messenger saw the rockets sent off from the Tower of London on the execution of Anne Boleyn, while the King himself was waiting in a house near by. The vista is still kept open, but it is seldom clear enough to see the tower through the smoky London air of to-day. Soon there arrived Lord and Lady Selborne and their daughter and Lord and Lady Cardwell. These, with Colin Campbell, a stranger who left immediately after dinner, Lord and Lady Russell, Lady Agatha, and Rollo, made up the company at dinner. (Rollo Russell later became distinguished as a scientist, specializing in meteorology and still later in aeroplane work. He died in the early part of the Great War and during his life published many valuable treatises. See "Who's Who," 1914.)

While it is not common to introduce people in England, you are always at liberty to talk with any one who is a guest of your host, though I found they frequently made an exception in my case, and did introduce, I being a stranger from America. If the name of a guest does not come out in the course of the conversation, the usual custom is to inquire of the butler, who always knows. At this dinner I sat between Lady Cardwell, who was on Lord Russell's right, and Lady Agatha, who was next to Lord Selborne, so I heard the best of the conversation. They spoke of a wonderful dog, about which I have read in the papers while here. It is now being exhibited and seems to have an almost human intelligence. This led to a little talk with Lord Selborne on animals, instinct, idealism, and the nature of matter, in which, from my interest in philosophy, I took an active part. They spoke of spirit photography, which seemed to mystify them. I told them some stories about it and explained two processes by which spirit photography could be easily and cheaply produced.

Very few of the English educated men know about chemistry or the action of light or science generally. Science is only just beginning to be taught at Cambridge and hardly at all at Oxford.

After the ladies left the room Lord Russell called Lord Selborne to his right and I sat next to him and Lord Cardwell on Russell's left. They got talking about old politics. From what Lord Russell said, it is to be inferred that the "Greville Papers"[1] were true about William IV and George IV. Many interesting anecdotes they told of Lord Brougham, one about his going to sleep through an able argument of an hour and a half to have a decision reversed. Brougham woke up at the end, saying, "The decision is confirmed."

Lord Russell said that William IV was very good-natured, easy-going, and pleasant, but that he liked to play the king at times, especially if his companions treated him too familiarly; that he was fond of a "jaw," and sometimes said things at Windsor worse than any one would like to repeat. This was all pretty well known in history and has been enlarged on by Thackeray. Russell only confirmed it. The general society of the Court was, as Lord Russell put it, about on a level with a dancing-hall barroom.

Lord Selborne told a story of how a Frenchman who knew Lord Brougham's reputation for being so great a judge, and who, in trying a case before him, suddenly discovered that his lordship was asleep, said in astonishment, "Mon Dieu! Il dort."

Lord Russell gave an account of the intemperance existing in London society during his younger days. He

[1] Extracts from the journals of Charles Cavendish Fulke Greville (1794–1865), great-grandson of the fifth Earl of Warwick, and clerk of the Council in Ordinary, having intercourse with royalty and the chiefs of all parties.

said that when the ladies left the dining-room the host would arise, lock the door, fresh bottles of port would be brought in, and almost every man drank until he was under the table. With the exception of one or two men who kept sober, they never joined the ladies again, and a page, towards the end of the drinking, as the men slipped from their seats, would loosen the neck-cloths of the prostrate guests, and it was a regular custom for the valets to come in, carry out their masters, put them in their coaches, and escort them home. Lord Russell said some curious incidents arose when some of the valets were not themselves sober and substitutes had to take their places, and some of the masters were put into the wrong coaches and carried to the wrong houses about midnight or later, much to the astonishment of the wives and other members of the households. The recollection seemed very vivid and Russell chuckled over the memory. Whether he actually saw these incidents or only heard of them, he did not say.

Lady Cardwell and Lord Selborne both urged me to let them know when I come back to London next year, as I plan to do, so they may invite me to dinner. They are soon to leave town and I am full of engagements to the end of the season, when grouse shooting begins, three days hence. Lord Selborne said to me of Lord Brougham, that putting a powerful leader of the House of Commons into the House of Lords was like cutting off Samson's locks. I knew that it had sometimes been called "kicking a man upstairs." As Lord Selborne himself had been Attorney-General, as Sir Roundell Palmer, and was himself given a peerage and promoted to the Upper House, he must have known whereof he was talking, and, indeed, probably had in mind his own exclusion from active statesmanship.

Lord Cardwell is a viscount, created such only a little over a year ago. He took a double first at Oxford, was called to the Bar in 1838, has been Secretary of the Treasury, President of the Board of Trade, etc. He was Chief Secretary of Ireland at one time and later Secretary of State for the Colonies from 1864 to 1866. Again he was made Secretary of State for War and has been member of the House of Commons for about seventeen years.

Saturday, July 31
PEMBROKE LODGE. Read and took a walk in the park before lunch. Afterwards drove with Lady Agatha and Rollo to Kew Gardens. The outside of this was not very different from our Public Gardens in Boston excepting for its larger size and the superb foliage of the big trees. The conservatories, however, were beyond anything I have ever witnessed. I saw for the first time the Venus Fly Trap, a plant which catches, closes over, eats, and digests small flies as they alight. The properties of this plant have been made use of by Darwin in the development of his theory of evolution by natural selection.

Before dinner we played three games of lawn tennis. At dinner were the family and a young Irish barrister. After dinner we played whist, and I did some tricks with cards and coins which I had learned for the entertainment of children and which were entirely new to all present, who seemed to think them more wonderful than they really were.

Sunday, August 1
WENT to the Richmond church, which was of an old style with square pews, and there was a beadle dressed in a parti-colored gown. The singing was very plain

and the sermon still more plain, mere words strung together without any apparent purpose.

Lady Ribblesdale and her son (who later married Mrs. John Astor) came in for lunch. At dinner we had the same party as yesterday except that Rollo was away, and we had two members of Parliament, one an Irish Catholic. I sat between Lord and Lady Russell and took Lady Russell in to dinner. We spoke of Edmund Burke, and I told of Rufus Choate's reading Burke so constantly and how he particularly liked the "Letter to a Late Noble Lord," and to my horror I suddenly remembered that Earl Russell was descended from that very Duke of Bedford concerned, of whom Burke spoke in no very complimentary terms. I, however, turned the conversation to the literary merits of this great speech, leaving out any reference to the rights of the case. Lord Russell said that Burke's son, who died and was so lamented by his father, was so highly esteemed only by the father and not by others. He also said that one of Burke's best speeches was against employing Indians in the American or Revolutionary War with the colonists, and that this speech was lost and, of course, not among Burke's published works.

He talked much about the great speakers and orators of Parliament in his time, of the French and Russian imitations of Parliament, and commended the wisdom of the founders of our American Constitution, and mentioned some changes in it which he thought necessary. I told him that, though the American Constitution is nowadays held in such high esteem, it came very near being defeated; that many of the leaders in the country opposed it; that my great-grandfather, Francis Dana, contended for it with great earnestness in the Massachusetts Convention against Samuel Adams, Elbridge

Gerry, and others, where it was adopted only by a very close vote, and had it been defeated there it would have failed of adoption.

Lord Russell agreed with my grandfather Dana's idea that a king and nobility in America would be a great blessing, believing the American people needed something to look up to. Of course this was only a fancy, for Russell knew well enough it would never work in our country. The people would never accept it. We shall in time outgrow our bumptiousness and cocksureness, which is sometimes so offensive to other nations, and do better in the end than if helped by any such artificial institutions, for, as I suggested, a bad king and dissolute members of the nobility might do more harm than good ones could offset.

I continue to be surprised at finding how much the English ladies know of, and how well they talk on, national and political questions in comparison with the American ladies I have known. (Nowadays this is greatly changed in the United States.)

Lord Russell showed much strength of mind even in discussing modern problems, and his memory for the past is very clear, but not always so for the present as to names and dates. He forgot that he had seen me a week before and repeated some things I had said, as told him by "an American he had lately met."

The guests coming down to Pembroke Lodge for dinner are, by a long understanding, excused from dressing, the men appearing in their frock coats worn in the daytime in London.

Monday, August 2
READ a little and played lawn tennis a good deal more. I saw Lord Russell again at lunch. He repeated his re-

mark of the other day that Washington was the greatest man of the age. He talked about the American trade with Japan and its growth and size, and when I told him it was carried on almost entirely in English vessels, he was greatly amused and chuckled to himself for some little time.

Went "up" to town directly after lunch. London is always "up," except in relation to Oxford and Cambridge when it is "down," and the universities are "up."

Found Tom Felton at Mrs. Brooks's. He was rather lonely and I was glad to cheer him up. He is the son of the late president of Harvard College, Cornelius Conway Felton.

To-day I took my first dinner at my own expense since July 15th, when I delivered my first letters. I went to the famous Simpson's Restaurant with a Harvard classmate. There they wheel up to your alcove table huge joints on warmed platters and before your face cut slices just as you direct. I visited again the Royal Art Exhibition and liked some of the pictures better than at my first visit. I looked up Millais's work with special interest since I have known him. Some of his portraits certainly seem to be of a very high order.

Tuesday, August 3

CALLED on Lady Pollock, whom I found in, and who gave me addresses and advice for Paris and France generally, which I am to visit this autumn. She reads and talks French easily.

Called on Sir William Vernon Harcourt, whom I missed, as he was off for six weeks or more in Switzerland. Dined at the Savile Club. Parliament soon closes and the London season was brought to an end by the opening of the grouse shooting. I surely have had great opportunities in meeting so many of the distinguished men — many more than I have mentioned in this journal by name — in seeing the procedure of Parliament, and hearing all the men of mark there. I also went to the House of Lords and to some of the courts several times under good introductions, and I am now off for a trip in the country and to make a series of visits in big houses. Lord Frederick Cavendish asked me to visit them during Christmas season at Chatsworth, having secured an invitation for me from his father, the Duke of Devonshire. There is to be a large and interesting party there, and as Chatsworth is the finest country house in England it is a great opportunity. However, I planned to be on the Continent, where I want to learn French, and it would upset those plans to come back for this one visit, and would also add greatly to the expense which I do not like to put upon my father. So I declined this invitation, attractive as it was. (Afterwards I regretted having declined, as it was an unusual opportunity to meet the Marquis of Hartington, the eldest son of the Duke, who was, I understood, to be in the party, and other prominent guests, and to see the Christmas festivities in an old family. Had I stayed but a week or two more in Paris than I did, perfecting my French, I could have run back to England in short time and at small cost.)

On one of my visits with Lord Russell I presumptuously brought the conversation to bear on the Trent Affair, boldly asking him why he had not stated to Parliament the grounds on which Seward had returned Messrs. Mason and Slidell, summed up in the end of his letter. Lord Russell said that this letter, like all Seward's communications, was so long and involved that he could not have read it to Parliament. This did not seem to be quite a satisfactory answer, but I did not press the question further. The Trent Affair was in short as follows:

During the early days of the Civil War Captain Charles Wilkes of the United States Navy, in command of the *San Jacinto*, a United States war vessel, took off from the *Trent* (a British steamer running between neutral ports) Messrs. Mason and Slidell, two Confederate envoys sent out respectively to England and France, with their secretaries. It was done without any authority from or knowledge on the part of the United States Government, but under the principle always contended for as legal by England up to the very moment that the capture of these gentlemen became known in London. The British Government, however, Lord John Russell representing it in the House of Commons, demanded, in conjunction with Lord Palmerston, under threat of war, the immediate return of Mason and Slidell. We had always contended that the English principle was wrong, and one of the issues of the War of 1812 against Great Britain was on this very subject.

At the end of Seward's letter he took the stand that we willingly surrendered these gentlemen on the ground that by England's demand she "disavows" her old claim of the right to do the same thing and "assumes now as her own" the ground on which we always stood. Had the dozen lines of Seward's letter, showing the why, been read by Lord John in Parliament, or their substance stated, it would have helped to allay the ill-feeling that naturally came from our being made to appear in the eyes of Europe as frightened into surrendering those men, instead of having achieved a victory thereby for our own principles. I think, however, this climax to a far too long and elaborate letter may have escaped Lord John's attention, as it has that of some historians.

Lady Russell wants to substitute "Britannia" or "British Isles" as the name for "England," and "Columbia" for the "United States of America." In a note to me she says: "England is, properly speaking, only one portion of Britannia and hence arise confusion and awkwardness in speech and writing. Depend upon it, when you and I have peaceably brought about these weighty revolutions, there will be an end of all the bickerings, bitterness, and broils which have disturbed the mother and daughter countries under their old names!"

During my stay in London there had been much talk about Moody and Sankey, who had recently come to England, as to their influence for good and the after effects of such revivals. The general opinion seemed to be here, as it was in America, that while a few were permanently improved, who might be called the survivals of the revivals, many were only emotionally carried away and soon went back into old ruts, and with some individuals it might be said, the last state of that man was worse than the first.

There were also echoes of the Tichborne "claimant." Sir Roger Charles Tichborne was supposed to have been lost at sea, and a man from Australia declared that he was the rightful Sir Roger and claimed the baronetcy and estates worth about $120,000 a year. He got much sympathy from the common people in Great Britain because he was a rough person, and if he was not the true Sir Roger was the son of a butcher. It was a curious mixture of mind. If he had been the original Sir Roger, he was an aristocrat, but if he was this son of a butcher, he was n't the rightful claimant. His original claims had been settled adversely to him three years before, but he and some of his witnesses had been tried for perjury last year and convicted, and this longest trial known in England still remained in the public mind, especially as attempts were being made to secure the pardon of the claimant and his witnesses.

General C. R. Schenck, our United States Minister to London, was several times mentioned, but always and only as having taught the English our American card game of poker, which had been taken up as the great gambling pursuit of the fast set and by others for amusement at small stakes.

The London post-office has been a marvelous surprise. Sir John Kennaway told me that letters would be carried about as quickly by mail as by special messenger, and this I found to be true. To notes that I posted in a "station" in a small store near my lodgings in the early forenoon to persons even two or three miles away, I often got replies on the same afternoon and not infrequently in the middle of the afternoon, incredible as it may seem to one used to our mails. The London post-office has many of these small stations where stamps, money orders, and postal cards can be bought and mail weighed. When posted in these stations, the stamps are immediately canceled, the letters sorted and made ready for the first letter carriers that come along, instead of lying idle in a letter box for one, two, or three hours and then taken to a central office to be assorted and later sent out for delivery, often traveling, metaphorically speaking, down one spoke of the wheel to be carried out on a parallel spoke, instead of being taken right across, without delay, as in London.

I have omitted one important incident which I witnessed in Parliament. Sir William Vernon Harcourt, in reply to one of Disraeli's speeches, quoted from one of the latter's works showing that Disraeli had changed his views. Disraeli disappeared into the library, and soon afterwards returned bringing a copy of the book and read an extract which did not quite sustain Harcourt's statement. It happened that the very next time I went to the House of Commons, I think it was the following day or later the same day after dinner, Sir William Vernon Harcourt got up and read from the first edition of the same work, which fully sustained his quotation, and then showed that Disraeli had read from a late edition in which he had amended the statement, and intimated that Disraeli must have well known of the amendment and was trying to mislead the House.

This would have been enough to smash the reputation of any ordinary Englishman. I looked to see him fall "down and give up the ghost" and to behold the young men arise and carry him out; but not at all. Disraeli only made some amusing remarks and the whole matter passed off like drops of water from a duck's back. The truth is, from what I learn, that Disraeli, while he has many charming qualities and is very true to his friends, is not really taken into the inner circles of the Tory Party, but is considered by them more as an adroit barrister who can represent their side in Parliament than as one of themselves.

(A story was privately circulated in England, which came to my ears and has recently been published,[1] that Disraeli wrote a beseeching letter to Sir Robert Peel asking for an appointment in his government and soon afterwards denied in Parliament in the most explicit language that he had ever asked for anything of the sort. Sir Robert, though Disraeli had been attacking him

[1] See George Earle Buckle's *Life of Disraeli*.

in rather an annoying way, did not divulge the begging letter. I was recently told by two eminent authorities, one a Liberal and the other a Tory, who were in a position to know, that Sir Robert had this letter in his pocket when Disraeli made the denial, and hesitated for a few moments whether to read the letter or not and that Disraeli had banked on Sir Robert's clemency. Another story I have heard is that at the moment Sir Robert could not find the letter and for that reason let the matter pass.)

CHAPTER IV

ALTHORP HOUSE: EARL SPENCER'S VIA WARWICK AND BIRMINGHAM

Wednesday, August 4

THIS morning I left London for a series of visits at great country houses.

Arrived at the Warwick Arms, Warwick. Put on my walking shoes, strolled about the town, and then started for Guy's Cliff. Saw Guy's Cave and the monument to Giles, Baron of Cornwall, slain here in 1312 "by barons as lawless as himself." At the Cliff the family were at home, so I was not admitted. Walked close to the castle on the other side of the Avon and visited the old mill.

Thursday, August 5

WALKED to Warwick Castle and got there before the crowd, so I saw things pretty much by myself. I might easily have got a letter of introduction to the family from some of my English friends, but have never asked for any introductions. I was surprised at the excellence of the collection of pictures by many great masters. Walked from there to Kenilworth, where I lunched at the Queen's Arms. I was enchanted with the old ruins and could hardly tear myself away. I climbed over the wall and went out by the old passage by which the Earl of Leicester and Queen Elizabeth came in to the castle nearly three hundred years ago. The romance of Amy Robsart lent wonderful pathos to the whole scene. The old way was closed by piles of ruins, and hard climbing was necessary, but I was too much worked up to mind that.

On arriving at Warwick yesterday I found a letter from my good and faithful friend Rawlins to a Mr. Lloyd, of the Priory at Warwick, which I delivered that evening, and on returning to my hotel to-day I found a note from Mr. Lloyd asking me to dine at the Priory. It was thirty minutes after his dinner hour and I was not dressed, when I got the invitation.

I found also an invitation from Sir John Kennaway to visit him at his splendid castle at Ottery St. Mary, Devonshire, which I cannot accept on account of other engagements I have already made, and one from Lord Coleridge of which I can avail myself.

Called at the Priory in the evening. It was magnificent and old with a superb great hall and galleries about. There was Prince Rupert's bed and Queen Elizabeth's stairs. The hall opened up through three stories and was almost all in dark oak wainscoting, with many family pictures and armor, swords, and shields about. The family were one and all very hospitable, and I had a delightful and romantic evening in this historic house. Ghost stories were told, but none of them very convincing or first hand, though all related to the house and its past owners. Talk drifts on spiritualism, which is receiving much attention in Great Britain.

Friday, August 6

WALKED to Stratford-on-Avon, eight miles, under heavy, low clouds with occasional rain. To-day, Friday, was market day. The market carts were about and wares spread on the ground in the middle of the main street. I went, of course, to Shakespeare's house and visited his tomb, passing on the way the school where he learned to read and write. The memorials and curiosities were many, but not a few of doubtful authenticity; in fact, there seemed to be some dispute about everything, even as to whether Shakespeare was Shakespeare or Bacon, or Bacon was Shakespeare.

Returned to Warwick by train after dinner and went over the old "Leyces Ter" Hospital. Parts of the gateway are very ancient, said to be of the seventh or eighth century. Saw some worsted needlework of Amy Robsart's, claimed to be genuine. It was very touching to think of her working on it in her expectation of a happy meeting with the Earl just before her tragic ending. Saw several autographs of Dudley, Earl of Leyces Ter, spelt as is the hospital.

Saturday, August 7

WENT to the morning service at Leyces Ter Hospital before breakfast. It was quite appealing. There were eight old soldiers who responded with so much earnestness and good-will that it was a lesson for us Episcopalians, even of the Church of the Advent, where responses were much better than elsewhere in Boston. These services are held twice a day, day after day, with rarely any strangers present. It quite stirred one's heart and made it worth while getting up early for this service, held in the old chapel over the still older gateway. The services were read from a prayer book given by Leicester. The devotion of these old men, their close attention, and their full, manly voices, with so often no one but their Maker to hear them, I shall not soon forget.

Left Warwick for Birmingham and delivered a letter given me by Mr. Ferguson to a Mr. Chance of this city; but as chance would have it, he was out of town. Smalley had promised to get me some letters to the leading manufacturers of Birmingham, Manchester, and elsewhere, but he must have forgotten his promise, for I have received none. Merely seeing pigs of iron go into one end of a machine and come out in knives, forks, spoons, bedsteads, or electroplated silverware, etc., at the other, is not half as educational as a few moments' talk on the management of the works, the methods of economy, and the labor questions, with the practical manufacturer and with some of his workmen themselves.

Walked about the town in a hard rain for an hour or so. The people in general looked less earnestly intent and careworn than our working people at home. Yet I should say they were hardly as healthy. There was a great prevalence of drunkenness, and skin diseases seem not uncommon; at least they were obvious. The few healthiest were fine specimens of human nature, but I hoped to see both in country and in town life, among the unprivileged classes of England, more strong bodies and ruddy cheeks than I have seen yet. It may be that the very healthfulness of the climate tempts people to its abuse. If this is so it is something of a compensation for our less favorable conditions.

I read Hartington's speech on the proceedings of the Government, which is manly and straightforward, and then "Dizzy's" answer, which, to me, seemed to show a great mastery, not of abstract style nor solid worth, but of just the sort of oratory to engage the attention and carry along the inert thought of the House to his side. In substance it seemed to me to consist of glittering generalities and catching phrases. I wished I could have heard both these speeches.

Sunday, August 8
ST. PHILIP's in the morning. Choral service. The text of the sermon was, "And does Job serve the Lord for

naught." It was well arranged, spoken in rich, melodious tones, and so put as not to arouse any one's conscience beyond the point of good-breeding and self-content. The clergyman certainly is not getting hold of the people. I walked through the city and saw miles of signs of continuous, heart-breaking poverty. On this day, Sunday, drinking-shops and tobacco stores were open; the former in great numbers. All other "places of amusement" were shut; no picture galleries were open, no libraries. You could not send a telegram even in case of illness or death, and trains were few and there were no mails.

The houses were mostly in three stories, though some of only two. I saw some partly built which had only the thickness of one brick between the houses and of only two bricks in front and rear. The bricks, however, were five inches broad instead of our narrow ones; but it was at best very flimsy construction. (The building laws of England have been very much improved since, as are the dwelling conditions for the poor in all its cities.)

Monday, August 9
I GOT from the landlady of the Inn a card to the Elkington Silversmiths, Electroplaters, and Bronze Founders, the largest manufacturers of the sort in the world. I told these people that I was an American studying the conditions in England, and they gave me cards to McCallum & Hodson, Papier Maché, Pearl, and Japan Goods; to Gillott's Pen Works; and, what is very hard to get, a letter to Taylor's Pin Works. I also visited a factory for making shoe pegs. The process of making these pegs was interesting and instructive. They were cut out roughly by machinery and then put in an immense caldron and jostled back and forth and up and

down till they became smooth and polished. Were this smoothing and polishing done to each peg separately, it would make their cost prohibitive. I said to the man who showed me about, "Is n't that something like a large family where the children rub off each other's rough corners?" He smiled and said, "It is." I saw to-day all but the pin works, which I shall visit to-morrow. At the pen works the hands were paid by the piece. The man showing me about was unwilling to tell what the laborers were paid or earn and avoided answering my other questions. Some of the laborers looked tired and unhealthy, but there were enough contented, well, and strong hands, both men and women, to make one believe that with temperance, fair amount of industry, and proper preparation of their food at home, they might have been on the average much better off than they were; indeed, I was told that almost all those who were temperate and saving did pretty well and a few became capitalists themselves. This I heard from both employer and employee. Still the share of these laborers in production is pretty small.

Tuesday, August 10

I STARTED for Althorp House, leaving the "Hen and Chickens" Hotel, Birmingham, where I had been staying, not without a feeling of satisfaction, for it was not as cheap as it was bad, or, as Longfellow said of a hotel called "The Raven," "The bird has a very foul nest and a very, very long bill." I traveled second-class, as usual, to Northampton. It was a closely built town, rather old and dirty, with a little admixture of modern improvement. I hired the best-looking cab at the station, a shabby four-wheeler, with a horse that was in keeping with the old trap behind him. I made a bargain for seven shillings to drive to Earl Spencer's, about seven miles away. The drive was over a good road with rather quiet English scenery on either side.

One notices here, and almost everywhere in England that I have been, except in the suburbs of the cities, that the houses are few and far between — not scattered along the road as the farm buildings are with us. Sometimes there is not a dwelling-house in sight, and yet the fields about are all ploughed or planted, or are well-kept pasture lands. I drove up to the house about four in the afternoon.

Althorp House has no architectural beauty or pretensions. It is plain, but large, and placed low to the ground, as are almost all English houses. It is built of brick, painted, and does not look as picturesque as the stables, which are of stone. The house is so well proportioned that one does not take in at first glance from the outside its great size, with its magnificent ballroom, its long picture galleries, spacious libraries, and broad, grand stairs. But on entering and going to my room and asking questions, I soon perceived it. At the door I was met by the butler who, when I gave my name, said he was awaiting me, and ordered my "luggage" to be carried up. I was to have the "Mignard" room.

The butler said that Lord and Lady Spencer were out on the cricket ground and that "his Lordship" had left word for me to come there if I liked. I was put in charge of a quiet young manservant or valet who showed me to my room where soon my luggage was brought up and unstrapped, hot water appeared, and I was asked if I wished anything else. I washed and got ready — but what clothes should I wear? I had on a rough Scottish suit of mixed color, while in my trunk I had nicer clothes that I had worn in town. I had never heard what was worn in the country, but I concluded to wear what I thought was the most sensible thing, and, at all events, to avoid being overdressed. So I kept on my rough things, put on my thick shoes, and donned my cloth hat. On coming downstairs I met Lord Charles Bruce, Lord Spencer's brother-in-law, and to my satisfaction, he had on clothes very much like my own in general appearance and cut, and he had also a soft cloth hat. He took me out to the cricket ground, a beautiful, level, grassy spot of oval shape, with fine old trees on the margin, containing about eight acres or more of well-rolled turf. The game was over and all the household had gone to the kennels, so we went on in a path between tall trees till we came up with the party. Spencer had on a cricket suit with a red handkerchief tied about his neck and a flannel shirt. Countess Spencer was plainly dressed and as handsome and charming as usual.

In the kennels there were about one hundred and fifty dogs. The keepers said that they knew each hound by name. On going to my room to get ready for dinner I found that my luggage had all been unpacked, and my things neatly put away, well and conveniently arranged in drawers, on the dressing-table or the washstand. I found laid out my dress suit, a clean shirt, white tie, handkerchief, my evening shoes, and black silk stockings. Hot water was at hand, and on the writing-table were paper, pens, ink, wax, and a card of the departure and arrival of mails. The room was high and the walls covered with portraits of distinguished persons mostly by the celebrated French painter Mignard. There was one tall window looking out upon a terrace, well-kept flower gardens, and more distant grove and park. The room was the one King William IV slept in and Spencer said the bed was the one he used. On com-

ALTHORP HOUSE: EARL SPENCER'S

ing down to dinner I found the curtains all drawn and candles lighted, though at eight o'clock, the hour for dinner, it was still plain daylight with sun shining brightly out of doors. The waiters were dressed in a quiet sort of livery; their hair was not powdered. At dinner were Lady Charles Bruce, Lady Clifden, sisters of Lady Spencer, Lady Spencer, Lord Charles Bruce, and Lord Spencer. I took in Lady Spencer, Spencer took in Lady Charles, and Lord Charles, Lady Clifden. After dinner the ladies went out leaving the men behind.

The conversation during dinner and in the evening was light and agreeable and such as to put a stranger perfectly at his ease. They did not talk, as people so often do before strangers, about their personal friends, speaking of "Will" and "John" and "Susan" and "Jane," or using nicknames, which would mean nothing to the stranger, but if they did speak of friends at all, they spoke in such a way that I was able to understand to whom they referred. Consideration and good manners here are second nature, not forced or laid aside on familiarity; nor is there anything formal or unnatural. All retired about eleven o'clock. Breakfast is when we like in the morning. I decided to have mine with Spencer and Lord Charles at half-past nine. The ladies are to breakfast in their rooms.

As we retired candles were handed to us and we said good-night on the broad hall stairs. In my room I found my clothes that I had worn during the day taken away and my night things laid out for me, and the shutters fastened to, the curtains drawn, and the window closed. It is so strange that in this country of fresh air they so universally close the windows at night. I can understand their wanting the curtains drawn as the dawn breaks so early, but I managed to open my window and arranged the curtain so as to let the air in and yet keep the light out. By the way, what we call window "shades," they call "blinds"; though we use the term Venetian "blinds" in the English sense; what we call "blinds," which in England are only on the inside and are without slats, they call "shutters."

Wednesday, August 11

I WAS awake at eight and three quarters or a quarter "to" nine, as they say, instead of our quarter "of" nine. The young valet, the same who always waits on me, brought my clothes all brushed and folded, and shoes I had worn the day before, blacked. He drew the curtains fully aside, spread open the shutters, brought in hot water, prepared a large cold bath in a movable bathtub, — for there are no bathrooms with set tubs in the house, — put my washstand in order, folded up the towels that were sufficiently clean and put out some fresh ones, laid out a clean shirt and collar, and took away my things worn the evening before.

All this was done quietly and quickly, while I was in bed, though without haste. On asking about the weather, he replied, "It's a fine day." Out of my window I saw three or four men working on the flower beds, and what beautiful flowers they were, with green shrubs or small evergreens to set them off! Breakfast consisted of coffee, tea, fresh eggs, with "Tuesday, August 10," written on them, fish, chops, orange marmalade, etc. All was very informal, and we mostly waited on ourselves, even getting up to get things from the side table.

Spencer was to go to Northampton to sit as judge in a county court. Many of the small cases are decided, not before a regular court with a judge, but before a tribunal of the Lord of the Manor and some of the local magistrates, aided by a young barrister. There are no formal papers signed or what we technically call "pleadings," but they hear the story of each party in person unrepresented by barristers or solicitors, and decide on general principles without much pretense at legal technicality. This proceeding settles many a small question at little or no cost to the parties, while the more complicated ones, or those involving larger amounts, or such as either party wishes to appeal, are taken to a regular court.

Spencer serves without pay and for no political advantage, and certainly not for the sake of renown in such small cases in a country town. I wonder how many a Cleon or Ben Butler would do as much for the people from a sense of duty alone?

Lord Charles spent the morning with me in the wonderful library. The catalogue was written alphabetically in small parchment-bound books. Numbers were added to the names and these numbers referred to a large book giving the locations, so that in changing the location of a book it was only necessary to change the number of the shelf in the latter book, and the original catalogue remained untouched.

I saw Dr. Johnson's copy of the last edition of his dictionary that was published during his lifetime, with notes in his own handwriting. In the room of treasures I saw some of the very earliest specimens of block printing before movable type had been invented, and some of the old blocks themselves. Several of these were on Bible subjects for teaching the illiterate by pictures. In this room I also saw the first edition of the first book ever printed. We looked over many old German and Italian books, examining the paper and type. Cicero was the first *classic* ever printed. This library has the best collection of block printing and early books anywhere in the world with the exception of the British Museum. (The next spring, when going over the old Library in Milan, they showed me a rare early book and said there is only one other copy in the world, and I replied, "Yes, and I saw it at Althorp House." To this the librarian added, "If you have seen that collection we have very little to show you." Some years afterwards Lord S. sold all this rare collection in order to make up for heavy losses caused by a dishonest agent. It was bought as a whole by Mrs. Ryland and made a part of the Ryland Public Library at Manchester, England, and is kept all together under the title of the "Althorp Collection.")

There I saw the earliest edition of Shakespeare printed soon after his death under the direction of the very players he had taught by mouth. They and Ben Jonson did not hesitate to ascribe the plays to Shakespeare in the most open terms. Ben Jonson's comment in his well-known poem on the portrait of Shakespeare also appears in this edition. When one sees Ben Jonson's admiration of Shakespeare, a person whom he met so frequently and with whom he conversed so often, it seems incredible that he should have believed him to be the author of these great works unless he, Shakespeare, had the mental capacity and showed it in his conversation; and then, too, we must remember that many of these plays were not fully written out when they were first acted, but Shakespeare, in the presence of his actors and friends, would often make suggestions and alterations, and if he was capable of that he was capable of writing the first drafts. It is true Jonson says that he (S.) knew "little Latin and less Greek," but we must remember that Jonson was a marvelous scholar and he would have said the same of almost any Harvard graduate who had elected the classics — if we except the high honor men — and that the historical plays are but adaptations of well-known English literature and did not require original research. However, I cannot enter deeply into the argument, but when we actually saw the first edition with the portrait of Shakespeare and Ben Jonson's reference to it, it was far more convincing than merely reading of it in dissertations.

In the afternoon Lord Charles and I set up the lawn tennis. It involved pretty hard work and a good deal of stooping in marking off the lines with whitewash by means of a brush and long strings. Countess S. said she was sorry to have us work so long and tediously, but they had no servants at hand who could do it. This is another illustration of the English domestic system. There were standing about an abundance, both outdoors and in, of men quite capable of doing this work; but not one was found, within whose duty it would lie. Neither the gardener nor the footmen nor the valets nor the bootblacks nor, of course, the maids would help. Our hostess knew this so well that she did not even ask them, for it would have meant point-blank refusal. They had one man-of-all-work for such odd jobs, but he was away in a distant part of the enormous grounds, somewhere, perhaps, in the 27,000 acres Spencer is reputed to own.

I played a game with Lady Spencer, and getting too much ahead, I left one half of her court for her to tend while I tended the whole of mine; with this advantage she beat me. I played three close sets with Lord Charles and was beaten in two out of three.

Thursday, August 12

THE morning was spent largely over the piano. Lord Charles, who had made a study of musical theory and composition, explained many interesting musical laws to me and played very agreeably. After that we adjourned again to the treasure room of the library to spend a couple of engrossing hours over some valuable books. In trying to open one of the windows I broke a pane of glass. I feared that it might injure the valuable treasures, but they assured me that it would not.

In the afternoon went over to a chapel some distance off where were the Spencer tombs and monuments. In going through the fields Lady Spencer and Lady Clifden did not hesitate to walk through a herd of black oxen and were not at all troubled as the lazy brutes lowered their heads and swayed their large horns as they sullenly turned off the path. At the further gate we met Spencer who had been waiting for us, and there the ladies turned to walk back again alone through this drove. I complimented them on their courage, but they said that there was no danger and that they were used to the cattle.

In the chapel Lord Spencer showed me the tombstone of the Washingtons with the family coat of arms on it. The design was a shield with three stars above and three horizontal stripes below. These stars and stripes led Spencer to think that Washington had his coat of arms adopted, with a slight change, for the design of the American flag and shield. This did not seem consistent with Washington's character and above all with his modesty. Spencer said he had shown Charles Sumner the same, with the same comment. On getting back Spencer and I looked up the only American histories I could find in the library, but no light was thrown on the subject. (On returning to America I found a complete account of the adoption of the flag, with which Washington seems to have had nothing to do.)

There were in the house the two children of Lady Clifden, her son (the present Viscount Clifden), and a daughter, called Lady Lilah. They were about thirteen and fifteen, but did not appear at table except at lunch. I noticed that the governess carefully corrected the pronunciation of the Clifden children and modulated their speech. I had always remarked on the fine voices the English had, but presumed it was a product of the climate. I asked about this and they told me that all the well-to-do English children were carefully taught to speak, almost as people are taught to sing, and to avoid all nasal or harsh utterances. With us in America children as a rule have been allowed to talk with little or no correction of this sort for fear of making them artificial or unnatural. As a matter of fact, they usually imitate people and are quite as artificial and unnatural in a bad way as they might be made natural, by second nature, in a good way. Every afternoon we had the tea now so fashionable all over England. It consisted of tea, very hot, bread and butter, cut very thin, and a few light cakes. It was very refreshing and helped one amazingly till eight o'clock, yet without spoiling the appetite for dinner. The lunch hour was two.

Friday, August 13
LORD SPENCER at breakfast asked me if I would like to ride with him to visit some farms. "Riding" in England always means on horseback, and "driving," in a carriage. He gave me a very handsome mount, a really splendid horse. We rode mostly through the fields or country lanes and had to open many gates. Spencer,

a noted horseman and huntsman, complimented me on my bringing the horse to the gates and opening them. He is a splendid manager of horses I readily see. I wondered how far his leaning a good deal forward, with back curved and rather short stirrups with knees bent, helped him. This very likely gives him power and control in rough riding.

We met a stranger, apparently a well-to-do farmer, with a broad, ruddy face and side whiskers, sitting erect on his saddle, with a self-confident air. Spencer asked him about his horse, if it were not such and such a one, and inquired as to how it went. The man at first was a little gruff and almost rude, as if he thought that the person addressing him had no right to be so familiar. Another horseman coming up addressed Spencer by his title. Immediately the poor farmer was in consternation. He blushed to the roots of his hair, stammered, and apologized; and yet he really had neither said nor done anything which was not perfectly proper; but such is the deference, amounting almost to obsequiousness, ingrained into the English people for the nobility.

The pastoral views were charming. The wheat was not yet harvested, but was yellow and made a striking contrast to the green grass of the pasture lands and the brown of the freshly ploughed fields. The lowlands were soggy from recent rains; all the work of St. Swithun! In the early afternoon I made a small sketch of the house in black and white. Spencer recommended my taking up colors as so much more rich and interesting.

This afternoon Lady Spencer invited me into her *sanctum sanctorum*, a prettily furnished den on the first floor. The door to it was so successfully concealed in the paneling on the side of the great stairs that I had not known of its existence. She showed me the many conveniences of her writing-table, the pretty furniture and settings, and we had an hour's delightful chat on friends and leaders in English society and on books and authors.

I forgot to say that on the previous Thursday we played some games of "go bang," a game something like the reverse of checkers. Lady Clifden beat Lady Spencer, I beat Lady Clifden, and Lady Spencer beat me, a result very like the celebrated championship at cricket between Harrow, Eton, and Winchester. One year when Eton beat Harrow with an inning to spare, Harrow beat Winchester also with an inning to spare, and then, when Winchester came to play Eton, to everybody's surprise it won also with an inning to spare.

The Spencers are evidently very fond of each other, kind and considerate, and plan to be much together in their daily arrangements. (On the death of Lady Spencer I received a letter dated the 9th of December, 1903, from the Earl in reply to one of sympathy from me, saying: "Yours is the third letter which I have received in a week from your country, and I assure you that it touches me much to know that my good friends in the United States valued my beloved wife's character and charm and sympathize with me in my great sorrow. It is a terrible thought that my constant helpmate and adviser for over forty-five years has left me and that I have to face the world alone without her. But I must face it. I must be thankful for long and blessed years of happiness and peace." It truly seemed as if his desire for life and active work had departed with her, for he did not accomplish much after her death. He outlived her seven years.)

During lunch the Spencers were discussing some plans for altering Althorp House. There was one that I preferred, for which I spoke favorably and hoped they would adopt in preference to the others. It showed up the grand stairs, while the two other plans gave less space from which to see them. In the afternoon Lord and Lady Charles Bruce left us.

After dinner, in the evening, Lady Spencer and I played two games of "go bang," one of which lasted over two hours, as each of us tried hard to win, Lady Spencer having beaten me in the first game. We did not get through till a quarter to one, when at last, on account of the lateness of the hour, I gave the game away. I was for stopping sooner, but Lady S. was for having it out if possible. Poor Spencer sat up all the time and was very sleepy, but was unwilling to retire and yet was most polite and kind. I felt awkward at having kept him up so late.

During this visit, though warned by my father to use titles as little as possible, I made an unnecessary use of one in speaking to Lady Clifden. I saw she fairly cringed, so I learned my lesson.

Saturday, August 14
IN the afternoon Lady Spencer left in company with her sister Lady Clifden and the two children for the up train and I half an hour or so later for the down train, "down" in this case means north-bound and "up" south for London. (Lady Clifden was married, a second time, soon after this and may have been going to London with her sister for her trousseau.)

I was sorry to leave where they had been so kind and where I had enjoyed the visit so much, but I must not outstay my welcome. I had got to have a feeling of real affection for Spencer, as for a kind and generous elder brother. This afternoon as the ladies were departing I noticed that he had tears in his eyes. Something had happened which moved him very much, I could only guess what. He has no children, and it may be that saying good-bye to his sister-in-law's children, one of them a boy and heir to the Clifden title and estates, made him feel his own deprivation. I was sorry, too, to leave the house with its wonderful library and its five hundred beautiful oil paintings, and my own room with its portrait of Molière by Largillière, 1656–1746; Seigneur de Saint-Evremond and Hortense Mamini, "Duchesse Mazarin," by Godfrey Kneller, 1648–1723; Louis XIV; Colbert; Julie d'Argennes; Mlle. de l'Enclos; Anne of Austria, "Soror, mater, filia, et conjux regum"; Lucy Barlow, *alias* Walter; Henrietta of Orleans; Madame de Montespan as Diana; and Marie Angélique de Roussille, Duchesse de Fontanges, all by Mignard, 1610–95. In the gallery is said to be the best private collection in the world of portraits by Sir Joshua Reynolds. There were also some portraits by Van Dyck and a very beautiful Madonna by Raphael.

Lord Spencer sent me to the station in an Irish jaunting car, I perched on one side, over the wheels, and my baggage balancing me on the other. He had picked this up when he was Lord Lieutenant of Ireland between 1868 and 1874. One felt the motion of the horse a good deal, and going round curves one had to hold on to the back of the seat; but it went rolling and jouncing along very fast and seemed to be easy on the horse.

CHAPTER V

LORD YOUNG'S VIA YORK AND EDINBURGH

I took the train for York and stopped a few hours at Peterboro to see the cathedral, one of the most important Norman churches in England. The choir aisle has on one side the tomb of Queen Catherine of Aragon and on the opposite side the former burial-place of Mary, Queen of Scots, her body having been later removed to Westminster Abbey. The chimes were ringing. Inside I seemed to feel the sound more than hear it, and outside, the bells, even close to, were more mellow, soft, and harmonious than any I had ever heard before. In the streets the people were selling their goods, one fishmonger outcrying another or running down the quality of the other's fish. Arrived at York in the early evening.

Sunday, August 15
Attended morning service at the Cathedral. They were mending the organ so the choir sang without accompaniment. The choir was of men and boys and is reputed to be the best now in England. I preferred it to the choir of the Temple. We had a full choral service. The pitch was perfectly kept, and as the beautiful chords died away among the arches, I fully realized my very dream of cathedral singing. How I can recall the notes all day long as the monotone of a response broke into a rich, harmonious chord or how the solemn chants were sung antiphonally, one side confirming what the other sang or adding to the thought! It was the praise of God sung by His most perfect instrument, the hu-

EDINBURGH

man voice, cleared of its defects and artificialities — and all in one of His most beautiful temples.

Edinburgh, Tuesday, August 17
I WAS very much struck with the picturesqueness of the city on my arrival last evening. The castle, right across a park and close at hand and yet so high up, was but dimly marked against a cloud-flecked sky, and the few lights shining here and there with a full moon over the castle, so still and calm and steady between the flitting clouds, gave one the idea of feudal times and of deep mystery and unreality. It all looked so like a picture, and so quiet, that it made a great contrast to the street and the moving crowd of people nearer by; and altogether it gave me a new idea of how beautiful a city might be. In the new part the buildings were handsome and solid; in the old part, high and dirty. I saw one block seven stories high, besides attic and basement.

I noticed a large number of recruits to the army in all the cities and read in the papers that the army and navy were both to be increased. In the evening the streets were crowded, and the people seemed to be jolly and the children played their games. There was a general air of neatness, cheerfulness, and good-will. A grand view of the city, the Firth, and the land between I got from the top of Nelson's Monument about four o'clock.

I came across a wandering preacher standing on a light movable chair or stool. He was assisted in singing by a young man who sang in unison with him. The preacher read texts and short printed sermons while all the time the audience was attentive and quiet, although composed largely of rough-looking men. It was in the poor part of the city in the old town about eight o'clock in the evening.

Wednesday, August 18

AFTER lunch drove to call on Lord Young who, when I met him in London, had made me promise that I would look him up on coming to Edinburgh. He has a superb house on Moray Place, but is now living in his country cottage about five miles from here on the shore of the Firth. I was lucky enough, however, to find him in his town house, though it was nominally closed. He asked me to come to dinner at his country house and I accepted. "No dress suits, and everything informal." The life there is simple like our way of living at Manchester. He does not keep up the formal servants of his town house. While he has a butler or valet and some maids, he himself brought me my hot water. He told me he has just visited the Duke of Argyll, and said that Inverary, where I am going soon, is the pleasantest place on earth, people and all. I missed the Duke of Argyll in London, but I have since received a letter from the Duchess asking me to visit them for a fortnight in September. Lord Young has fourteen children, of which number Lady Young speaks with pride. I met there a Miss Goldie, sister of the famous Cambridge University stroke oar, said to be the best there ever was in that University. Passed a pleasant evening and was invited to come to-morrow, an invitation I readily accepted.

One of the daughters sang with a good voice, sweet tones, and a natural ear, but needed some cultivation. A beautiful sunset and exhilarating six-mile walk before dinner along the shore. Lord Young is noted for his keenness of intellect and yet is kindly. He is a smoker, but does not believe in smoking. He is said to be one of the best wits in Scotland and an eminent judge of more than ordinary ability among the able judges of Great Britain. I said, "Smoking must sometimes do good. It quiets the nerves." "Yes," said he, "it does quiet the nerves *of a smoker*." I thought that perhaps very near the truth. A beautiful moonlight drive back to Edinburgh.

Thursday, August 19

AFTER lunch went to 28 Moray Place. (They pronounce it Murray, as home is pronounced hume, and gold, gould.) The library and stairway were the handsomest private ones I have yet seen. There I met Lord Young, who is Lord Advocate of Scotland, his wife, and one daughter. They showed me over the house. Walked about the city with Lord Young, who pointed out Sir Walter Scott's house where most of the novels were written, now barristers' rooms. We went to see the National Gallery, but found it closed. Back of Lord Young's house in Moray Place there is a garden overlooking a steep dell. Several of the neighbors, but none else, have admission to it, and it makes a delightful private park. Drove to Silverknowe, Lord Young's cottage. Took a short walk with Young and was glad to have him say that he did not think the knowledge of Roman law was worth the expense of a year's study; for I had been considering taking a course at Oxford, Cambridge, or Germany in that subject, but hardly wished to give the time to it. I asked him if he thought the knowledge of the Roman law might not be useful in settling doubtful points which arise in our law. He said it had been useful to a certain extent, but that now it was a cake with all the plums taken out. He said that slavery and the social laws which made a large part of the Roman law, of course have no application nowadays, that New York and London probably had more commerce and commercial questions in a year than Rome had in one hundred, and that the mode of establishing testaments was very clumsy, while their land was held by an entirely different system. He said he believed far too much has been made of the Roman law. His opinion is all the more valuable, as in Scotland they make a point of knowing and quoting the Civil or Roman law and he, himself, is well up in it.

He spoke of Mayne's "Ancient Law," and thought it not worth reading, not because Mayne did not know his subject or did not write well, but because the subject itself was not a fruitful one. (I met Mr. Mayne at Sir William Vernon Harcourt's dinner in London and he is considered the best authority in the world on ancient law. Indeed, Mayne not only wrote the masterpiece on ancient law, but developed the important theorem in the history of law; that law is in the main the embodiment of the customs of peoples.) Lord Young approved of Stevens and Brougham highly. At dinner we talked of John Stuart Mill's writings.

After the ladies retired I explained our caucus system of nominations in America. Lord Young told me several very amusing stories. One story told of Lord Young is this: As he was presiding over the trial of a very important case in which the water board was a party, there entered the court-room a stout man with a red nose and blurry eyes, who pushed his way forward to a conspicuous seat in the front. Lord Y. leaned over his desk and in an undertone asked a young barrister who that was coming into the room. The barrister replied, "He is a trustee of the water board, my lord." Lord Y. then said, "From his looks, I do not know of any one to whom I could more safely trust water." (I later heard the following story: Lord Young chancing to meet Austin, the poet laureate, asked him what he was doing. Austin replied, "I am writing a few verses to keep the wolf from the door." Lord Young, quick as a flash, replied, "Do you read the verses to the wolf?" — a bit cruel considering Austin's uncertain reputation, but Young knew him very well and their acquaintance would admit of chaffing.) Lord Young's humor was not biting or sarcastic. He made very firm friends and his relatives and in-laws liked him well. He complimented the best American wit as fine and delicate. In the evening there was family singing and they made me sing a negro song, hearing that I knew some. I selected "Stop that Knocking at the Door"; I also sang the Irish song, "I learned Both Readin' and Wroitin'." Passed a very pleasant social evening and have made, I think, some real friends in the family. They asked me to come again when they are to be in town and could entertain and present me to the Scottish Bar and social leaders. Lord Young gave me a copy of Mackenzie on Roman Law, writing his autograph in it. Lord Young, three of his daughters, and Miss Goldie walked with me part of the way back to Edinburgh, I going alone the rest of the distance. The moon was just past the full, and the sight as I approached could hardly be surpassed in any city anywhere, unless at Athens.

CHAPTER VI
ROSSIE PRIORY: LORD KINNAIRD'S

Saturday, August 21

LEFT Edinburgh for Inchture where I found Lord Kinnaird's carriage waiting for me, and I drove to Rossie Priory by a very picturesque route. Met Lord and Lady Kinnaird in the study. Lord Kinnaird took me out for a stroll. He is interesting, communicative, and extremely kind. We had a most pleasant and varied talk. He showed me his gardens which he had planted and his rockery and artificial waterfall. The park was full of people whom he allows to come out from Dundee and roam all over it. He had swings put up for them and they made good use of all their privileges.

Speaking of Plimsoll he said he could sympathize with him, for he himself had worked hard over a bill for improving the condition, health, and safety of miners, and though all the while men were dying from bad management which could have been prevented by legislation, yet it was ten years before he could get the bill passed, and that he, Lord Kinnaird, well knew the feeling when others would not take any interest in so important a measure.

Telling him of Lord Young's opinion of Roman law, Kinnaird said I might well trust it, for no one in Scotland knew better than he what was important in the study of law. At dinner we had Lord and Lady Kinnaird and a young man who is studying farming on the estate. Lady Kinnaird is much interested in geology and paleontology, about which we talked a little.

Apropos of trusting people in order to bring out their

ROSSIE PRIORY: LORD KINNAIRD'S

best, I explained our Harvard Dining-Hall Association system. When in the old, bare room of the association, which was a converted railroad station on Holmes Place, there was much noise and disorder, and sometimes rolls of bread were thrown about. The question came as to allowing the association to use the new Memorial Hall with its fine inside architecture, old portraits, and stained-glass windows. I was then in my senior year in College and President Eliot consulted me. I told him I believed that with better surroundings the men would behave better and rise to the confidence placed in them. He said he believed so, too. I was appointed the first president of the association on its going into Memorial Hall, the following year, being my first in the law school. Our predictions proved true. No damage has ever been done to pictures, stained glass, or architecture.

Sunday, August 22
EARLY service in the chapel of the Abbey at 8.15 after which we had breakfast at 9.30. Walked alone until the second service at quarter-past eleven. After lunch looked at some of the pictures in the Priory. Many of them are by old masters such as Raphael, Michael Angelo, Van Dyck, and Velasquez, and some held to be unusually good specimens. There are also antique busts and altars from Italy. The old English families had a great opportunity to secure Italian works of art in the early part of the century when they could be got at reasonable prices. In the main corridor leading from the front door are some ancient mosaics of the best classical period brought with great care from near Rome. One of these is quite large and as beautiful as the mosaic of the Battle of Issus in the Vatican. Pictures, mosaics,

and other antiques were bought abroad jointly by the Duke of Bedford and the father of the present Lord Kinnaird years ago. The collection was divided between them on their return to Great Britain.

At the luncheon were all the grandchildren of Lord K. and his son-in-law Mr. Ogilvy. After lunch the children took me to see the fernery and set all the fountains playing. They showed me King James's bed, which is really very handsome, with carved and inlaid woods. Took a long walk with Lord Kinnaird and his grandchildren. Visited the fruit gardens, where the cherries and gooseberries were under nets to protect them from the birds. The peaches and plums were either trained on the walls or were in greenhouses. The fruits will not otherwise ripen in this climate for want of sun. I saw figs growing under glass. I got to be great friends with the grandchildren. All these are the children of a daughter, so none of them can inherit the title, which will go to his brother whom I met in London.

Dinner was at 7.30. The Kinnairds are very religious and have three services on Sunday, but to-day there was no evening service, as the clergyman, Mr. Simmons, was unwell. They belong to the Church of England. They have morning and evening services on week days and all of these are in the chapel of the Abbey close by. Passed a quiet Sunday evening with pleasant and varied talk.

Monday, August 23
No early service this morning, as the chaplain was still under the weather. Drove with Lord K. and his son-in-law, Mr. Ogilvy, to Dundee. First we went to a sort of reform school. Lord K. is on the committee to carry out the work. They receive as an advance three shillings sixpence a week for each child from the National Gov-

ernment. This money is collected from the parents of the children if they are able to pay; otherwise the money is made up from the poor-rates and, as I understand, then returned to the national treasury.

The committee has authority by Act of Parliament to take in any boy or girl whose parents are so bad as likely to lead the children into crime or injure them through neglect. The child, either boy or girl, on being examined by a magistrate and found in that condition, can be kept in the school until sixteen years of age. In the school they do useful work such as making their own clothes, sewing jute bags, making scrubbing and blacking brushes, splitting wood, and the like. Of course they also study and play and the boys undergo military drill. If they behave well, they are given a chance to make money by their work, but this is not given them immediately; instead it is put in savings banks and they can draw at stated periods on the deposits when they come out. They are generally treated with kindness and the more trustworthy are allowed to go about the streets for certain purposes, and several are apprenticed to trades or to farmers.

They got up a special drill on my behalf, and when it was over, the spirit and eagerness with which the boys resumed their work and their evident happiness showed the success of the scheme. Boys convicted of smaller first offenses are also allowed to be taken in, though they do not admit criminals. There are some 150 boys there and the school has worked well for thirteen years. The boys are said to be kind and helpful to one another. This was all a project of Lord Kinnaird's.

I next went to see some linen works, where from the flax in an uncombed state they spun and wove all sorts of stuff from the fine linens to sail cloth. About 700 children between the ages of seven and fourteen were employed by the mill, but by a recent Act of Parliament they can work only four and a half hours a day during one week and six the alternate, and they are obliged to go to school every day but Saturday. For carrying out this law they are divided into squads or shifts. I went to the half-time school where these children were taught. I examined their writing and heard some of them read and recite while others did long multiplication for me. Some of these children were bright and on the average not unlike our public school children. The building was not quite up to our public school standard. They said the children are no more troublesome than those of a better class.

I went to the library in the Albert Institute and saw an ingenious arrangement for showing instantaneously whether books were in or out. It was a device that seemed well worth copying. It also told automatically when a book was out overtime, so that the librarian could see, without moving from his seat and at a glance, when any one was overdue.

Visited the Museum and Royal Exchange. I was taken about by an agent of the committee of the "Prison Aid Society" for employing discharged convicts. A month before a convict who has behaved well in prison and seems worthy of trust is to be discharged, the jailer reports him to the agent, sending photograph and statement of character. If the case seems worthy, it is reported to the committee. If the committee approves, the agent then goes to the managers of the various mills and makes arrangements to have the man employed without having the owners of the mills, the overseers, or the fellow-laborers know anything about the man's career.

According to an Act of Parliament the discharged man has to report to the police weekly, but to save him the disgrace of this and the chance of his status being made known in this way, the committee has made special arrangements that the police shall be furnished information as to the man's whereabouts by the committee. This was all Lord Kinnaird's work and it has so far been successful. It has been in operation three years.

Lord K. has also started coffee houses, very much more successful than those we have in the United States, as far as I know of them. There are fourteen regular and thirty branches and they make money by selling coffee at a penny a large cup and soup at twopence a plate. The management is put in the hands of a committee from the poorer classes and the manager of each establishment has a slight interest beside his salary.

Those coffee houses that we have started in America are run from above as philanthropies, and naturally the working-man does not like to accept charity and takes little interest in the success, but here by giving him a control he feels independent and self-respecting.

Lord K. told me that the last thirteen have all been started from the profits of the first and succeeding ones. As a result of a recent Act of Parliament which shuts up all liquor shops at 11 P.M. till 8 A.M. the next day, the coffee houses are made still more successful.

Drove home by way of a farm and saw steam ploughing machines and a reaper at work. Lord K. showed me a farm so bad a few years back that his tenant gave it up. Lord K. took it himself and by draining and subsoiling it and using suitable fertilizers, it has now on it the best wheat and barley crops in the neighborhood.

Played lawn tennis from tea to dinner. In the evening played bezique with Lord and Lady K. and Angus Ogilvy, Lord K.'s eldest grandson, an Eton boy. Lord K., who is sixty-eight years of age, occasionally drops asleep, but wakes up again bright and ready to play his hand well. He and Lady K. get up early for chapel services before breakfast, work very hard all day for their tenants and over charities, and go to bed rather late, and it seems to me they do not give themselves enough rest.

Tuesday, August 24
IN the Dundee "Advertiser" was a notice of my visit to Dundee, speaking of me as the son of the popular writer of "*Three* Years Before the Mast" and the grandson of Dana, the American poet. This is St. Bartholomew's Day. We had a full service at 11 A.M.

After service I worked over an idea of mine for a machine to gather up and bind the barley and wheat lying on the ground. Every other process of harvesting is done by machinery except this, and it requires a number of laborers to be temporarily employed who have no other useful work on the farms at other times.

After lunch went to a flower and vegetable show at Inchture got up by Lord and Lady Kinnaird. I was made judge and awarded the first, second, and third prizes for cut flowers arranged in beds, which I was to consider as to taste in arrangement and harmony in color as well as the quality of the flowers. Drove back and played cricket from tea to dinner. After dinner bezique again with the same as last night.

Wednesday, August 25
RAINED almost all the time before lunch. Cleared up later and Lord K. drove Lady K., the Reverend Mr.

Simmons and myself to see Macbeth's castle or rather the site of it. It was on the top of a very high ridge of hills with almost inaccessible sides except from one direction. The castle must have looked grandly and have been as secure as Edinburgh or Stirling. Saw also the place where Macbeth met the witches and the Birnam wood which, to Macbeth's horror, came to Dunsinane castle.

After tea played lawn tennis with Angus who would not take a handicap, though I beat him badly. He is a plucky young fellow. I have seen a good deal of the Ogilvy children the last few days and have become a great crony with each of them. They are clever, jolly children, and very easy to get on with and readily amused. Played cards again in the evening. I have breakfast in my room as a rule, and take up some fresh figs, apricots, and grapes the evening before to eat in the morning. There are very extensive hothouses for raising fruits of all sorts at the Priory and they occasionally have some rare kinds at dinner.

In the afternoon, before tea, Lord K. showed me some of his cottages. The newer ones were built of concrete. Concrete is one part Portland cement and seven parts clean, small stones or gravel. This is laid in solidly so that as it petrifies, the house becomes from foundation to ridgepole, where the roof is of the same, one solid stone. This concrete becomes harder and harder in the course of years. It is said to be practically waterproof. It dries quickly, more so than ordinary plaster. I saw one which was papered and the paper was perfectly smooth, although it had been on the walls all winter without a fire in the house. This construction does away with all mason's work and with plaster and lathing. Lord K. showed me one cottage that had been built by one man and two boys, none of them skilled masons, in twenty-one days. Kinnaird had a new method of ventilation which he had invented from the principle of the inverted siphon and connected with the chimney flues. He showed me how it worked. He has put this device in all his newer cottages.

Thursday, August 26
WE drove to a flower, fruit, and vegetable show at Dundee. There I met the American Consul, who kindly introduced himself. Went to see an engineer at Errol about my invention. I explained the details and he gave me encouragement. He said that if I should succeed I could save half the hand labor and perhaps all of it in this gathering and binding. I lunched in this queer, dirty little town of Errol and got back to the Priory at half-past five. There I found Lord Kinnaird playing lawn tennis with his grandson. I played cricket till dinner. As usual I took Lady K. in to dinner. She is bright, well-informed, and entertaining. It turned out afterwards that she was suffering all the while from a splitting headache and had to give up after dinner and go to her room. Talked over American politics in the evening with Kinnaird and Mr. Ogilvy. (I did not have time in these visits to have this machine built after my plans, and soon after returning to the United States some fourteen months later, I heard that the device or one very like it had been patented and was being put on the market.)

Friday, August 27
LEFT the Priory to-day. I drove to the station at twelve and rode on the train as far as Perth with Lord K. I had taken a second-class ticket as usual and he had

bought a first-class, but he insisted upon sitting with me in the second-class carriage so as to talk. He showed me from the carriage window a high precipice on the land of Lord Gray which he (Lord K.) very nearly fell over during a hunt.

Lord Kinnaird is an instance of a useful member of the House of Lords. Not being so mixed up in active politics as members of the Lower House, he had more time to give to useful legislation. For example, he gave years of time to laws for abolishing the smoke nuisance in large manufacturing cities in England. He was one of the pioneers in this movement. He told me that it was very discouraging, and he thought beside general apathy and the opposition of those who would be put to expense, one of the chief obstacles to getting anything done was that so few educated Englishmen had any scientific training. He thought there were not more than two or three members of both houses of Parliament put together who know enough chemistry to understand the burning of the candle. I have already mentioned some of the other projects to which Lord K. has given much time.

I may say generally that the members of the nobility do not use titles in talking to one another and do not expect their friends or visitors to use them except perhaps on first meeting them. It is only the servants, persons who have business relations with them, and tradespeople, who use the title on all occasions, and, when it becomes necessary to use a title in calling their attention, the title should not be emphasized. Friends call them Spencer, Kinnaird, Sir John, etc. I think they like to be spoken to in just the same way that one would speak to distinguished Americans, such as Lowell or Longfellow.

Beside a lack of scientific education I was surprised to find how little those I have met know of English history outside the few things with which their family and neighborhood may be associated or which have some recent political significance. I had assumed that every Englishman would know his country's history by heart and could give the dates of all the kings, but I found they were not all Lord Macaulays by any means.

The Kinnairds belong to a very old family dating from 1176, Radulphus de Kinnard, under King William the Lion. The first Baron Kinnaird was created in 1682. The family used to live in the old Kinnaird castle, which was of mediæval type and uncomfortable. Rossie Priory, built of stone, was begun in 1807 on the Braes of Carse. It is on a high terrace, is extensive and imposing, of delightful proportions, and the chapel especially beautifully finished with carvings, stone mullions, and tasteful doorways. There are fine specimens of rare and varied firs, some very large. One, they told me, extends its branches in a circumference of one hundred fifty feet.

The view from the house or Priory is varied. In front, and to the left, one sees the valleys of the Carse and of the Tay with cultivated fields, and in the distance the smoke of Dundee, often colored by the sunlight and purple from the effect of its remoteness. The ruins of Moncur Castle, "hoary with age" and rich in legends of Pictish wars, is near by, but dearest to me is the memory of these good, kind people who have had their sorrow as well as their joy. They lost an only son and heir when he was a young man, but they make the most of their daughter and her husband and children — rather pathetic, it seems to me, with all their outward

PICTURES AT ROSSIE PRIORY

smiles and cheery words. The pictures, mosaics, and books in the Priory are worth admiring study.[1]

[1] A list of some of the pictures at Rossie Priory:
Angelo, Michael. Head of a Slave.
Bassano, 1510–1592. Announcement to the Shepherds. Adoration of the Wise Men.
Bramantino, 1460–1529. The Nativity.
Correggio, 1494–1534. Virgin and Child with Angels.
Caracci. Ecstasy of a Saint.
Dürer, Albert, 1471–1528. Virgin and Child.
Dolci, Carlo. Head of the Virgin.
Gainsborough. Sir William Pulteney-Johnson (married a Miss Kinnaird).
Hogarth. Portrait of the artist.
Jan Steen. Dutch interior ("Saying grace").
Lely, Sir Peter. Duke of Monmouth.
Luini, 1475–1533. The Colombine.
Van Dyck. Lady Van Dyck's child. Prince Rupert.
Velasquez. A servant. A page.
Leonardo da Vinci (probably by a pupil). Venus. Portrait of a lady.
Morland, George. Pigs.
Meissonier. A greyhound.
Northcote. Charles, 8th Lord Kinnaird. The Artist's Brother or the Falconer. Pope Pius VI.
Poussin. Four landscapes.
Raeburn. Portrait of an old gentleman.
Reynolds, Sir Joshua. Sheridan. Lady Hamilton. A banished lord.
Raphael. The Resurrection.
Rembrandt. Portrait of the artist. A lady with a ruff.
Rondinelli, 1480–1500. Two heads.
Romney. Lord Kinnaird. Lady Kinnaird.
Solario. Descent from the Cross.
Spagnoletto, Giuseppe Ribera, 1589–1656. Virgin and Child.
Titian. Portrait of a lady of Colonna family.

CHAPTER VII

INVERARY CASTLE: THE DUKE OF ARGYLL'S (PRINCESS LOUISE) VIA THE TROSSACHS

Saturday, August 28

DROVE by coach to Loch Katrine, passing on the way Coilantogle, Loch Achray, and then through the picturesque and romantic entrance to the Trossachs. I put up at the Trossachs Hotel, a very pretty stone building, once a shooting lodge. Sketched Benvenue across Loch Achray and Ellen's Isle on Loch Katrine, sitting near the beach called the Silver Strand where fair Ellen had her first interview with the knight of Snowden.

I shall not go into the details of scenery, but must mention the intense and brilliant coloring. The sun broke forth after a rainy forenoon and lighted up spots of green grass, red heather, and warm brown shrubs, all sparkling with showery drops in the sunlight; while as the sun conquered the day, the shadows of the few clouds still in the sky passed rapidly over the hills like troops of dark horses and the glens purple in the middle distance, the gray blue of the more remote peaks of Benvenue, and the cobalt of the sky brought down to the sparkling waters of Loch Achray and Loch Katrine thrilled me with an ecstasy of delight I have never felt from nature before.

Sunday, August 29

WENT to chapel in the morning where they had the service of the Established Church of Scotland. We sat while hymns were sung and stood in prayer. There was no organ, but a clerk pitched and started the tunes. We sang "Martyrdom," and had a good sermon on "Put My Tears in Thy Bottle." In the evening we had Church of England service and a very eloquent sermon from a Presbyterian (!) minister who told two stories after the manner of Moody. When the service was over there was some general singing of hymns in which all joined. This latter was very homelike.

Monday, August 30

HARD rain. Old St. Swithun again at it! Very little to do as the bedrooms were too small for comfortable reading or writing. There were no bowling alleys, no reception rooms, and no piazzas. In the afternoon I tried to sketch in water-colors a lovely view from my window, but the damp air would not let the colors dry and the mist kept obscuring the sight of Benvenue. Before dinner I braved the rain and started out on a footpath leading round the hills and close under the foot of Benvenue to Loch Katrine. It was a rough path and seldom used by tourists.

I passed an old ruin of a Highland cottage. It was built of the rudest stones, held together with mountain bog mud. The builder, to save himself trouble, had taken advantage of two boulders to form a large part of his walls. This gave a good idea of the former poverty of the country. Before I turned to go back, after a walk of two miles, the sun suddenly came out over the mountains and produced again, as it were for my special benefit, rapidly changing but very beautiful effects as it topped first the tallest trees and then shone on the glistening heather and on nearer and then on more distant hills. I passed several gurgling water-courses coming down the mountain-side and felt well repaid even for the thorough wetting which I got.

Tuesday, August 31
ROWED over to Ellen's Isle and wandered about for an hour there. It reminded me a good deal in shape and woodiness of the island off our beach at Manchester-by-the-Sea. Left the Trossachs Hotel, called for short "Ardcheanacrochan Hotel," to walk to Inversnaid, my luggage booked to go by the next coach. I walked to the pier and took a steamer across Loch Katrine, as there is no road round it. Bade farewell to Ellen's Isle and to the pretty Loch Katrine and walked from the landing on the other side to Inversnaid.

Took a row on Loch Lomond in the evening with some young Englishmen who sang, "By yon bonnie banks and by yon bonnie braes." My luggage did not come because no coach came and no coach came because there were no passengers. The hotel was near the pretty waterfall plunging into the Loch. They put me in a very magnificent room of huge proportions and I was without even night clothes or a toothbrush.

Wednesday, September 1
TO-DAY I began my visit to the Duke and Duchess of Argyll. Sailed by steamer from Inversnaid to Tarbet. I took a fifty-minute start of the coach and walked through Glencoe to "Rest and Be Thankful," a distance of nine miles from Tarbet, and then waited ten minutes for the coach, which labored very slowly up the last mile or two of steep ascent. I secured a seat on the top of the coach, which I liked better than the driver's seat, as I could look from there both forward and backward. It was very exciting going down the steep hills

INVERARY CASTLE, SEAT OF THE DUKE OF ARGYLL

ARRIVAL AT INVERARY CASTLE

with the brakes all set. I felt in exuberant spirits after my walk.

We had a very jolly guard, who, as well as the driver, was dressed in red coat and looked very old-fashioned and picturesque. He wound his horn at every occasion and "set the wild echoes flying," and as the horses rested and all was quiet we heard the "horns of Elfland faintly blowing." On going up the long hills the men got off and walked as is the custom riding in these Scottish coaches. I arrived at Inverary, a quiet little village on the west shore and near the head of Upper Loch Fyne, where is the Duke of Argyll's place.

There was no carriage from the castle so I took a local cab and drove up. The footman at the door, dressed in Highland costume, did not know that I was expected. I was sure the Duchess specified the first fortnight in September for my visit and that I had replied I would come on September first. I took her letter out to make sure and then sent in my card. I had not mentioned the hour of my arrival, as there was no exact schedule for the coaches. The servant came back saying it was all right, and the Duchess immediately met me at the door with a word of welcome, saying that she had been looking for me.

I was shown to the drawing-room where soon the Duke appeared. It is very cordial and pleasant to find the head of the house ready to meet one, but it is really more convenient to be met by servants and shown to one's room first, as was done at Althorp House and I am told is usually the custom; especially convenient after my long walks on muddy roads. Having been separated from my trunk for nearly two days, I should have liked to have been in my room first, with razor and access to clean linen, before being presented. I saw Princess Louise[1] for a moment.

The Duke asked me to go out with him after lunch to shoot some deer which were doing damage outside the deer park, from which they had escaped. Off we went, the Duke, myself, and the keeper. The Duke stayed on one side of a wooded hill while I stood on the other, both with our guns ready to be used at the shortest notice; while the "beaters in" drove the deer toward us. I saw two roe, neither good shots as both were in thickets running fast. I fired at one of them, but did not hit, so I failed to keep up the reputation of my family, my father twenty years before having made an unusually difficult shot at very nearly this same place. No deer came near His Grace and at the second beating in no deer at all were started.

The gamekeeper was with me, and when he saw the sport was over he started me back by a path in the woods through thick underbrush higher than our heads, I walking in front of him. I had on a gray suit, not very unlike the color of a deer's breast and neck. We suddenly emerged from this thicket, between the leaves, and there I saw the Duke in front of me with gun leveled and hand on trigger ready to shoot, as he took me for a deer, and yet, as he said afterwards, there was just something queer enough about our motions to make him hesitate before pulling the trigger. The Duke was very angry and rightfully so. He said the keeper should have warned him by calling, as we were going in a runway much frequented by the deer, and had the Duke not been remarkably cool-headed and

---

[1] She is a royal princess, daughter of Queen Victoria. In Europe the title of "princess" represents a standing sometimes below and sometimes just above that of a duchess. She is the wife of the Marquis of Lorne, the eldest son of the Duke.

experienced, the affair would doubtless have ended fatally.

On the way home, at the Duke's request, I made a long standing shot at a heron some four hundred yards away on the edge of the Loch. It was a good liner, but just under the bird. On returning home we all had tea a little after five. I read the papers and talked with the Duke and the two very pretty children of his second son, Lord Archibald, until time for dinner.

A bagpipe was heard playing outside and His Grace said that was their way of announcing time to dress for dinner — a rather short notice, for I changed my things as fast as I could, but was even then just a little late. I sat at the Duchess's left and probably was to have taken in Lady Elizabeth, the eldest daughter, now twenty-three years of age, who was on my left. I apologized for being late, only a moment, however, as I arrived just as they were sitting down. At table were Princess Louise, the Duke and Duchess of Argyll, the Marquis of Lorne, Lord Edward Cavendish (the father of the present Duke of Devonshire) at the right of the Duchess; Lady Elizabeth, Lady Edward Cavendish, Lady Victoria, a woman artist, and lastly a sister of Lady Edward. The Princess was on the Duke's right. She is good-sized, well developed, with a German cast of face and a slight German accent. Her r's are guttural, for example, instead of lingual. Her table manners are not at all German. After the ladies went out the conversation was mostly on deer, and on this I had not much to add, so did not join in, otherwise than to be a listener, who, in a certain sense, joins in the dovetail of conversation as he keeps the others talking.

I am much fascinated with the Marquis of Lorne. He is handsome and strong, with delicate features, bright complexion, a small mouth, very light hair, and blue eyes, and a manly and kindly bearing. In the evening Lady Elizabeth played on the piano very well and softly so as not to prevent conversation. The Princess talked pleasantly and easily and showed me some etchings of hers drawn for embroidery patterns. They are original and really very graceful. She disclaimed one as being only a copy and would take no credit for it at all.

(James Russell Lowell told me, when I returned to America and spoke about my visit, that he thought Princess Louise was the most gifted both artistically and intellectually of all the royal family.)

We all retired about eleven. They told me that breakfast was to be at ten in the morning. Arrangements in the evening were made to go grouse shooting to-morrow at eleven. Before going to bed I looked over some autograph letters of Queens Mary and Elizabeth, of Charles I and James I, which the Duchess had brought out to show me. Some of these were historically important as proving some points of history otherwise unsettled.

Thursday, September 2

THE valet appeared with clothes, hot water, bathtub, and shoes, at 8.45, thus giving me ample time to dress for breakfast. It was raining hard. At breakfast were the same persons as at dinner. The breakfast was very informal here as in so many of the houses. The Princess wore a dark green, well-fitting dress of some woolen material, and all had on rather rough clothes, which they wore until dinner-time at the end of the day, when of course dress suits are *de rigueur*, except that the Marquis of Lorne wore Highland costume — kilts and long stockings and his knees were bare. The Princess has a

PRINCESS LOUISE

straight back and carries her head well without having the slightest appearance of stiffness.

At breakfast the servants disappeared after putting the food on the sideboard and we helped ourselves or waited on one another. The ladies seemed to expect to wait on themselves, even the Princess. They start from their seats towards the side table, but of course accept assistance from one with grace, but rather as a bit of Henry Esmond gallantry than as really necessary. It was all so very simple and informal. The talk at breakfast was cheery and pleasant. After breakfast I read the "Times" and wrote letters. About 11.30 I came down and, meeting the Princess, asked her what it was usual to do on so rainy a day, and with that she proposed that I try fishing, for it was far too wet for the grouse shooting, which had been postponed to another day. She went to the front door or vestibule, selected me a salmon rod, and looked about for the flies, but could not find the fly book at first. The Duke brought it, and then Princess Louise got out some flies from the book, showed me how to tie them on, doing a couple herself, and then made me do a few to see that I fastened them properly.

The Duke, however, thought I had better wait until there was more rain and the river higher, when the sea trout would come up. I then read Charles Kingsley's "Westward Ho!" which the Duchess suggested and found for me.

At lunch the same as at breakfast with the younger children added: Lady Constance eleven, Lady Mary sixteen, and Lady Frances seventeen. After lunch Princess Louise spoke to Lord Lorne, her husband, asking him some question. He did not hear at first, as he was talking to some one else, and she put her hand on his shoulder to draw his attention in a gentle, loving way which struck me quite pleasantly. I fell a bit in love with Princess Louise, for besides her most agreeable manners, she has many fine traits of character and is amiable with all and not in the least demanding attention, modest without being retiring or sensitive. When she first appears in the morning all the ladies courtesy to her, even the Duchess, the courtesy being the short bend of the knees, not the long backward, graceful movement.

After lunch Lord Edward Cavendish and I went out fishing. He did the upstream, which had much swollen, so as to use the fly. I stayed lower down and used bait for the most part, for the fish, my guide said, will not rise to the fly in this section of the river under these conditions. We each had a guide, or gillie as they call them here, with us who showed us the best spots, unhooked the fish, changed the flies, or baited the hook. I got a pretty fair mess — sixteen in all — but only two over a pound and large enough to require the use of the reel. Lord Edward caught three fine fellows of two or three pounds each.

I came back in time to read for a while and dress for dinner. I saw Lady Evelyn for the first time. She is just twenty years of age. At dinner I took in Lady Elizabeth and sat at the right of Princess Louise who had the Duke on her left. Next the Duke on the other side were Lady Edward Cavendish, the Marquis of Lorne, Lady Edward's sister, Lady Victoria, the Duchess, opposite the Duke, then Lord Edward Cavendish and Lady Elizabeth in order. Princess Louise had one large beautiful ring, beside the wedding ring, on her left hand and two small ones on her right. She wore a handsome cross hung from a black velvet band round her neck and two plain pearls for earrings. Her dress was fine white silk trimmed with glossy white satin. Her hair was well dressed and the whole effect tasteful and quiet. Her features are regular and she has a distinguished air.

The conversation turned on American subjects. The Duke could not be persuaded that the Fall River boats go outside in rounding Point Judith. He said he was sure they could not because these boats were built out on guards, and he thought it would not be safe to sail in the open sea even for a short distance, that it would not be allowed, and so I must have been mistaken in saying they did. He has a way of disbelieving what you say, I am told, even in a case like this where I had sailed on these boats myself several times, knew the map well, and was aware that the rounding of Point Judith in the open sea was proverbial for its roughness.

After the ladies left us the talk was on fishing. As my knowledge on that subject was far behind an ordinary Englishman's, I again did not contribute much to the conversation except as a listener.

The Duke sketches in oils and one or two of his things are rather good. Lord Archibald, his second son, has even more talent than his father and has done some paintings on door panels about the house. He has also made some funny caricatures of his father, illustrating his pursuit of geology, philosophy, and the study of birds. After dinner there was some pretty good conversation at times, but as yet the Duke has not come out on any abstruse, scientific, or highly intellectual subject, up to his reputation, though I tried to start him on some of these topics, especially scientific and historical.

During the day the Duke pointed out to me a hill, I think he called it the Gallows Hill, where executions in olden days took place, and he told me that his predecessors used to have the absolute power of life and death.

Friday, September 3

BREAKFAST at ten; all down as usual. None of the ladies here breakfast in their rooms. Lady Edward asked me about the passage over and how we entertained ourselves. When I mentioned singing to my guitar, the Princess asked if I had brought it with me to Inverary, and said she was sorry I had not when I told her I left it behind in London. She wanted to hear some of the negro and American college songs. It might not have been a bad idea to have carried the guitar on these visits, as the English are fond of anything new.

Fishing at 11.30 took me out with Lord Edward who went up one branch of the river and I another. Lorne lent me his salmon rod and sent after me his fly book and flask. How kind and attentive they are! Under the instruction of my gillie I improved much in casting. Before three days were over I was able to throw the fly some eighteen yards or more. A large salmon weighing between eight and ten pounds I managed to hook and had to play him for more than ten minutes before he could be taken in the landing net. The rod and line would not bear its dead weight at the end of it. Walter Brackett, the celebrated American salmon and trout sportsman and painter, once told me that it was important to keep the line taut as much of the time as possible so that the fish could not rest and get its breath, and that I must remember the pressure at the end of the pole was not nearly so great as it would seem to be from the amount of effort put out at the handle; so I kept the pressure up good and strong. He said this lack of sufficient pressure was why it often took so long to land the fish.

My guide complimented me on the whole, for on this visit I had my first experience in fly fishing except the fishing for some rather small trout when I was at St.

THE DUKE OF ARGYLL

Paul's School as a boy. Beside the salmon I caught three fair-sized sea trout. The lunch which I had carried with me I shared with the guide and took some nips from Lorne's flask which proved to contain some fine Scotch whiskey, and got back at five o'clock in time for a refreshing cup of tea which the Princess poured out for me, and then read "Westward Ho!"

Before going into the castle Argyll came out and met me and the guide, inspected the salmon, told me its probable weight, and asked the guide how I had been getting on, and then told me that Charles Francis Adams, our American Minister, tried salmon fishing several times, but could not manage to cast the fly. The line, Argyll said, always got into a tangle at Adams's feet, though he struggled hard and got very red in the face. Adams, from what his sons say of him, never took part in sports or games of manual skill and was therefore at a disadvantage in trying to learn this very difficult art.

The Duchess talked most agreeably with me for a quarter of an hour, speaking of my father's visit in 1856. I spoke of his admiration for her mother. She told me about Queen Victoria and her wonderful sympathy, kind-heartedness, and interest in all that was going on. The Duchess is the eldest daughter of the celebrated Duchess of Sutherland, the mistress of Stafford House, London, who was so great a favorite of Queen Victoria, was the acknowledged leader of London society in her day, and who was so hospitable and gracious to my father in 1856. The Duchess of Argyll was Mistress of the Robes to the Queen some few years before my visit. The Duke has been Lord of the Privy Seal, Postmaster-General, Secretary of State for India, President of the Council of India, member of the Council on Education, is hereditary master of the Queen's household in Scotland, Lord Lieutenant of Scotland, and has held other important positions.

The Duchess of Argyll is somewhat diffident, and talks in so low a tone and with such slight articulation that I find it hard to understand her at times. This was caused in part by a serious illness not long before. She is kindly and thoughtful of those about her and democratic and liberal in her public and political views. I saw the two perfectly lovely children of Lord Archibald.

The Marquis of Lorne and Princess Louise have no children, so Lord Archibald is heir presumptive to the dukedom after the death of Lorne and his knightly little boy is the next in line. Lord Edward returned about 6.30 and had not had as good sport as I, for he had got no salmon and but two two-pound trout.

Many of my friends here, as in London, drop their *g*'s in the words ending in "ing," saying "talkin'" for "talking," and few make hardly more than three syllables out of "extraordinary," saying "extrornry."

Earl Shaftesbury, the celebrated philanthropist, came in the afternoon with a son and a daughter. At dinner Shaftesbury took in the Duchess, who as lady of the house, as always in Great Britain, they tell me, and certainly wherever I have been so far, waited till the last. The Duke took in the Princess and went first. The Marquis with Lady Edward came next, I followed with Lady Edith Ashley, Lord Edward with Lady Evelyn came next, and then Honorable Mr. Ashley, son of Earl Shaftesbury, with Lady Elizabeth, followed by the Duchess and Shaftesbury himself. I had a pleasant, talkative, and well-informed neighbor in Lady Edith Ashley, four years my senior and daughter of Shaftesbury, and quite pretty, too, she is. Earl Shaftesbury, who is now seventy-four years of age, looked overworked and tired and seemed hardly up to much conversation. He and his family came round in the Duke's steam yacht, which now anchors off the castle in the loch.

After dinner several of us played a game of billiards. There were seven balls and four persons on a side, the Princess being one of them. It was called "battle." The game was exciting and brought forth a good deal of merriment. Talked mostly with Lady Victoria.

Lady Ashburton was expected all the time during and after dinner. A maid appeared with the luggage by coach. The horses had given out some sixteen miles away and new ones they could not find there, so on the maid's report of the dilemma, two of the duke's horses were sent off to help out. At every sound of carriage wheels or ringing of a bell they said, "There she is!" and a footman was sent to the door; but all proved false alarms.

On account of so many new and unexpected arrivals and many of them ladies, I had to be changed from my large guest chamber to Lord Colin's room with thoughtful apologies from the dear Duchess. Lord Colin was away. All retired at eleven except the Duke and Duchess, who sat up for Lady Ashburton.

Saturday, September 4
LADY ASHBURTON arrived at quarter after eleven last night, we learned, and yet did not seem a bit tired at breakfast after her long, fatiguing journey and annoying delays. She is the widow of the second Lord Ashburton and is between forty and fifty years of age (nearer fifty I find from the "Peerage"), but looks hardly forty, she is so hearty and bright.

We went shooting after breakfast, Ashley, Lord Shaftesbury's son, and I. We stayed out till after four, taking luncheon in a farmhouse. Weather was "a wee bit soft," which translated into American meant steady, fine rain all day, and we had a wet time of it, indeed, with grass and heather dripping and got no game for our pains. We saw some deer in the park which the Duke had enclosed this spring, but they were not to be shot just now or at least we were not asked to shoot them.

Tea as usual at five. At dinner there were the same persons as the night before, with the addition of Lady Ashburton and her daughter, Honorable Mary Florence Baring, a tall girl or rather young lady about sixteen, but looking nearer nineteen, and Lord Colin, who had arrived during the day. On my left was Lady Edith Ashley, and Lady Edward's sister sat at my right. After dinner we played battle again at billiards, and after that I played a regular game with Colin who more than doubled me, but I was content not to be worse off, for I play billiards so seldom.

Got a pleasant letter from Lady Russell at Pembroke Lodge. After the billiards we all went out to hear the echoes, tried by shouting through long horns. It was all so pretty, wild, and romantic with a bright party from the house, and this answering to the peculiar Scotch cries, the near echoes sharp and quick followed by the dying vibration over the water —

> "The devil mocks the doleful tale
> With a merry peal from Borrow Dale."

I had the pleasure of helping the Princess put on her shawl as she came out to hear the echoes. The ladies courtesy in saying good-night to the Princess as well as in greeting her in the morning. All retired at eleven.

Sunday, September 5

WENT to the Kirk, where services began at 11.45. The Princess and some of the family did not go, as the ritual was Scottish — very like our Presbyterian — and not that of the Established Church of England. Walked home with Lady Edward and had an outdoor talk with her, the Duchess, the Princess, and other ladies who met us. For a time it stopped raining. It was still, however, cloudy and heavy. In London there are but twenty-six inches of rain in the year while the Duke tells me that in Argyllshire they have often eighty and never less than forty.

After lunch read and wrote and later in the afternoon all went on various walks. Lorne took me out to see his father's yacht. It is a steamer of about three hundred tons and one hundred and forty feet over all. It holds about forty tons of coal and burns five tons a day. It steams eleven knots an hour. It is handsomely fitted up with woodwork, curtains, cushions, etc. The Upper Loch Fyne is a salt water tidal loch directly connected through the Lower Loch Fyne with the sea and with endless channels between pretty islands on the west coast of Scotland, and the family take many trips in this steamer. At dinner were the same as yesterday, and Lady Edith Ashley I took in again and sat between her and Lady Ashburton.

In the evening were prayers, the house servants all appearing. There were eighteen maids and ten menservants present, and these did not, of course, include the stable hands or farm laborers. This shows what an establishment it is, and yet the Duke of Argyll is one of the poorer dukes. The servants all remained standing until the others were seated. After prayers and when the servants were gone, there was general conversation, but no hymn singing.

The Princess, by the way, has a separate allowance from the Government given by Act of Parliament amounting to £6000 or $30,000 a year, with a dowry of $150,000 besides.

The Princess asked me to explain a plan that I had thought out and said something about for raising the *Vanguard*. The *Vanguard*, one of the newest and most costly of the English battleships, was sunk in a collision in about sixty feet of water in the Irish Channel and the Admiralty had been considering plans for raising her. The possibility of lowering large tubes filled with water to be pumped out and filled with air so as to float her had occurred to me; but it flashed on my mind that these tubes were unnecessary, for if the water should be taken out of the vessel itself, she would rise of her own accord. In order to accomplish this I had thought of covering the whole vessel with canvas, or if not that, at least to calk all the cracks, cover the holes made in the collision, and make the vessel as tight as possible and then pump out the water.

But in order to pump the water out from pumps worked on the deck of a vessel near by (the only practical way of working the pumps), the water must be replaced with air just as is done in caissons sunk for foundations of wharves or bridges. I had worked out the whole question of air pressure. At sixty feet of depth, it would require three atmospheres in all, two beside the natural one, or air at a pressure of forty-five pounds to the square inch. Hydrostatics and general physics I had studied in college, getting maximum marks in my examinations, so I was extremely interested in the subject and felt confident that the plan was practical.

After I had explained my plan for raising the *Vanguard* to the Princess, Lady Edward, and some others,

PLAN FOR RAISING A SUNKEN SHIP

they got me to explain it in their presence to the Duke who happened to be coming along. He had had some scientific training and was generally looked upon as an authority in such matters. Knowing as I did that it would be utterly impossible to pump the water out, without forcing the air in at a sufficient pressure to take its place and to overcome the pressure of the outside water, and, assuming that the Duke knew enough about hydrostatics to understand, I told him exactly what pressure would be necessary. At this the Duke immediately said, "Oh, I see, you have the popular fallacy that as air is light itself, therefore, the more air you put in, the lighter the vessel will be." He said that this was "a great mistake" and "your plan will not work." I then tried to explain to him how impossible it would be to pump the water from the vessel without this air pressure.

This general theory is an elementary bit of knowledge to any one who comprehends the principles on which a pump works. It is only the pressure of the ordinary atmosphere that enables the every-day pump to raise water to the height of thirty feet below the buckets. I tried to explain that this air pressure was not for the purpose of making the vessel lighter; on the contrary, it would make it a trifle heavier, but so little that this extra weight could be ignored with safety; and that the pressure was solely for working the pumps.

The Duke, however, would not listen. He shook his head, smiled, and repeated again that I had "been caught by this popular fallacy," and gave me no chance either then or later, when I made a second attempt, to explain or call his attention to the pump theory.

(It is quite interesting to note that the method I then thought out has since been successfully used for raising sunken vessels over and over again. Sometimes a canvas cover has been used and sometimes they merely blocked all the holes. For example, there was the case of the *Yankee* in 1908, and the *Nero* raised at Newport. I have collected some twenty accounts of raising vessels in substantially the same manner. Even the Japanese have used this method with perfect success. The latest case is that of the *Leonardo da Vinci* in December, 1919. The account of this states, "The leaks were plugged and the water driven out with compressed air."[1] Since the World War the British Admiralty has built some great tubes of concave model on one side so as to fit onto vessels, to raise some of the merchantmen torpedoed by the German submarines, and where the holes were too large to be plugged up. The tubes are filled with water, then sunk into position, the water pumped out by "filling with air." If the Duke had comprehended the scheme and had given me a letter to the Admiralty endorsing it, very likely the *Vanguard* would have been raised and the method adopted ten years or so before it was.)

One day as we were entering the castle the Duke pointed out a very beautiful and rare specimen of pheasant with wonderful coloring, stuffed and set up in a glass case at the left of the front door. Shaftesbury and I were walking beside him. The Duke, pointing to this bird, said, "Darwin tells us that all these beautifully varied colors have come about by a process of natural selection; how manifestly absurd!" However, I observed that Shaftesbury did not assent nor did he or I argue the point.

The Duke is hospitable and kindly, but usually rather silent for long intervals at a time. He has reddish hair growing in a long cowlick over a high forehead. He is,

[1] See the *Boston Herald*, December 30, 1919.

I should guess, about five feet seven inches tall, slender and active. He was very friendly to the North in the Civil War and used his influence with that of others successfully to prevent England's recognizing the Southern Confederacy. He is an eminent and useful man. His description of the flight of birds in his book called "The Reign of Law" is one of the best, if not the very best, that exists.

The Princess is among those who fail to sound their *g*'s in the present participle, and I notice that Lord Edward says "ain't" for "are not" and "am not," and I think I caught the Duke using it also. Shaftesbury told some very amusing anecdotes during the evening. He thinks that the Church of England will in time become disestablished and that it will not suffer, but will, on the contrary, be made more vital and living, that the laymen will have more interest in it and it will have a greater hold on the masses.

Stories had been current both in the United States and England that the marriage between Lorne and the Princess was not a love match. These stories varied in detail and were somewhat contradictory. From my observation I don't believe a word of them. It is clear that the Marquis and the Princess are more than fond of each other. One reason that Lorne did not join in the fishing and shooting was that he drives every day with the Princess in their pony cart, choosing the hours when the rain holds up. They often chat together just because they like to, and their amiable ways together are too natural and spontaneous to be merely assumed for effect, and, moreover, it is evident that she is a happy woman. My father in 1856 had seen them playing together as children, Lorne then about eleven and Louise eight. These stories arise, I am sure, from the not uncommon desire to detract from the eminent, to make out the fortunate as ill-starred, and the apparently blessed as unhappy at heart.

Monday, September 6
THIS delightful visit has come to an end, as I leave at 12.30 to-day. I found, however, that I had seriously been expected to stay on according to my invitation, which read for a fortnight, and all, including the Princess, were kind enough to express regret at my leaving so soon and hope of seeing me again. I have been here just six days. The Duchess pressed me for the reasons of my leaving so soon and asked me where I was going next, and when I spoke of having accepted invitations from Lord Coleridge and Tenderden she proposed to write and ask them to postpone these visits to later dates. I told the Duchess I should love to stay, how pleased I was at her suggestion, and how hugely I had been and still was enjoying my visit, but that I did not like to have her ask Coleridge and Tenterden to change their plans when it might inconvenience them to do so. I felt also that a request from her would be tantamount to a command.

The Duchess gave me a copy of "The Reign of Law" in which she had written her name "with kind regards." I am the more pleased with all this friendly kindness, because the manner of all the family is a little stiff and quiet. Perhaps it is a Scottish trait.

Inverary Castle is of gray stone, machicolated and flanked with round, overtopping towers, with a background of a fine wooded park and steep hills. There are in it some very beautiful tapestries, several portraits, a collection of old arms, and many relics of the hunt.

THE ARMORY, OR FRONT HALL, INVERARY CASTLE

CHAPTER VIII
LORD COLERIDGE'S

THE Cavendishes left in the morning. I took a boat across Loch Tay to St. Catherine, thence by coach to Loch Goilehead, with a few miles of footing it up the hills ahead of the slow coach. We had a damp-smelling, red-faced coachman who was incessantly either jerking the horses' reins or whipping them, or both, and kept up all the time a continual "cluck, cluck — hiss, hiss" accompaniment.

From Loch Goilehead I went to Greenock on the Clyde by fast steamer, at nearly twenty miles an hour; then by rail to Glasgow. Tea at Glasgow and by night train and sleeping-saloon car to London. Very comfortable arrangements with more privacy than in our Pullman sleepers. What little I saw of Glasgow was depressing, indeed. The city was dirty and smoky, and I never saw so many drunken people about as I did that evening, both men and women, drunk and dead drunk, sitting or lying on the sides of streets.

Tuesday, September 7
FROM London went by afternoon train to Honiton, Devonshire, for my visit at Lord Coleridge's. Lord and Lady Coleridge received me cordially and had supper all set out for me. As it was late Lady Coleridge soon retired and Lord C. sat up with me, sending off the butler. As we started up the stairs he gave me my candle and then showed me my room.

This room was a fairly large one, about 22x18, with a fireplace, one large window with a dressing-table in front of it, and the sides all wainscoted to the ceiling with paneled oak. The evening had been damp and rather cool. A small fire was burning on the hearth, and I sat in the cozy, rather large armchair in front of it, musing over my experiences on this, to me, wonderful trip in England. At last went to bed and soon fell sound asleep. Some hours later I awoke suddenly with a feeling that some one was in the room.

I open my eyes, take in the situation, and remember my surroundings. The fire has gone out on the hearth, but I can clearly see the window and the dressing-table some three or four feet from it and silhouetted against it. The rest of the room is as dark as ink. I listen intently, and in a moment I hear a grating sound as of a chair moved along the carpet. The sound comes from my right side exactly in the direction of the armchair in which I had been sitting before I had gone to bed, on which I had put my clothes and which I had left near the fireplace. I am now convinced that some one is in the room.

I try to pretend I am asleep, but my heart is pounding like a triphammer and my breath comes and goes so fast and so noisily that I know I am betraying myself. I can't any longer feign sleep, and I fear the burglar or insane person or whoever it may be that is in the room will rush at me. I then turn over, take the bedclothes in my hand, throw them quickly off, and jump from the opposite side of the bed.

I then go towards the dressing-table, where I remember to have seen some matches, stumble over a chair, seize it in my left hand on the way, hold it above my head for defense, get hold of the matchbox, take out a match, break the first one in trying to light it, take another but the head snaps off, seize a third, light that, and then call, "Now, sir!" expecting to see before me at least a stalwart burglar, but to my amazement and horror the room is empty.

I look under the bed and behind it, under the dressing-table and in the large wardrobe, before which I am startled as my candle is almost blown out in opening its big door, glance up the chimney, and behind and under the armchair. This armchair is not where I had left it, but very much nearer the bed, in fact almost touching it. I then go round the wainscoting, examine and feel all the panels, but can find none that is loose or that indicates a secret entrance. Strange to say I find the only door of my room locked on the *inside*. I do not remember locking it and it is not my habit to do so except in hotels. Being locked with key on the inside, no one could have gone out by the door and locked it again. I sit down in the armchair and try to calm my thoughts. Just then I hear an old dog in the garden below baying and growling. Was it the ghost of the toothless mastiff of Coleridge's "Christabel," answering the midnight clock with "Sixteen short howls not overloud"? I again go round the walls, holding the lighted candle close to the panels. Finding no clue to the mystery, I go back to bed, blowing out the candle, putting it and some matches on a small chair beside me so that I can strike a light at the first sound of alarm. I meant to stay awake for the rest of the night. Strangely enough, I fell sound asleep immediately and did not wake up until I heard the household moving in the morning of

Wednesday, September 8
WHEN I came down to breakfast they inquired solicitously, it seemed to me, as to how I had slept and what sort of night I had passed. I wondered if mine was not

the haunted room. I said nothing of all this to any of the family, but merely replied that I had slept fairly well.

This was the nearest I have ever come to a ghost; all the other ghost stories I know of have come to me second hand and most of them third or fourth hand.

At ten minutes to nine we had morning prayers followed by breakfast at which were Lord and Lady Coleridge, Mr. Edward Coleridge, an elderly man and fellow of Eton, uncle of Lord Coleridge and nephew of Samuel Taylor Coleridge, the poet and philosopher, Mrs. Edward Coleridge, and Miss Mildred Coleridge, daughter of Lord C. They served me with some delicious Devonshire cream. I saw them spread it on bread very much as we do butter, only in thicker layers, and I did the same. Coleridge and his uncle told stories and capped verses and were very lively and entertaining. Coleridge himself is wonderfully quick and bright. He asked me into his study and I read while he was writing. I noticed that he sealed every letter which he wrote and this sealing took no little time. I asked him about this and he said it made a very good break between writing one letter and another and gave him an opportunity for change of thought.

Between his letters he read me two of Bacon's essays from an edition which he carries in his pocket; one was on the "Duties of a Judge" and the other on "Cunning." I took a walk about the grounds and inspected the flower gardens. This place does not belong to Coleridge. He has only hired it.

Lord Coleridge told me that his income from his professional work alone was lately about £15,000 ($75,000) a year and while Attorney-General he made annually £20,000 ($100,000). His salary as Chief Jus-

LORD COLERIDGE AT 56

tice of the Court of Common Pleas is £5000 with a retiring pension of £4000 after fifteen years of service.

(The very next year his salary was raised to £7000 and he was appointed in 1880 Lord Chief Justice of England, the first to hold that new title, which had been extinct for many years.)

He showed me about the stables, and after lunch took me to drive with his uncle and uncle's wife to see an old fort said to be an ancient Roman camp called Hembury. The country was beautifully green; the dark hedgerows and dense trees and bright flowers in the fields all came well up to my idea of "merry old England" in this rich South Devonshire country.

Speaking of the English feeling towards America, I said we were rather surprised in the North that England took so strong a side with the South in the Civil War while the South was built on slavery, which England abhorred, and it was slavery that had been at the bottom of the whole muss. He said that he personally was not on the side of the South.

(He had apparently forgotten his early war views, for in Coleridge's "Life," [1] in volume second, pages 1 to 34, it appears that at the very beginning he did side with the Southern Confederacy, though he was still anti-slavery, but soon changed his views and helped, with the Duke of Argyll and others, to prevent action hostile to the North.)

He said that the upper ten thousand in England had felt very jealous and bitter towards America, which they had lost through their own stupidity in the last century and now found to be so great a rival, and added to that, said he, was their "pig-headedness" and want of information in believing that all the gentry were in

[1] By Ernest Hartley Coleridge. D. Appleton & Co., 1904.

the South and only shopkeepers in the North. All this led them to take an attitude which had not surprised him.

He told me that Charles Francis Adams, our Minister to the Court of St. James in the Civil War, had had a very hard time during the first year or two of that war; that few others could have kept his position and dignity amid such scorn and sometimes insult, and that in the end he won very great respect. "Adams," he said, "and his work on behalf of the North are not half appreciated in America." He also added that the conduct of the North during the war won great regard for that side. As illustrating how high the feeling was on this subject in Great Britain during the war, he told me that the only time in his life he had ever known of a dinner party being broken up was when some one at table had taken the side of the North. It must be said, however, that this hostility was almost entirely confined to the majority of the aristocracy. There was never a public meeting held in Great Britain on behalf of the South, while there were several for the side of the Union, and even during the cotton famine, Lancashire stood faithfully by the North, notwithstanding the blockade which prevented cotton from leaving the Southern ports.

As to the aristocracy, it should be stated in justice to them that they had been impregnated by the diplomatic and consular service of the United States with the Southern pro-slavery ideas. They had been told that all the "gentlemen" and chivalry of our country were in the Southern States; that the Northerners were a race of shopkeepers; that the tariff and not slavery was the fundamental cause of the war; and that States had a constitutional right to secede.

No one had been appointed to a position in our foreign service during twenty years at least before the Civil War who was not in sympathy with these pro-slavery views, and the higher officials were almost always men of old family, good breeding, and charm of manner.

At dinner were the Right Reverend John Fielder Mackarness, Bishop of Oxford, and his wife Alethea, who is Lord Coleridge's younger sister, their daughter, Mr. and Mrs. Edward Coleridge, another Mr. Coleridge and his wife and daughter, Lady Coleridge, and her two sons, Bernard and Stephen, who had come down during the day. Lady Coleridge is quiet and reticent. She is artistic and has painted some pictures that have received high mention and some prizes in exhibitions. She has n't much small talk and only joins in when literary, artistic, or other subjects that interest her come up.

After dinner they had piano-playing and all retired at 10.30, after much interesting conversation, most stimulating to thought. On going to bed I reëxamined my room and again placed the matches and candle on the small chair beside me.

Thursday, September 9
I HAD no disturbance during the night and slept well, nor was the armchair again moved from its place. Lord Coleridge read prayers as usual at ten minutes before nine. The household servants came in. In reading a passage from the Bible, Coleridge paused and underscored or marked two or three special verses with the gold pencil he took out of his vest pocket. Played battledore and shuttlecock with Stephen, who is in his second year at Cambridge. Coleridge sang some English ballads and sang them well. He has a good, mellow,

baritone voice, correct ear, and a great love for music. It was really a pleasure to hear him. Bernard, the elder son, and Miss Coleridge played piano duets.

At noon Lord Coleridge and I started on horseback for Sidmouth, a distance of nine miles. The day was glorious. He was extremely affable and talkative, telling me all sorts of things about the effect of large and small landowners and of a nobility on the country and its people. He is quite democratic in his notions, at least in theory. He was knighted about seven years ago, and he told me that his wife, who was then first called Lady Coleridge, found she received far greater attention in the shops simply on account of her title and that the tradespeople would begin attending to her before others who had come in ahead, but she insisted upon taking her turn.

He told me also that at one time he went with the Duke of Wellington to a railway station and on coming to the booking office found there was some delay about the tickets, the man asking those in line to wait. Then Coleridge said, "I see, Your Grace, that they make us stand in line and wait like the rest." As soon as the ticket-seller heard that there was a duke in line he immediately stopped what he was doing and insisted upon giving them their tickets ahead of the rest, "all which very much amused me," said Coleridge.

At Sidmouth we saw the dwelling in which Queen Victoria was born. It was very simple, small, of only two stories, close to the beach, with only about two acres of grounds about it. Coleridge said, "Would any prince to-day live in so modest an establishment?" He pointed out a small house at Sidmouth and said that when he was first married he hired one half of it for the summer.

The Sid does not flow directly into the sea, but into a small pool just above the beach, and there the water wholly disappears, reaching the ocean unseen. Coleridge quoted from a poem on the River Sid by the Reverend George Kestell Cornish, illustrating from this our apparent disappearance in death before our souls reach the infinite immortal:

> "Yon stream, that from its furzy bower,
> Has toiled full many an hour,
> Yet with an onward course and clearly,
> And at her labour singing cheerly,
> Lies as a lake — and pebbles hide
> Her union with the rising tide.
>
> "And canst thou tell, thou loitering one,
> Where the waters are gone?
> They have not perished in the earth,
> But they shall rise in second birth,
> And soon, from all pollution free,
> Shall join the everlasting sea."

Coleridge unburdened his mind to me regarding the acts of a certain high personage and his own experiences and troubles therefrom when Solicitor-General and Attorney-General. He also told me a good deal about prison discipline and the great amount of hysteria among criminals, and many of the practical difficulties of keeping men under close restraint and how it had at times to be relaxed. We rode back over Downe Hill. There the road ran about five miles along the ridge, affording all the way very extensive views.

We dismounted at one of the finest points and, on calling my attention to the beauty and expanse, Coleridge suddenly remarked, "I suppose, however, this is nothing to you in your much greater country." I instantly replied, without thinking how rude it might be,

"You forget that the curvature of the earth there is just the same as it is in England and we have no more extensive views from the same elevation than you have." He burst out into hearty laughter, taking it in utmost good part. After I had made the remark I felt more as though I ought to have been whipped for such insolence from a youth to one of the most distinguished men of the realm.

Things had got, said Coleridge, into such a bad state in London society some years ago that the Queen was appealed to by the leading men and women of the kingdom to come back and give drawing-rooms and become again the leader of society. It had been her intention, after her husband's death, never to take part in society again, but she consented and her presence had a most wholesome effect.

We got back in time for tea at half-past five. At dinner were some friends of the family including a Madame ——, an English woman who married a Russian and whom I had the honor of taking into dinner, and who told us something of Russian society and peasant life, with the great contrasts of luxury and poverty between the upper and lower classes. There was some more singing in the evening, Coleridge doing his part.

Friday, September 10

TOOK a walk with Coleridge to a near-by church. After lunch tramped with Bernard, his eldest son, to get a famous view from a hill about three miles off. Bernard graduated this year from Oxford, and we found a common topic in rowing, for he was captain of his college boat and I captain and stroke of the Harvard University crew; he was too light to make the Oxford Varsity boat. The sliding seats had only recently been adopted in the great races, and he and I talked over the development of this stroke which has practically been the same at both Oxford and Harvard. Harvard first used the slides in 1872 and Oxford in 1873.

At four o'clock came back and dressed for a dinner with Sir John Taylor Coleridge at Heath's Court, Ottery St. Mary. Lord Coleridge drove me over. Sir John is his father. While waiting for dinner we went to the celebrated church of Ottery St. Mary, which is so remarkably graceful and delicate, and walked about the grounds with the beautiful turf so green and smooth. Saw the flowers, the church from all sides, many old headstones in God's Acre and the views, chatting all the while as we strolled.

At dinner were Sir John Taylor Coleridge, Lord Coleridge himself, the Bishop of Oxford, Miss Coleridge, a sister of Lord Coleridge, and the wife and two daughters of the Bishop of Oxford. These two daughters, the Misses Mackarness, are well-mannered, good-looking, modest and attractive. The younger I thought the prettier. (The elder, Mary, was next year, before I came back to England, married to her cousin Bernard, who in 1894 succeeded his father as Lord Coleridge and later was made Judge of the High Court of Justice, the only case in English history of father, son, and grandson occupying in turn that eminent position.)

Particularly glad was I to see Sir John. My father had told me that he thought he was the most perfect gentleman of the old school that he had ever seen, and in this I agreed with him. Sir John is now eighty-five years of age (he died the next year), but neither age nor feebleness prevented a most courteous attention to all. It sometimes gave me almost pain to see him rise with difficulty to bow to the ladies or to get a book. Every motion of his had grace and charm. He was a handsome man with beautiful features, almost feminine, and a winning smile, and yet underneath masculine strength of character was evident. He is a retired judge of the Court of the King's Bench.

Coleridge, his married sister, and her youngest daughter, Miss Mackarness, sang a trio very well. How much music does add to a family gathering! We had a beautiful moonlight drive home after this delightful evening, and on the way back I got Coleridge to tell me his views about the Trent Affair from the English standpoint. He admitted that taking Mason and Slidell off the *Trent* by the American naval officers was in accord with old English law and practice. He told me, too, about the probable effect of the new Judicature Act, especially on the procedure. The procedure, he told me, had been very much quickened so that no longer do the old scandals of the law's delays exist; no more Jarndyce *versus* Jarndyce. The procedure gives justice much more quickly than in the United States and has continued to do so. The English may be slow to reform their ways, but when once aroused, they generally make a thorough job of it.

Coleridge spoke about the Alabama Claims and the trial of these at Geneva under the Treaty of Washington. At one time the American claims for "indirect damages" were so enormous that it came near upsetting the whole arbitration. Coleridge told me we owed much to the tact of Lord Tenterden, to whom I go for my next visit, in preventing the whole affair from becoming an abortion.

He also told me about Lord Cockburn, who was the English judge or representative on the commission which

SIR JOHN TAYLOR COLERIDGE
FROM A PAINTING BY MRS. CARPENTER IN THE HALL OF ETON COLLEGE

was to decide the affair. Coleridge said that the Attorney-General's office had prepared full briefs so that Lord Cockburn might be ready intelligently to discuss with his colleagues these claims which arose from the loss of vessels, mostly merchantmen, destroyed by the *Alabama*, a war vessel which had been fitted out in England and manned by Confederates to fight for the cause of the Confederate States.

"Cockburn," said Lord Coleridge, "was so sure, in his positive manner," that the arbitration would never come off at all that he threw away all these briefs and when it was finally decided that the case was to go on, after all, Cockburn at the last moment asked for copies. They had no complete copy on hand (for these were before the days of typewriting and manifolding) and it took no little time to prepare these briefs from material on hand, and pretty much the whole force of those familiar with the case in the Attorney-General's office had to be set to work.

The briefs, however, by great effort were got to Cockburn in time to be of use, but when Cockburn got to Geneva, where the great case was to be tried, he so quarreled with his fellows on the commission that he made enemies and his information did him no good. Cockburn was also rude to the counsel, as I had heard from other sources as well as from Coleridge. When Caleb Cushing, one of the American lawyers who was a great linguist, asked in what language the court preferred to be addressed, Cockburn, who prided himself on his own linguistic powers, replied, "In Choctaw, in Choctaw."

The award of $15,000,000 Coleridge said he believed to be far too great. (It was so much too great that Congress has never distributed the whole of it on the ground that some classes of claims allowed by the decision were really invalid.)

After the case was decided, Lord Cockburn, said Coleridge, uttered many bitter and unpleasant remarks about the decision and against Americans. Coleridge said that $15,000,000, which was so large as compared to the merits of the case, would have been but a very small sum, indeed, to pay had England thereby regained the friendship of America, but Cockburn, by his words and acts, did all he could to prevent a consummation so devoutly to be wished.

Saturday, September 11
Up at 7.15; breakfasted at 7.45 and left at 8.15, some three quarters of an hour before the usual breakfast time, but dear Lord Coleridge got up early, breakfasted with me, and saw me off. How kind and attentive he has been to me, of course largely on my father's account, but I hope a little on my own. He has talked much and freely with me and has been like a good, kind uncle.

Coleridge is tall, I should judge six feet two inches. The most striking thing about him to me is his fine-shaped head and broad forehead, over deep-set, large, and handsome eyes. His nose is a trifle long, his upper lip short, with a beautifully moulded chin and mouth and very expressive lips, and he has an almost boyish freshness of complexion, though he is nearly fifty-five years old.

CHAPTER IX
LORD TENTERDEN'S

LEFT Honiton by early train on way to Lynmouth for my visit with Lord Tenterden. From Crediton to Barnstaple — some forty miles — I rode on the engine. On the locomotives in England they have no cabs, but only windshields. I asked the engineer about this, and he said that in cold weather they sometimes wished they had a covering, but on the whole they got hardened to their work. I told him about our American airbrakes worked from the engine, which they have not yet adopted in England, and in return I got some information from him of no little value to one so much interested as I am in mechanics.

I explained to him that our American railroads could not be built as thoroughly and well as the English on account of the greater distances to be covered in our country. We have some 70,000 miles of railroads, while in all the British Isles — England, Scotland, Wales, and Ireland — there are only 16,000; that is, the English railroads put together can go less than two thirds around the world while the American can go nearly three times around. Stopped for a half-hour at Exeter and visited the Cathedral where they were making restorations and improvements, some of which seemed rather finical in places, but, on the whole, the effect was very beautiful. The roof is all stone of the fan-tracery style. Stayed an hour at Ilfracombe, the end of the railroad, and looked out on the beautiful sea view.

After lunch left by coach for Lynmouth, catching on the way some glimpses of the sea between high cliffs and ascending and descending the steepest hills I was ever on in any vehicle drawn by horses. On the steepest descents they put under the wheels steel shoes held by stout chains. Lord Tenterden, whom I am to visit, met me at Lynton and drove me down to his pretty cottage, "Woodside," as it is called, at Lynmouth. I saw Lady Tenterden and the children. Lady Tenterden is pleasant, kindly, and humorous. She is Irish by birth and has Irish wit and fancy. We all drove over this first evening to dine with Mr. Bailey, the country squire of the neighborhood. His place is called "Lee Abbey." It is large and spacious and architecturally good. There I met two Mr. and Mrs. Pollocks, brothers- and sisters-in-law of Sir Frederick Pollock, the judge who was so kind to me in London and who has lately been appointed, as I have just learned, the Queen's Remembrancer, a sinecure office. The ladies are sisters of "Squire" Bailey. The late Chief Baron Pollock, the father of the three Pollocks I know, had twelve sons averaging over six feet one inch in height, so he is said to have had seventy-three feet of sons.

After dinner some of the ladies sang and then all played pool and billiards. We had a moonlight drive home through the Valley of the Rocks, a most desolate region, bare of any vegetation whatsoever and with huge boulders and square masses of stone piled recklessly on one another. The scenery of North Devonshire is very grand, a great contrast to that I have just seen in the south. The hills and high moors are nearly bare of trees except in clefts and narrow vales. At Lynmouth, on the other hand, shielded by high ridges, there are endless trees, brakes, and shrubs of many varieties, with a lovely, running river gurgling over rapids and under bridges to the sea. Southey, who

CASTLE OF ROCKS, LYNTON

NORTH DEVONSHIRE AND LORD TENTERDEN 137

traveled far and wide, said Lynmouth was one of the three most beautiful places he had ever known. The high moors of North Devonshire come to the very edge of the sea, which seems to have eaten into them so that they end abruptly in steep precipices from five hundred to eight hundred feet perpendicular. "Woodside" is nestled in Lynmouth valley, and has, on each side, lofty hills more steep than any I saw in Scotland, though not so high.

Sunday, September 12
WROTE letters, attended church, and walked to the pebbly beach in the morning. In the afternoon took a long stretch of seven miles partly over very rough ground. Tenterden had to take up some international affairs in the forenoon. The afternoon walk was with him through the valley of the East Lyn. "Ham" is a common suffix here for the names of villages, as "Middleham." The root is that in our word "hamlet." We saw some charming scenery of great contrasts — waterfalls, woods, ferns, steep hills, bare rocks of varied shapes, pretty bridges, quiet pools, foaming rapids, and much brilliant green, and many, many bright flowers.

On Sundays there are no mails in England and all the telegraph offices are closed excepting for the Government service alone. Tenterden showed me some telegrams that he, as the head of the Foreign Office, had just received this Sunday morning from Constantinople, with important bearing on the Eastern question. These had not been forwarded to the Foreign Minister, and it was great fun to read them in this confidential manner before any of the Cabinet knew of their contents. Tenterden has a wonderful memory and posts himself up on all the geography and names of persons as well as informing himself on the great issues, but with all his study, knowledge, responsibility, and influence, there is something more — a human side of cheer, tact, goodwill, fun, kindness, and laughter. I wonder if it was not more the human side than the intellectual that enabled him to preserve the Alabama arbitration from collapse. He is a man to win both admiration and affection.

Monday, September 13
STROLLED along the North Walk, as it is called, to Lee Abbey. This is a path cut in the side of the steep hills near the top, with a sheer precipice of five hundred feet or so below us and guarded by a low stone parapet. At the Abbey Tenterden and I lunched. After lunch we had a try at archery, in which the others were skilled, but I did fairly well for a beginner, they made me think. We then walked to Duty Point from which the only daughter of Sir Edward de Whichehalse threw herself down when she was deserted by her lover, a favorite of James II. The precipice is some five hundred feet perpendicular. We passed Castle Rock, a huge promontory six or seven hundred feet high, of square blocks of stone and looking very like a ruined, cyclopean castle of enormous proportions.

In the evening dined at Dr. Julius Pollock's, where were Lord and Lady Tenterden, Dr. and Mrs. Pollock, and Mr. and Mrs. Rowcliffe. Mr. Rowcliffe, a Queen's Councilor of much ability, has now lost his health from overwork. Mrs. Rowcliffe is handsome, witty, and a brilliant talker and *raconteur*.

(Some years later, the first Lady Tenterden and Mr. Rowcliffe having died, Lord Tenterden married Mrs. Rowcliffe and a delightful pair they must have made.)

Tuesday, September 14

DROVE to a meet at Exmoor. Exmoor is a high plateau near the sea and in places from 1500 to 1600 feet above high tide mark. Here is said to be the only place in England where the red deer is found wild. Only fifty years ago the country hereabouts was almost unknown, with no roads, only mule paths leading to the interior. It was for a long time, in fact till free trade came in, the haunt of smugglers, and as late as Queen Anne's time there were bands of robbers in the vicinity. We drove in a carriage together, Tenterden, Mrs. Julius Pollock, Mrs. Rowcliffe, and myself. About two o'clock a fine stag was started by the hounds, and, trying to leap across a sunken road just ahead of us, he struck on the opposite bank and broke his leg. He was easily caught and killed near our carriage. Later another start was made and off went the hunters, with here and there a red coat, over heath and heather, down one valley and up the opposite hill, following the hounds. Soon they all appeared silhouetted against the sky on the high horizon, then they disappeared slowly and left us to envy their enjoyment and plan for our return home.

Exmoor is the romantic setting for Blackmore's "Lorna Doone," of which they tell me the story, I not having read the book. Tenterden then took me to walk by way of Glenthorne, the seat of Mr. Halliday, where we called, but found them all out. We had a fascinating and wild walk, part of the way on a narrow path on the side of a precipice with no outer wall. On arriving home my pedometer registered eleven miles.

At dinner were Mr. and Mrs. Rowcliffe and Dr. and Mrs. Pollock. Mr. Rowcliffe was unwell and had to leave the table. There was some fear of his being se-

Wednesday, September 15

TOOK sketch book up the river to do a pretty scene; as usual, not so pretty on paper as the scene itself. The others tried the fishing, which proved to be poor. They always give curious explanations about this fishing and lack of fish, as that there is an east wind, or the water is too clear, or the weather too dry, or there is too much rain, or the water is too brown. The subject I chose for the sketch was an arched stone bridge and rapids underneath.

After lunch we went out sea fishing in a heavy rowboat and had fair luck, catching one cod and several rock whiting.

Dined at Dr. Pollock's, where were the usual quartet, with a Mrs. Rowe in addition. She is a widow and one of the three large landowners in the neighborhood, lively, bright, good-looking, and considered a great "catch." The good ladies, who, like most of their kind, are match-makers, got me to call on her and made several occasions to bring us together.

Thursday, September 16

AFTER lunch drove with Dr. Pollock and Tenterden several miles up the river Lyn and fished, but the river was too low and the water too clear, so we had no luck. We then drove to within three or four miles from home and about dusk began fishing in Long Pool. Long Pool is in a deep ravine between high, perpendicular rocks with a small fall of water at the upper end. The banks are wooded here and there on little shelves of rock with a variety of trees. At all times it is very picturesque, but the change from twilight to darkness and then to moonlight, with the moon itself at one moment behind clouds, at the next dimmed with mist, and again shining out clearly on the opposite bank, glistening to the water's edge and falling through the trees here and there upon rocks or water, was something surpassingly beautiful. It was a fairyland; the soft shadows and bright spots gave easy play to the imagination to picture all sorts of depths and heights, palaces and halls, while the falling water, with its babbling sound, put one nearly to sleep, until there would come a tug at the line to remind one of reality and to turn the mind from soothing dreams of the imagination to catching real fish, from castles in Spain to Long Pool, Lynmouth.

We had good luck for the state of the water, catching twenty-two trout and three eels. We stopped fishing a little past midnight and walked home by the banks of the stream. The moon had a highly colored ring about it and our path lay mostly in the woods, sometimes high above and again on a level with the stream which flows over a rocky bed with several waterfalls and frequent rapids. The whole scene was very different from anything I had imagined as existing in England. It is wild and not unlike some unfrequented parts of our White Mountains, if a variety of oaks, beeches, birches, and plane trees should be substituted for the New Hampshire firs. The ivy grows wild in great profusion and fuchsias and blossoming myrtles thrive out of doors all the year round. At half-past one we had a late supper or early breakfast, if you prefer to call it so, which was very refreshing and was brightened up with Tenterden's cheery talk and catching laughter.

Friday, September 17

AFTER lunch walked up the river while others fished and had a long talk with Mrs. Julius Pollock. Afterwards went in bathing in the sea and came near being caught by the tide under the cliffs. The tide rose to-day some twenty-two feet ten inches, and when it got started, it came up very fast, every wave being in advance of the last, during the rush. The cliffs were so steep they were impossible to climb and the beaches were very flat, so that a few feet of rise caused a rapid rush of the waters over long distances, and, with the strong currents and rough surface, it would have been almost impossible to swim round the point to the mouth of the Lyn and I came near meeting the fate of Mary in Charles Kingsley's poem "The Sands of Dee."

Fished from a boat in the harbor, but had very poor luck. The bad luck was, of course, explained. There is a reason for everything that goes wrong in fishing, only the reason is never known until after the fishing is over. The reason this time was distant rumbling thunder. There was a heavy shower during the night with loud claps and sheets of lightning and in the morning the river "came down"; that is, the water had come from the hills and the river rose. That is generally a promise of good sport, so we all, ladies included, started up the river before lunch, but the fishing was never worse. We could not even get a bite. The ladies went back for lunch while we men ate the "grub" we had taken with us, stayed until eight o'clock in the evening, and went home for late dinner.

In the afternoon the luck was as bad as it had been in the morning, though in the early evening Tenterden succeeded in landing a sea trout, a salmon peel of about one pound and a half, a few eels were caught, and one or two smaller trout. The reason given this time was that the fish expected more rain, though exactly why they should have been less hungry in that expectation or why they had any power or cause to expect anything, was not explained. Another reason was that the water was not fine enough. I thought that was a very clever excuse, for no one really knows exactly what "fine enough" is, so it has the advantage of being indefinite. Some said the color was too brown or too yellow or not brown or not yellow enough, but strange to say, in this case as in the others, they did not find out that the water was the wrong color or the fish were expecting anything till after we had been several hours without catching a thing.

After dinner Tenterden and I went over to Dr. Pollock's and they made me do several sleight-of-hand tricks with cards and coins. Lady Tenterden has been unwell since the first two days of my visit. Tenterden told me he prized very highly my father's notes to Wheaton's International Law and said he and others use them all the time at the Foreign Office as the best authority and expressed with remarkable clearness and precision.

Sunday, September 19
WENT to church in a very pretty chapel with a good clergyman, a tourist, and no choir, but fair congregational singing. In the afternoon went to Lee Abbey where I met a Mr. and Mrs. Wilde. Wilde is a barrister, and the son of Lord Truro. Mr. Wilde is father of Mrs. Bailey.

On the way over I discovered that Mrs. Julius Pollock was an authoress. She wrote a book called "Lissadel" which was published this spring and had been favorably criticized. The scene of the novel is laid in the vicinity of Lynmouth. We took a walk to Leemouth where there is a sand beach, all the other beaches being more or less stony. As we were walking along the shore they pointed out an overhanging cliff. It seemed almost directly over the water and yet they told me that from above, it was almost impossible to throw a stone into the sea.

I knew they would ask me to try and at the top of the cliff there would be only jagged stones, so I slyly put some smooth, large, flat ones into my pocket. When at last we wound our way up to the top, surely enough they challenged me to try, and making use of the best one of the stones from my collection, I threw it off toward the water and succeeded in reaching it, where we saw it splash, much to their astonishment. The feat, they told me, had been done only one or two times before and that I beat the former throws by a fair distance. I suppose the others did not have the forethought to supply themselves, like David when going against Goliath, with "smooth stones from the brook," or, in this case, from the beach.

It was a beautiful sunset over the water. We walked home by the North Walk. The great height at or near the tops of the cliffs gives a very extended horizon which seems so high as to be almost a hill of water and adds much to the charm of the sunset. The ships on the large waves below seem like toy vessels on the ripples of a duck pond.

Mrs. Pollock asked if she might make use of me as her hero in the next novel. In my conceit I said that I would hardly do for a hero and got a deserved answer: "Oh, it does n't do to have a perfect hero or he would be laughed at by the critics."

A moonlight walk up the Watersmeet Road. Sang songs.

Monday, September 20
MR. and Mrs. Rowcliffe left in the morning and I waited to see them off. They asked me to be sure and come and see them when in London. It threatened rain in the afternoon and just before I left it began to pour in torrents. On bidding Tenterden good-bye he gave me letters of introduction, which he had prepared, to the British ambassadors in the various capitals which I was to visit: Paris, Rome, Athens, Cairo, and Constantinople. He told me that these were more than "soup tickets."

Went to Ilfracombe by steamer. There is no wharf, so passengers and luggage have to be rowed out by boat. Lord and Lady Tenterden and children and Dr. and Mrs. Pollock came down to the beach to see me off. Rather a wet farewell. This is the first time I have seen Lady Tenterden since she was ill. The steamer passed as close to the cliffs as possible so as to avoid a strong head tide and we caught occasional views which were grand, though soon shut off by rain and mist. All the friends at Lynmouth had been so kind to me that I was sorry indeed to part from them. I hope to meet them all again next spring when I return to England.

CHAPTER X

HURSLEY PARK: SIR WILLIAM HEATHCOTE'S AND GENERAL REVIEW

Tuesday, September 21

THE weather cleared off and I finished "Lissadel." The trains were so scheduled that it was impossible to stop over at Salisbury and yet be able to call at Sir William Heathcote's at Hursley Park near Winchester. I had got ticket and had my luggage marked for Winchester, but the guard of the train told me that Chandler's Ford station was nearer Hursley than Winchester, and on his advice I had my trunks taken from the van, got out of the railway carriage in a fine rain, and told the porter to call me a cab. He said there were none about. I asked him where was the nearest place I could find one. He said, "The nearest place is Hursley." "How far is Hursley?" I asked. "Three miles," was the reply. Then I looked down the track at my train and saw it was disappearing rapidly "beyond recall." I asked him if there was any other kind of trap to be got nearer, a farm wagon or anything of the sort, and he said "No." I then had my trunk sent by parcels express to Winchester and started on foot for Hursley.

I arrived in the park with wet and muddy shoes, a cloth cap, and rough clothes, inquiring my way as I went. I walked up the avenue and by mistake took the turn to the stables. I then asked one of the coachmen which was the way to the house and he pointed to me a path which I innocently took, but found it led to the back or the kitchen door only, so I turned and had to pass the stable again, much to the amusement of the coachman. To add to my discomfort I found Lady Heathcote and somebody else driving away in a carriage from the front door just as I reached it. I was afraid that that somebody was Sir William, but the liveried footman at the door told me that Sir William was in the house.

I thought altogether I had made a pretty bad entrance, and the majestic menial at the front door did not offer to take my coat or hat or ask me into the front hall, but simply told mé to wait in the vestibule. He looked at the letter of introduction and my card, leisurely walked off, and apparently took his time about it, for he did not appear for many minutes — it seemed to me at least half an hour — and then, when he came again in view, asked me to walk up. I found Sir William in his library; he was expecting to see me, for I had sent him word by mail that I should call. He was most courteous and insisted upon my staying overnight, sent for my trunk at the station, and had a message telegraphed to my London lodgings, saying I would not arrive till Wednesday. After a pleasant chat with Sir William, who was affability itself, I read and wrote till five o'clock when I was shown into the drawing-room where they were having afternoon tea. There I met Lady Heathcote, several children and grandchildren, and Archdeacon Mildmay of Chelmsford, his wife and children. At dinner I took in a Mrs. Heathcote and sat on Lady Heathcote's right. Lady Heathcote still preserves her charm, both of person and mind, which my father described.[1] I talked with the Archdeacon after dinner for an hour or so on Church and State, education in America, college life and influence.

[1] *R. H. Dana. A Biography.* By C. F. Adams (Houghton, Mifflin and Company, 1891), vol. II, pp. 89–96, 106.

The servant in charge of my room made a mess of my leather portmanteau, which he had believed, I think, to be some strange outlandish American invention. He took the canvas cover all off and indeed every buckle and strap he could see. As a matter of fact, it was an English trunk from Last's in London, and when he learned that, he seemed to gather his wits together and managed it all right afterwards.

The house is large and spacious. There is a grand stairway and broad halls and long rooms with fine, well-painted family portraits dating back one hundred and fifty years when the baronetcy was created. The present Sir William is fifth in line, and there are some old masters, rare engravings, and good statuary about and an air of substantial affluence moulded by good taste and culture.

Sir William, who is now seventy-four years of age, took highest honors at Oxford and a doctorate of civil law, was in Parliament for many years representing Oxford University for part of the time, and has been a leader in philanthropies and good works both in Winchester in particular and in the kingdom in general. Though holding no cabinet position, his many years in Parliament, his high character and good judgment, give him unusual influence in the affairs of Great Britain.

Wednesday, September 22
BREAKFASTED with all the family and then took a walk with the Reverend Mr. Heathcote, a younger son of Sir William. He was very cordial, repeatedly urging me to visit him in his rectory if I should be in that part of the country. He showed me the Hursley church and rectory where Keble preached, lived, wrote, and died, and I saw Keble's tomb and the house where lived Charlotte

KEBLE'S CHURCH AND VICARAGE AT HURSLEY

Yonge, the author of "The Heir of Redclyffe." How I loved that book and how I wept as a schoolboy over the death of dear Guy! Mr. Heathcote spoke to me of primogeniture. He said that though he was a younger son, he would far rather his elder brother should have the estate and keep it up, retaining all the family portraits and heirlooms so that the estate and the family dignity might be maintained, than to have everything divided equally and each child get only a small share. My father in 1856 spoke of the old estate as sure to be in the family for generations to come.

(Curiously enough, soon after this, Hursley passed out of the Heathcote family. The elder son was a Catholic and a Jesuit and, if I am correctly informed, broke up the entail and gave the bulk of the proceeds to his Church. I thought he and the incidents in connection with Hursley might have furnished the character and plot for "Helbeck of Bannisdale," but Mrs. Humphry Ward, in her "Writer's Recollections" (1918), tells how the suggestion for that book came from another family and other scenes.)

Archdeacon Mildmay also asked me to visit him and told me to write him and let him know when I came back to London. How hospitable, genial, and kindly these people are, just as my father found them to be when he visited Sir William in 1856!

Sir William drove me to Winchester in time to escort me over the hospital personally and to let me see the Cathedral before the train left for London. He explained the system of nurses, probationers — that is, nurses on trial — their training and education, and also a system of outdoor or visiting nurses, which he said worked admirably and seemed worthy of adoption in America. One thing struck me particularly in the hospital. In many such places the intimacy with death and the frequent post mortems make the managers careless and hard, but here Sir William had a special place set apart and at the head of the room erected a marble slab with this text, "When this corruptible shall have put on incorruption," and does all he can to secure reverential treatment in autopsies. Sir William showed me over every part of the hospital, pointing out any improvements over other hospitals, and then sent me off to the Cathedral in his coach while he stayed for a meeting of the trustees. I spent an hour in the Cathedral, lunched, and left for London, having said good-bye to Sir William at the hospital door.

One hears occasionally of dull English dinners, but it has been my good fortune not to have been present at a single one. The conversation has always been interesting and sometimes brilliant. I noticed, too, that there was habitual courtesy to and consideration for the domestics: "Please hand me this," or, "Be so good as to get my overcoat," etc.

I believe I have never given a menu of the dinners. They have been bountiful, with many courses, generally two of meat, one perhaps being of game, and usually there have been from four to six kinds of wine; sherry, champagne, claret, and port appearing the most frequently.

At the five o'clock afternoon teas the prevailing fashion is to take the tea rather strong, with milk or cream and no sugar. It is always some kind of black tea. Thin slices of bread evenly and slightly buttered, and usually folded with buttered sides together, are served and sometimes some cake. The full dress of the ladies at dinner is rather open, rather low and broad in front, sometimes though not always higher in the back, and of handsome light material, and with long trains. In the daytime the dress is high.

I have been asked whether a great deal of this cordiality of the English is not superficial. I have sometimes met Englishmen traveling where I thought the good wines and well-cooked dinners had aroused a temporary expression of hospitality which was more gastronomic than heartfelt, but even among these chance travelers I have made firm and enduring friendships; but with all those English men and women with whom my lot has been cast for nearly three months, the acts of kindness have spoken even louder than words. As I shall show later, on my return to England the following spring they by no means forgot me, and often by letter or by kindness to friends I have sent to them, and by hospitality later they have shown a warm-hearted friendship that is by no means superficial.

The English method of entertaining guests is worthy of consideration. Our hospitality at home has been too much of a burden on both host and guest. A three-days' visit is a burden; a week's is torture. It is considered necessary to devote practically all the host's time to the guest; all other matters are in abeyance, conversation must be kept up, even the short time given to housekeeping has to be apologized for, and it is hard for either guest or host to find time for rest or writing necessary letters. Excuses have to be invented and white lies told. This is continued from hour to hour so that before three days are over every one is fatigued and talked out, no matter how agreeable are either the visitors or the host and his family.

The English, on the other hand, have carried hospitality to a fine art. Life goes on pretty much as usual. At breakfast the host says such and such things are going on or suggests certain plans for the visitors. What would the guests like to do? Perhaps the guests plan something between themselves and the host and hostess are free to join or not as they please. Then at lunch and afternoon tea there is a gathering of those who happen to be about and perhaps more plans are talked over. It is only at dinner and in the evening that all are brought together and conversation is kept up. This makes hospitality easy and therefore frequent.

I left England September 25th for Paris.

CHAPTER XI
PARIS SALONS, AND ENGLISH EMBASSY

Paris, September 28

DELIVERED letters all the forenoon till lunch; among others was one to the Honorable Elihu Benjamin Washburne, United States Minister to France. He gained a reputation for courage and diplomacy in the Franco-Prussian War that will always be a credit to our country. He was the only foreign minister to stay at his post during the Siege of Paris and the Commune and gave shelter and protection to nationals of other countries as well as to citizens of the United States. He also protected those unfortunate Germans who were unable to leave Paris during the war and altogether won the admiration of all.

He was "at home" and insisted upon seeing me at once, and then later took me with him in a carriage on his way to some public business. He has a rough exterior and rather nasal voice, is tall and commanding in appearance, has a way of going straight to his object, and his talk is sensible and sincere. With all his stay in France he has not yet learned to speak French well. He called out to the coachman, "Cocher, allez au coin de la rue," pronouncing "coin" like the English "coin," "de" with a flat "e," and "rue" in two syllables like "rou-hey."

He could not have been more kind to me than he was and spoke most pleasantly of my father, his character, ability, and writings. Washburne had been called the "father" of the House of Representatives in Congress, being, I believe, longer in that body than any other member of his day. He was appointed by General Grant first as Secretary of State for the United States and soon after as Minister to France. (He wrote "Recollections of a Minister to France" and died in 1887.) To come back to his cabman, that man comprehended the directions that Washburne had given him, badly pronounced as they were. The French are wonderful at understanding.

Thursday, September 30

AMONG the other letters of introduction I had for Paris was one to Monsieur Xavier Marmier given me by Professor Henry W. Longfellow of Cambridge. In reply to an invitation from Marmier I went to his apartment at half-past eleven. I found him taking his morning coffee. He does not speak English well, so my small store of French had sometimes to be called into requisition. No one could be more charming and gracious than Monsieur Marmier. He showed me numerous American books on his shelves and complimented American literature. He has a great love as well as admiration for Longfellow. He asked me if Miss Edith were married and was surprised to hear that she was not, and then said, "One so pretty *and* so good," with his hand on his heart, all which set my pulses beating with pleasure, for my wish at the Wishing Tree at Pembroke Lodge was about that same young lady.

His rooms are plain and furniture a bit shabby, but the books which line all the walls make up for everything else and give an air of coziness and intellectuality. He is one of the forty Immortals, an Academician or member of the Institute of France. He has written many books of travel. He lives with his little old housekeeper and his dog, who made friends with me, contrary to the usual custom of this little animal as Monsieur Marmier told me. His rooms are on the third floor according to French counting. The wooden part of the furniture is old and handsome and floors are all bare excepting the library, which is the only one carpeted. He was surprised that I, being an American, did not smoke.

He dressed or rather finished dressing while I was in the room. It was very good of him to speak so kindly of America, for I had been told that in his journeys in the West he was much disconcerted by the roughness of some American travelers, especially on one of the Mississippi flatboats. There they crushed his tall hat over his eyes and made fun of his broken English, though, to be sure, in the eastern part of the country he was well received and properly appreciated. He took me to see Monsieur Mohl, another member of the Institute and a friend of Professor Longfellow, to whom also he had given me a letter.

Madame Mohl has the reputation of being one of the brightest and wittiest ladies in France and is the last one to keep up the old-fashioned "salon." She was not up, but Monsieur Mohl was; dressed, however, in a long, loose gown and slippers, although it was quarter after one. His dressing-gown was of a brown woolen stuff and he wore no collar. Indeed, I suspected from the looks of the arrangement that he only had his nightshirt under the dressing-gown. He was reading a ponderous, unbound book which was lying on the top of a pile, about a foot or two high, of old half-cut pamphlets and leaflets. They appeared more and more dusty as my eye descended to the bottom of the pile. His hot-water jug was still on the fireplace. His letters were in hopeless confusion on a table near by. I judged the correspondence of the whole year must have been there, and how it was possible for him to find anything in particular or tell in general what notes were answered or what unanswered, or what bills paid or what unpaid, I could not make out.

He speaks English pretty well, for his wife was English by birth, though she has been so long in France that she speaks French better than English, which she has partially forgotten. The celebrated Academicians soon got deep into literary conversation, of which I could get no connected idea. At one time they became very much disgusted with some one's presumption and made up faces to correspond to the disgust they felt. Monsieur Mohl invited me to come to-morrow evening in time for tea, when Madame Mohl and some friends would be present and Monsieur Marmier offered to send me a ticket to the Théâtre Français, and two to the opening lectures of the Institute. Both sets of tickets, he informed me, he gets free of charge. Monsieur Marmier walked back with me as far as the river. Both he and Monsieur Mohl live on the Latin Quarter side, Monsieur Mohl at 120 rue du Bac and Marmier in the rue St. Thomas d'Aquin, No. 11.

Marmier, although an old man deeply interested in literature and a distinguished member of the Institute, found great youthful interest in the shop windows before which he would stop in admiration. He told me to be sure to look at the shop windows in the Palais Royal for amusement. Several times as we were walking he would stop in the street and take my arm to explain something more fully, talking all the time. He put his hand over his heart and said, "Professor Longfellow is very close here."

Friday, October 1
IN the evening, after dining at a nice, clean restaurant where we had a good selection of soups, entrées, meats,

vegetables, and fruit, wine included, for two francs (forty cents), went with Monsieur Marmier to Madame Mohl's for the evening tea. French was spoken almost wholly.

Madame Mohl said she was very sorry that it was so much out of season. She regretted not to have more society to offer me. However, it gave me an idea of one of her salons. She boiled her water for the tea in a kettle on the wood ashes on the hearth. She has a small, quaint figure, gray hair very carelessly put up, and loose-fitting gown, and all the time she is apparently much absorbed in keeping up the fire, boiling the water and making the tea, and yet I see she is listening, for she breaks into the conversation with a few words now and then, to which all listen, often causing a bright laugh or stimulating a quick answer. There were several literary people and bright talkers, I was told, but no one of them of very great distinction this evening.

Madame Mohl's salons are famous and distinguished foreigners passing through Paris are glad to be asked there to hear this bright little lady — more brilliant than her distinguished husband — the other intellectual talk, "the flashing play of French" wit, and to meet *littérateurs* gathered in these quaint, crowded, and unkempt rooms. It all seems a triumph of mind over matter, about which latter there is rather too much of "never mind." (Her letters have been published and widely read.)

Saturday, October 2
ANOTHER morning in the Louvre Galleries. Dined with Mr. F. Ottiwell Adams, the English *chargé d'affaires* at Paris. Lord Lyons, the English Minister, to whom Lord Tenterden gave me a letter, was away and Adams entertained in his place. At the dinner I met Mrs. Abbott,

Lord Tenterden's mother and daughter of the late Lord George Stuart. She had a very beautiful young lady under her charge. There were also a Mr. and Mrs. Hugh Wyndham (later he was knighted as Sir Hugh Wyndham, was British Minister to Servia, Rio de Janeiro, and Bucharest, and *chargé d'affaires* at St. Petersburg). He had just received a promotion to the position of Secretary of Legation at Athens. Beside these were a number of others to whom I was not introduced. I took in Mrs. Wyndham.

Mr. Wyndham explained the methods of examination for the British diplomatic positions. These are not open to all, but only to persons who are nominated; that is, it is a limited competition. He said also that they would have to pass subsequent examinations to show that they were keeping up with their work. For example, he would soon have to pass an examination in modern Greek, after being a certain number of months at Athens.

Monday, October 4

MADE calls in the afternoon. Found Madame Mohl at home. She was cutting out a dress for herself and that led to talking about American young ladies. It relieved her mind for me to tell her that several of the young ladies I personally knew at home could sew and cut out dresses and trim hats and that a few of them did a good deal of this for themselves, especially those of moderate means who were still in society, daughters of Harvard professors and the like. It is not an uncommon impression among foreigners — an impression which Madame Mohl shared — that all well-to-do American women did nothing but sit with hands folded, neither taking exercise nor doing anything useful. Madame Mohl kept on with her work, carrying on the conversation all the while in her bright, quick, natural way. Natural is just the right word, for she says what comes into her mind, setting it off with droll figures of speech and odd comments. She stopped her work just long enough to give me a good cup of tea made from the hot water boiling on the wood fire.

Tuesday, October 5
To the Théâtre Français in the evening and saw "Demi-Monde," by Dumas Fils. Croisette took the part of la Baronne and acted it supremely well. On the whole I think the most perfect thing I have seen since I left America, the one that had the least flaws and gave the least disappointment — apart from personal friends — was the acting at the Français. It came up to my ideal. Every character was well done. Even servants' parts were taken by finished actors, one of the best in the world taking one in which there was very little to say, but in which there was a chance to show suppressed emotion. Nothing was overdone, while, when the part called for it, there was fire and spirit enough. There were no useless motions, no comic attitudes just to produce an irrelevant laugh, and no unbefitting dress. Every actor was attired simply and looked and moved like the character represented, just as you would have seen such a person if you had met him or her in a parlor or walking the street in real life. In fact, all the success was made to depend upon good acting alone, for there was not even an orchestra, and yet the theatre was filled and the audience enthusiastic.

Received a present from Monsieur Marmier of his book "Les Fiancés du Spitzberg," with his name in it and these quaint words, "To Mr. Richard Dana friendly offered by the author."

Wednesday, October 6

To the grand opera in the evening at the invitation of Mrs. Abbott, who had Madame d'Erlanger's box, which is one of the best in the house. We saw in one of the proscenium boxes the old Queen of Spain, stout and dark, and three of her offspring. Our box was large and roomy, number 25-27. Some Englishmen in the box thought it necessary to put on the *blasé*, and not only went to sleep in the back of the box during some very interesting portions, but what was worse, talked and laughed quite loud during others. The opera was "The Huguenots," and the general effect was very grand, although there were no great soloists.

Mrs. Abbott is bright, cheery, and humorous. I now see where her son got his cleverness.

After the opera was over the English gentlemen seemed very slow about getting the carriages, so I undertook, with my limited knowledge of French, to find on which side of the building the carriages were, how to get there, then to find the right ones, and put the ladies of the party in them.

Friday, October 8

IN the evening I dined again with Mr. Adams, who is now full British Ambassador to France, at the Embassy, and there met a large company, mostly French. It was truly an enjoyable occasion. The conversation was interesting and largely in the French language. Mr. Adams said that the Japanese were inferior to the Chinese in power of organization especially. He said that in Japan — and he was in the embassy there for several years — his head servants were always Chinese. He and others who had been long in Japan agreed that the Japanese civilization was only external, a mere

AN ENGLISH OPINION OF THE JAPANESE 161

veneer. Great proclamations had been made and nothing but change in dress and a few other externals were ever carried out.

He said that it was a great mistake to have them so cried up in the newspapers all over the world. They had not even the quickness of the Chinese. They could only do what they were told and shown how to do.

(This was a very interesting opinion considering what the Japanese have done in the forty-five years following. About the time Adams was leaving Japan, its Government was laying the foundation for solid improvement. It sent its brightest young men to study in the great universities of the West, specializing in the various subjects for which they showed adaptability, and with this foundation of education they then investigated every industry and profession on its practical side, each one pursuing his specialty in various countries, made reports to their Government and were put in charge of the needed reforms.)

A period of great material prosperity all said was in store for America. It was generally acknowledged that it would be impossible to guarantee European peace for a longer time than till next April (1876). The Frenchmen scoffed at the idea of an empire in France before ten years at least. They agreed that the political and social advance in France was far less than the material. It was hoped that the new Assembly would be more conservative and that a senate, which it is now proposed to add, will cause a great improvement over the single assembly.

Bismarck, they said, ate not only in a slovenly manner, but also ate and drank enormously and the Frenchmen thought that he had been "greatly overrated."

The East Indian question, the future of India and what to do with it, troubled the Englishmen not a little.

Saturday, October 9

BREAKFASTED at 11 A.M. with Monsieur Marmier. There were present a French admiral and two MM. Fouret, the heads of the largest classical publishing house in Paris. One of them spoke English pretty well and knew of both father and grandfather. There were, besides these, a member of the French National Assembly and also a man rather younger than the rest. There was much conversation, most of it in French, some of which I could not understand. It seemed to sparkle with wit, to judge from the rapid-firing remarks and bursts of laughter.

There is a saying that Frenchmen can never meet together without talking of mistresses. Strangely enough, and even in such a circle as this, made up of literary and distinguished people, some of them in middle and past middle life, that turned out to be the case. They went quite into detail, with names and descriptions and some stories had a comic touch. They discussed these subjects with the frankness and simplicity which we should use in talking of rare books or beautiful bindings.

They asked me about the Senate of the United States and how the senators were chosen, for the composition of their senate, which they are about to create, was one of the problems they were trying to solve. They could not well copy the United States method of selection where senators are elected by state legislatures, for the nearest approach to state legislatures are their department governments, which are only executive with very limited administrative powers. These department governments can only suggest to the Assembly, they can never make laws as our States do, so the department governments have not the dignity of our state legislatures nor do they represent such distinct local interests. So they thought the French will have to adopt some other plan.

Monsieur René Fouret gave me the name of a good tutor and said I would probably find a cultured family who would take Paul Dana and myself in. We wanted to have just such an opportunity to improve our French. He said, however, it was not the custom in France to take strangers into families.

He spoke to me apart about the subjects of conversation which I have already alluded to, and I told him of the different ideals among American men as a rule. He said he had heard of the same difference before and wondered whether, present company excepted of course, there might not either be a lack of virility among American men or of full blood among American women, or perhaps, he suggested, a certain amount of decorous custom or a sort of hypocrisy that kept these subjects in the background. I had heard somewhat the same suggestions from some Englishmen as accounting for the better state of affairs in American society than in European.

I urged it might be accounted for by the fact that our men were more busy and occupied, we not having so large a class of idlers of wealth who were seeking excitement and diversion. In France, too, it is with some few exceptions presumed that a young man is to go wrong, while in the United States he is expected to keep straight. Moreover, with us most fathers have set a good example, while in Paris the sons too often learn that their fathers are not above reproach; but most of all, I suggested that the influence of the American young ladies over the young men of their own class was wholly for good. Our young men have played with them as children, have met them as friends, have got to know and respect them, and to have affection for them or perhaps even to feel that they are or are beginning to be in love. Such feelings keep the young men up to high ideals which no preaching, no beatitudes, or no moral precepts alone would do as well. The American youth were fortunate too, I said, in having for their national heroes such high-minded men as Washington and Lincoln.

Marmier was kind and even affectionate to me.

Monday, October 11
RECEIVED a kind note from Mrs. Wyndham, wife of the English Secretary of Legation recently appointed to Athens, whom I met at the English Embassy dinners, giving me the name of a nice French family she recommended for us to live with. Went to call on this family.

Tuesday, October 12
ENGAGED two places with the good people recommended by Mrs. Wyndham. They consist of Monsieur, Madame, and Mademoiselle Laya, and they live in a two-storied apartment at 36 rue Montaigne, Faubourg St. Honoré. Madame Laya is English by birth and is related to persons of distinction in her native country.

Thursday, October 14
IN the afternoon we moved to our new rooms and had dinner at seven o'clock. The cooking was excellent, and altogether it bids fair to be a pleasant place and a good opportunity to become familiar with the French language.

Monsieur Laya's father was one of the forty Immortals of his day, a member of the Academy, the author of many plays. Monsieur Laya now lives with the family. He was an advocate and later a professor of Roman and International Law in the Ecole at Paris. Mademoiselle Laya is somewhat over forty years of age and her parents probably about sixty-five. She is a teacher of singing of considerable reputation in England, where she goes during the London season. She has herself obtained the degree of Bachelor of Literature from the University of Paris after having passed the regular examinations and written her thesis just as is required for men.

The whole family was quite bright, lively, and entertaining and our first dinner passed off pleasantly. Monsieur Laya is writing a history of the American Revolution and has published two volumes on English law. I think he puts in the mouth of General Washington the things that he, Monsieur Laya, wishes to prove rather than what Washington ever did or probably would have said, in my humble opinion. Monsieur Laya knows the present Lord Chief Justice Cockburn, and several prominent barristers in England. We seem to be very lucky in our French family. The ladies are both able to speak English so as to explain when necessary, but they are very good about talking and making us speak in French. Monsieur Laya never talks in English, though he is able to read it.

Friday, October 15
WE engaged a French tutor for one hour every day at the price of thirty-six francs a week for both. Called at Monsieur Marmier's, who was out, and left a copy of my father's book "Two Years Before the Mast" for him. He had read it, but did not have a copy in his library.

Sunday, October 17

A CALL from Monsieur Marmier. He thanked me for "Two Years Before the Mast" and complimented it very highly. He is going to send me a ticket to the opening of the Academy, of which he is a member as I have already said, and he promised to get me admission to the Assembly or French Parliament, which opens next month. He has met and knows the Layas with whom we are staying.

Tuesday, October 19

THIS evening Madame Laya had her weekly reception. At dinner were two young Irishmen, and also the Vicomtesse de Pérusse. She was very bright, clever, and genial. She looked so young that I hesitated at first whether to call her Madame or Mademoiselle. Later in the evening her husband and two daughters appeared. Her two daughters were just over twenty and looked but little younger than Madame. One of the daughters is considered a beauty. We were not introduced to the young ladies and Madame Laya explained to me that no young men were ever introduced to young ladies in good French society. The young ladies sat by their mother almost all the evening except when in a game or to play the piano. We spoke to them a little and they appeared intelligent and sensible. But it is customary for young men not to speak much with them. They tell me that as a general rule the French young men only ask for a turn at a dance or remark on the weather or about art or the last new play, by way of conversation, and even that little is always carried on under the mother's eye and generally within her hearing.

There was a good deal of music, vocal and instrumental, and they made me play on my guitar. I sang some German and negro songs. They apparently liked them. "Omne ignotum pro magnifico." We played "How, When, and Where do you like it?" — in French, of course. When the ladies got up to go they said goodnight to us all, but it is allowed only to the married ladies to shake hands with men, young or old. Is this what the good influence of young ladies on society is confined to by the French etiquette? On the whole we passed a very agreeable and instructive evening.

Wednesday, October 20
FOR breakfast café au lait, eggs, and bread and butter at nine, being awakened and having our hot water served at eight-fifteen. I fence for exercise on Mondays, Wednesdays, and Fridays and paint on Tuesdays, Thursdays, and Saturdays, all with French teachers who can speak no word of English. The fencing-room, or *salle d'escrime* of M. Varille, is conveniently just across the way.

Sunday, October 24
IN the afternoon called on Monsieur Marmier to thank him for two tickets of admission for the opening of the Assembly which he had just sent us, and found him at home. He was kind and affable as usual. We talked French almost all the time and he was good enough to compliment me on my improvement. His manner is leisurely, his subjects of conversation, though mostly literary, are varied, and kindness, consideration of others, and good-breeding prevail.

Monday, October 25
AT the opening of the Institute I "assist," as the French say. It took place at two in the afternoon. Our tickets

were very good ones in the centre. There were many distinguished people present, but we had no one to point them out to us. There were four addresses and one of them, "La Maison," was by Monsieur Marmier.

More than two thirds of the members of the Academy present were bald. Only five or six had really good heads of hair — furnishing an argument for the theory that excessive brain work causes baldness.

All the speaking or rather reading was somewhat artificial and much after the same manner. The voice was held long on one key and the antithetical sentence was spoken on another. In stating statistics or matters of fact, the voice was somewhat plaintive.

An account of the expedition to the Island of St. Paul to observe the transit of Venus was received with great enthusiasm. There was pretty general merriment at the mention of some mistakes on the part of the English expedition to the same island.

The audience was of the best French families and composed largely of ladies. The dress was plain and simple like that of the good Boston families rather than of New Yorkers.

Of the members of the Academy only the presiding officers and speakers appeared in full dress. This consists of a dress coat, a vest embroidered with bright green, a sword at the side, and all their honors on their left breast.

The building in which are housed the forty Immortals of the Academy, the old Collège des Quatre Nations, now called the Institute of France, is remarkable both for its architectural beauty and its prominent situation. It is placed on the border of the Seine, on the Quai Malaquais, opposite the gardens of the Louvre and the spires of St. Germain l'Auxerrois, with a view of the fine bridges, towers of Nôtre Dame, and having altogether a situation emphasizing the dignity and importance of this centre of art, literature, and philosophy, and showing the estimation in which France holds her Academy and Academicians. It is a building of wonderful harmony of proportion and beauty of architectural composition. Its extended open arms seem all-embracing.

Tuesday, October 26
THIS is the evening for the Layas' reception or "little salon." This time we had a Mademoiselle Tribout, who was very cultivated and intellectual, sweet and unobtrusive. She is about forty-five years of age. There was a young man named de la Roselle and a Monsieur Montucci. The latter is the examiner in mathematics and science for admission to the military school of St. Cyr. He is an elderly gentleman of the old régime. He told us that the candidates for admission must pass in arithmetic, algebra, plane and solid geometry, plane and spherical trigonometry, analytics, physics and chemistry, and while at the school they study still further in all these subjects. St. Cyr corresponds to our West Point only that it is devoted exclusively to cavalry and infantry including only light artillery. The system of education in every department of France seems to be very thorough and the examinations hard.

Friday, October 29
To the opera in the evening to see "William Tell." It was very well done. Salomon, the tenor who took the part of Arnold, sang splendidly. Madame de Reszké had a voice of good quality and great compass, but it was cold, as was her acting. The choruses were well trained and sang perfectly. I thought the ballet in the

last scene very much out of place, for it interrupted the thread of the plot and let the interest drop and had singularly little to do with the sturdy Swiss of that day and occasion.

Saturday, October 30
WENT to the Institute at Marmier's invitation to hear a new musical composition played before the Academy and to see the award of some prizes. In two cases prizes were awarded to sons of members and the sons, after receiving their diplomas for music or art, went up to and kissed their fathers on either cheek in the presence of all the people. That might appear very simple, spontaneous, and affectionate as an impulse of the moment did not one know that the programmes were all printed beforehand with the names of the successful competitors, and that the fathers sat near the president who gave the prizes in a convenient place to be kissed.

Monday, November 1
TO-DAY is All Saints' Day and we went to the great mass at St. Roch, where is said to be the best ecclesiastical singing in Paris. The church was pretty well filled and people were passing in and out during the service. There was no programme distributed and from my neighbors I could not find whose mass was being played and sung, but it was certainly very grand. As we entered there was a tenor solo sung with full, rich chest notes. The violins kept up a running accompaniment, and after the solo the whole chorus joined in, and after they finished the grand organ at the other end took up the air and was again answered by chorus, orchestra, and smaller echo organ. All over the church were seen great numbers of small candles and tapers burning in

the dim light. These were in supplication for the souls who are passing through Purgatory.

Tuesday, November 2
IN the evening went down to the Layas' "little salon." There were present Mademoiselle Strada with her married sister. Both of these ladies were daughters of Marquis Strada, who was a master of horse under Louis Philippe, but lost his title and head, I believe, in some of the rows since. They were both very pleasant and dignified, with quiet manners. Monsieur de la Rosalie also came. There were music and games of words.

Thursday, November 4
HAD a long talk on French politics in the evening. The French are hard to understand. They are not practical but theoretical in their politics. They do not act on reasoning from the real state of affairs, but are moved by certain *a priori* illusions and generalizations and get wrought up into states of mind of which we can hardly conceive. There are many French of the middle and lower classes especially who have an intense hatred of having any one over them in State, Church, or even in Heaven. There are also several instances of persons of this sort who had been crying out for Liberté, Egalité, Fraternité, in the press and in public speech, and then as soon as they are given office and power have acted in a manner more arbitrary than king or emperor would dare to do. They take perfumed baths, surround themselves with luxuries, and demand a respect from inferiors which just before and as applied to others had been their *bête noire*.

At present France is more prosperous than ever in her

past history. The Republic has suppressed the Commune without any assistance from king or emperor. The measures of the Assembly have been in the main wise, yet the French press and very many people are calling for a change. The Legitimists, to whose party belong the ladies of this family, say the Republic means reign of terror, commune, murder and theft; they point back to 1789 and 1792, to 1848 and to the last Commune, but do not notice the present satisfactory state of affairs. The Imperialists or Bonapartists form a strong party and are quietly watching the growth of a youth of nineteen now living near London. (This young Prince Napoleon was killed in the Zulu War in South Africa, thus giving the final *coup de grace* to the Bonapartists.)

There is a talk of a dissolution of the Assembly. A great deal of this is talk only and makes itself heard more by its noise, I believe, than by the number or strength of the talkers, but still the discontented elements are not few or altogether weak. There is still a large number of Communists among both rich and poor who desire actual division of property, and the troubles and discontent in Paris are sufficient to make the Assembly still think it safer to meet in Versailles, although Paris is more convenient for the members and is really the capital of the country. The French are quiet enough just now externally, but it is said they are in a state in which it will take but little to cause an eruption of the subterranean fires. It is easy enough to say this, but I wonder if there are any great fires really smouldering underneath — whether there is anything more than the smoke and small flashes of light caused by cabals and political intriguers.

Friday, November 5

In the evening the Vicomte de Pérusse with his wife and two daughters called; a very pleasant evening. The Vicomte de Pérusse thought it very strange that we allowed physicians to practice in America without having passed public examinations. I told him that as a rule the people hired only the best doctors who had graduated from the best medical schools and if any one practiced without sufficient knowledge he could be sued if he caused any damage. The Vicomte remarked that it would be rather late to sue a physician for malpractice when one is dead. The French system must be a great advantage to strangers, poor people, and those who have no way of judging physicians' ability to know that any practicing doctor has at least sound professional knowledge and training.

Laya Père read a scene between Christ and the devil from his play. Some parts rather shocked the good Catholics but the Vicomte courteously gave an appreciative purr whenever he thought it possible. Monsieur Laya is a radical and agnostic if not an atheist. I asked one of the daughters, who was still at the Sacred Heart Convent, at what age young ladies finish their education in Paris. She said that young ladies generally left the convents at seventeen or eighteen and sometimes even at fifteen, but that when they left at fifteen, they usually studied a year or two afterwards.

The Vicomtesse is very bright, lively, and has an interesting and almost handsome face when lit up in conversation. She was a great friend of Mademoiselle Laya when they were at the convent as girls together and hence the intimacy.

Tuesday, November 9

IN Paris there are reminders of the Commune not yet removed, such as the Tuileries with its gaping windows and blackened walls. These are kept, I suppose, to remind the citizens of the dangers of anarchy. Dined with the Charles A. Dana family. In the evening a Mr. Huntington called. He has lived in Paris twenty years. He was here during the Franco-Prussian War and the Siege. He said it was only during the last ten days when there was any difficulty about food and that then all able-bodied persons got on well enough. It was only the old, the sick, and the infants who suffered. He witnessed the tearing down of the Colonne de Vendôme. It was done peaceably and quietly. During the week of barricades he was once entirely shut up in his street, but he said the excitement was so prolonged that fires and deaths caused him no alarm and that he slept as well as ever.

Paul Dana and I left about ten o'clock and came back to the Layas' salon, where we found the room full. We had playing, singing, and some original verses read. At the reception were Vicomte and Vicomtesse de Pérusse and their two daughters and several others; in all about eighteen.

Wednesday, November 10

MY father had sent me a letter of introduction to Monsieur Laugel, who had asked me to dinner. I dined with him this evening and there met Mr. Washburne, our American Minister to France, Mr. and Mrs. W. W. Story, the American sculptor of Rome, their daughter, and Mr. and Mrs. Edward Dicey of London.

Monsieur Laugel is a writer, the private secretary to the Duc d'Aumale. He is a publicist of high reputation and considerable influence, and his wife, an American, is by general consent one of the sanest and cleverest of women.

Story has varied talent. He wrote "The Conflict of Laws" and two other valuable law books, so well done as often to be attributed to his father, the celebrated Judge Joseph Story, of the Supreme Court of the United States. He also wrote a collection of poems, some of them quite good, and several prose works, as "Roba di Roma," the only one I know. (His daughter, Miss Edith Story, afterwards married a Florentine of the old family of Peruzzi dei Medici.) Story was very kind and cordial to me. Took Miss Story in to dinner.

During the dinner Sir William Vernon Harcourt was discussed. I said from what I could gather while in England I did not think, with all his ability, he would ever be made Prime Minister. Laugel also thought that he had no chance for the place in quiet times, yet in times of great excitement or public stress his party would look to him on account of his unusual powers. Perhaps that might be so, I replied, in case of war or any great difficulty with another country, but I thought he was too radical to be chosen a leader on any internal issues. He had frequently said in the House that he wished to destroy primogeniture and entail, and such a man with such opinions the English were the last people to trust to settle their home affairs.

While in England I heard a story, whether true or not I cannot say, that a company of three well-known men, talking over the unpopularity of certain persons, decided to write down those whom each thought the most unpopular of any distinguished person in Great Britain. They did this separately on pieces of paper, folded them up, and when opened, it turned out they had all written "Sir William Vernon Harcourt."

His manners are rather rough on the exterior and he is rather careless in expressing his opinion freely of everybody and everything without regard to whose feelings may be hurt, but I believe him in reality and at bottom to be as kind-hearted and as altruistic as he is powerful; indeed, I think his altruism is at the bottom of many of his radical opinions.

Mr. Story says the Italians are overtaxed, their industries checked, and all the public funds badly wasted. For example, to sell land under a mortgage foreclosure, the duty to the Government is twenty-odd per cent. There are heavy duties on all buying and selling and the income tax, municipal and state, in Florence is forty-one per cent; that is, he says that with an income of 100,000 francs a man has left to spend on himself but 59,000. There was much interesting conversation on French politics.

I like Monsieur Laugel, for he is very intelligent, polite, and self-controlled. He shows, I think, what might be made of the French character with its natural vivacity, brilliancy, and fire when moderated and held in hand. The Storys told me to be sure and see them in Rome.

Thursday, November 11
AT one o'clock went to the French Academy. Sat very close to the speakers in the inner circle of all and close to the desk. Monsieur le Baron Vieil-Castel presided. The order of the readings was:
1. Report of the perpetual secretary on the work of the preceding year.
2. A poem entitled "Livingstone," by Monsieur Emile Guiard.
3. On "The Price of Virtue," by the President.

The President's address was read very indistinctly. The seat on which I sat was made for three, and after it was full a little man came in and insisted on sitting next to me and crowding us all. He sat on the edge of the seat, was fidgety, had rather a bad complexion, and wore boots which were much broader at the toes than anywhere else. I was as polite as possible, but at heart could not help feeling a little contempt for the man. After the *séance* Monsieur Marmier presented me to him as Henri de Bornier — fifty years old — the author of "La Fille de Roland," etc. I was much surprised, for his head looked very ordinary as well as his face and general appearance. Of course my opinion of him was changed as greatly as it was suddenly. "La Fille de Roland" is a popular patriotic drama aimed against traitors and for the encouragement of devotion to country. It has just come out this year. The author's name is on everybody's lips. I was presented to the secretary also, who promised to give me a ticket to the Théâtre Français.

Saturday, November 13
IN the evening went to the Comédie Française (the same as the Théâtre Français) on ticket given me by Monsieur le Secrétaire through the request of Monsieur Marmier. Three pieces were played: "Tartuffe," by Molière, "Julie," by Octave Feuillet, and "Les Deux Ménages." Mademoiselle Jonassain took the part of Madame Pernette in the first piece, Mademoiselle Favart, Julie in the second, supported by Febvre. The third piece was a light comedy and had no celebrated actors. Only one actor appeared in any two of the plays. The number of actors they have to draw from must be very great; twenty-two took part this night and only two of these

acted in the "Demi-Monde" the other night. All three plays had the not uncommon French plot — inconstancy of some sort, yet, as in most of the best plays, none of the interest is made to come from the vulgar side, but from remorse, anger, jealousy, mystery, and revenge in tragedy, and in comedy, the discovery. The acting was perfect. In the ordinary scenes the actors talked in quiet, natural tones, suitable to the occasion and just as one would hear in a drawing-room, at table, in the garden, or wherever it might be. Strutting, striding, unnatural voice such as some of the best English actors, even Henry Irving, affect, do not exist here, and yet in suitable scenes there is plenty of action. But, in general, the best actors seem to prefer to express the most violent fear, remorse, or hatred by but little bodily motion; there is a reserve of action, a half gesture, a rigid stare, or an uncertain step. There is very little hair pulled out. They do not tear to tatters; they spare their own heads and the stage boards and furniture.

Sunday, November 14
IN the afternoon called on Monsieur Marmier who gave me his poems, a private edition copy. Evening at home. Monsieur Laya, hearing that I had gone to the Hôtel des Invalides earlier in the day, told the story of the visitor who, having seen the old soldiers with the "jambes de bois" and "bras de bois," asked where were the men with the "tête de bois," and was answered: "Les hommes avec les têtes de bois sont à l'Hôtel de Ville parmi les conseillers." That suggested the English story of securing block pavement for the streets by putting together the aldermen's heads.

Tuesday, November 16

CALLED on Monsieur Laugel after lunch. The ladies were out, but Monsieur Laugel was at home. I enjoyed the call hugely and only wished I had more opportunities to meet so interesting a man as Laugel and were able to take down accurately more of what he said. He was at the Assembly lately during the discussion of the "scrutin" and said that the "arrondissement" — that is, voting in small districts, each electing one member, which was adopted on that reading — he thinks will be adopted finally and will give a more conservative Assembly, for then the country members will have more chance, for each district will be likely to send its prominent man, while by the "scrutin de liste," or electing many members from large districts, it would be possible to elect as country constituents candidates unknown to whole sections of voters.

He also liked the method of electing senators. The only difficulty was that the Senate would be too large, having from 350 to 450 members. The municipal governments, he said, by whom the senators were to be elected, were responsible, dignified bodies of men with other important functions to perform. The senators are to go out by thirds as with us and to be elected for five-year terms — rather an odd number of years to divide by three. He was, on the whole, very much encouraged by the wisdom and good sense of the Assembly. He still thought there may perhaps be further trouble, though he hoped that he had good reason to believe not. He said the French were excitable and often unreasonable.

He said there was no real cause for the late Commune. The leaders knew that they could not succeed and only hoped to get off before they were captured. It was a great mistake to think that the Commune was, as some supposed, "patriotism gone mad," but he said that the leaders had communications with the Prussians. During the Communist conscription his servant saved his house and valuables by saying that she was not sure but that Monsieur Laugel was a German, for he was born in Alsace. The Communists never touched anything which belonged to the Prussians, and what is more their leaders invited a large number of Prussian officers to be present at the pulling down of the column in the Place Vendôme. He said a friend of his has the order signed in due form for so many carriages to be at the railroad station to take the "Prussian officers" to the Place Vendôme and back. The communication with the Prussians was constant. They caused damage to Paris and made the Commune the scapegoat.

He said that the bank escaped pillage because the leaders of the Commune were bribed and the others did not know how to break in without being directed by leaders and without being supplied with the proper tools. The Commune, he repeated, was wholly unreasonable and was without any hope of success in any respect. The whole thing was like a set of schoolboys off for a "bat"; they knew that they would be punished, but wanted to be as wicked as they could when they had a chance.

In the evening the Layas had their reception, but not so many people as at the last. A Monsieur Rosalie played on a kind of French horn about two feet in diameter with eight or ten twists. It was played with the lips at the small end and the hand at the large end, with no stops of any kind. It was a very sweet instrument. His mother played delightfully on the piano.

Wednesday, November 17
NOTE from Monsieur Marmier enclosing a letter of introduction to the secretary of the President of the French National Assembly at Versailles, where I shall go on the first pleasant day of next week.

Friday, November 19
IN the afternoon went to the great Franco-American affair at the Palais de l'Industrie. It was too late to hear the speeches, but heard the singing and music. In the evening the Vicomtesse de Pérusse was at dinner at the Layas' and a Mr. Knox, an Englishman whom I had already met. It was Madame Laya's fête day; not her birthday, but the day of her patron saint. After dinner the Vicomte de Pérusse and his two daughters came in. The Vicomtesse charming as usual and ready to do anything for Madame and Mademoiselle Laya. She has delightful manners, speaks the best French with a distinct pronunciation, is very clever and a devout Catholic. Neither of her daughters is as clever as herself, but they are sensible, intelligent, above the average in looks, and well behaved, cultivated, and religious.

Saturday, November 20
THIS evening went to the Opéra Comique which is not in the least comic, but has, in fact, many of the best operas played, has always some great singers, and is under government patronage. The opera was "Le Val d'Andore." Madame Chapuy took the principal part, Rose de Mai, and sang and acted splendidly. The opera was very touching and very nearly tragic but for an unexpected ending. I went by invitation with Mademoiselle Laya to the Vicomtesse's box.

Monday, November 22

IN the morning went to the Messe Annuelle de Ste. Cécile at the church St. Eustache. The church, at half an hour before the service, was almost "as full as an egg," and many persons had been there for two and a half hours to secure seats. I could not get a good one and had to pay a franc for the one I got. The mass was composed by Weber and was directed by Monsieur E. Deldevez. At the offertory Monsieur I. Cargin, the most celebrated violinist in France, played; the organist was Monsieur E. Batiste, and the leading solo singers were Messieurs Hottin and Proust. A beautiful hymn to Ste. Cécile by Gounod was sung.

During the service a contribution was taken up in person by Madame General MacMahon, the wife of the President, a handsome, dignified, and beautifully dressed lady. She and her young lady companion, each attended by a gentleman, went round the church, in all the crowd and during all the prayers and praises, to get money for poor musicians and their orphans and widows. The music was indeed grand and impressive and sounded superbly in that large church. Oh, "the height, the space, the gloom, the glory"! After the service was over I went round the church and came unexpectedly upon the tomb of Colbert. It seemed like a new discovery. It struck me with delight to come across something connected with one I had read of and cared about in history, not being directed to it by guide-book or custodian.

Tuesday, November 23

IN the evening Madame Laya had her usual little salon. The Vicomte and Vicomtesse de Pérusse and two daughters, and two daughters of Marquis Strada, one married and one not, and among others a very odd American woman. When this latter entered the room my heart sank within me for fear of the reputation she would give my countrywomen. She was tall, rather stout, nearly fifty, I should say, but with dress and hair done like a young lady of twenty-three. "She dressed like twenty, but looked like sixty." She had too much paint on her face, spoke in a loud voice, wore the extreme *décolletée* fashion, and was plainly common and eccentric. She invited herself to the reception, so Madame Laya said, immediately upon being introduced by an English lady. Altogether she did and said so many strange things that she made me blush for my country, and the good French people stared in amazement.

She had left her husband in New York, her children in Germany, and is in Paris, as she says, to "amuse herself." It is by such women that foreigners judge American society. These queer people inform their new acquaintances that they are of the best families; of the "high aristocracy" of America; and the poor foreigners swallow this information with astonishing credulity and afterwards tell their friends of the *Américaine,* so none but the most eccentric get talked about and it becomes generally believed that our American society is made up of just such people; while the well-bred, cultivated Americans escape observation altogether. But for the constant dread as to what next my countrywoman would say or do, the evening passed off very pleasantly.

Thursday, November 25
DELIVERED letters to Mr. Healey's family in Paris. Mr. Healey was in Chicago. Called also on the Vi-

comte de Chabrol, who unfortunately was in Italy. Healey is an American artist and celebrated portrait painter who has painted so many distinguished Europeans, including royalty as well as Americans and English, and is a bright talker, with a large fund of anecdotes. The Vicomte de Chabrol, when in America some years ago, was considered the best possible specimen of a young noble. It was he who at our house insisted on giving the "pas" to Agassiz, and when Agassiz said, "I recognize your rank," replied, "What have I to offer to merit but rank?" I also called on Monsieur Marmier who was out, but I met him afterwards in the rue du Bac and had a short talk with him. Made arrangements to go to Versailles to-morrow to witness the National Assembly which has recently convened.

I omit all mention of the many pleasant meetings with American friends while in Paris and of all the usual sight-seeing.

CHAPTER XII
FRENCH ASSEMBLY AND LAST DAYS IN PARIS

Friday, November 26
LEFT the Havre station at half-past eleven for Versailles to "assist," as the French say, at the Assembly or National French Parliament. Arrived at twelve. At Versailles walked to the Palace. The town was stupid, dreary, and dirty. At the market the peasants, with their broad, clumsy figures and dull but rosy faces, were packing up their carts to go home or selecting some hats, clothes, or other articles in neighboring booths. The double rows of leafless trees on each side of the Boulevard de la Reine were uninviting and dismal enough, but must be quite beautiful in spring and summer. In the Place d'Armes were drilling a few small squads of recruits, some of them without guns. The sun, which had broken through the clouds, was drawing the frost from the ground, making the air damp and chilly and the walking muddy.

Arrived at the château about twenty minutes after twelve and was told that Monsieur le Secrétaire would not arrive till after one. In the meanwhile I visited the historical museum and saw the pictures and portraits. The pictures of Louis Philippe have no frames while those of Napoleon III retain them with the imperial arms. I used up all my spare hour in the museum and had but a moment to glance at a part of the park.

Monsieur the chief secretary of the President of the Assembly, whom I had met at lunch with Monsieur Marmier, paid the greatest respect to Marmier's letter. He said that the only place which was at his disposal he would most happily give me, but that it was not very good. I was conducted by a liveried servant up, and up, and when very near the stars of heaven, I was led into a little dusty, dark, unfurnished room where one had to take the greatest care not to stumble over some uneven steps. When I got accustomed to the dark I found that there was an iron grating on one side with some high-backed, uncomfortable benches behind the grating. This grating opened into the Assembly, close to the ceiling.

The present room for the meetings of the Assembly is a perfect theatre; in fact, it is the Salle de Spectacle built by Louis XV. The President of the Assembly occupied the stage. In front of his desk are some secretaries and reporters, and in front of them all and between the President and the members, about where the footlights would be on a stage, is the "tribune," or sort of rostrum from which the speakers address the house, for the members are not allowed to speak from their respective seats or from the floor as in the British Parliament or American Congress, but have to mount this tribune to speak when recognized by the President of the Assembly. The members occupy the ground floor or pit, while the galleries are filled with spectators, and ladies are allowed in full view and not kept behind a grating as in the English Parliament.

I was in my perch before the *séance* began. The galleries were crowded to repletion with spectators, for it is the third reading of the 14th article of the Constitution; the great question of whether it should be "scrutin d'arrondissement" or "scrutin de liste." The President entered a little after two and called the house to order. Very few members appeared at the ringing of the bell, but as soon as the speaking began, they poured in from the lobbies. The first to address the house was a near-sighted, elderly man, who had to hold his manuscript so close to his face that few could have heard him even if all were silent and trying to listen, while in the noise and confusion that actually existed, not one, even the nearest, pretended to take in a word he was saying. The man, however, persevered and read to the end of the last leaf of his manuscript, to his own great relief, I am sure. That long and doubtless carefully prepared speech was not written to affect the house, but for his own constituents at home, to appear the next morning in the country newspaper; that is, he was talking to "Buncombe."

The next member to get up was from the extreme Left — the left of the President, that is — from the radical side, and occupied about fifteen minutes. A few of his friends left their seats, stood near the tribune, and patted the man on the back when he had finished. He was evidently a man of no general influence, for the members, with the exception of these few friends, went on talking and writing and some even discussing loudly with each other, gesticulating vehemently and not listening at all to the speaker. I could hear nothing but occasionally a ringing of the President's bell and the tapping of his hammer or gavel. I could see the member who was speaking open and shut his mouth, turn over his sheets of manuscript, gesticulate, and drink sugar and water. I may say that they allow speaking from manuscript, which is not allowed in the English Parliament excepting for mere reference for data, permitted to Cabinet officers.

The third speaker was a young marquis of about twenty-five years of age. Before he began the President made a short address, begging the members to come to order. This young man made no less than four beginnings, three times giving up in despair of getting the attention of the members. The fourth time he went bravely on without it. Towards the end of his speech he made some personal remarks and accused the Left of some political crimes. That awakened some attention and called forth angry replies. One gray-haired republican got furious at something the marquis had said and made a rush for the tribune. He was held back by some of his friends. While flushed and heated he nearly burst with epithets against the young marquis, who had not been very wise in his language and who had more spirit than discretion. The poor President of the Assembly, what was he to do? He had already rung his bell four times during the last speech, had already besought the house to be more quiet, and had kept up such a continual tapping with his hammer that I ceased counting the number of times. The young speaker got more excited and the extreme Left also, until the President had to stop the speaking and talk to the house for about five minutes. The members listened in a casual manner to the President, but he has not a strong voice or a commanding personality and does not in the least know how to control a body of men. He was like a poor rider on a fiery and unruly horse. There was really a storm in the house. The members shouted out not only to question, but to interrupt the speaker with counter-argument, and several times in a passion such as I never saw in any intelligent Anglo-Saxon unless I except the case of poor Plimsoll. So great had become the disorder and confusion at this time that the President of the Assembly threatened to dissolve the session unless order was at once restored.

After this young marquis finished, I had the good fortune to see Gambetta, the great orator and leader of the Left, mount the tribune. The Assembly immediately quieted down and listened to him with the greatest attention, "*Conticuere omnes intentaque ora tenebant.*" He began his speech in a quiet, calm, slow manner and almost conversational voice, after having waited for the attention of the house for a minute, which seemed to be as long as five. He is blessed with good vocal organs and has an easy and distinct utterance. He has a broad, commanding figure, and a "lion head" which he threw back at emphatic moments. His speech was not at all radical or extreme, and the whole trend of his address was more conservative than I had expected. He explained clearly how the "scrutin de liste" was less open to corruption than the other, for in order to get any one person elected it was necessary to influence ten times the number of voters that would be required under the "arrondissement" plan.

(I believe there is no general rule applicable to all constituencies and that in the country districts the "scrutin d'arrondissement," as Laugel, who knew the farming region believed, is the best, and that in the cities or large districts including parts of cities, the "scrutin de liste" would work to the greatest advantage.)

Gambetta read some words of Monsieur Buffet, the Premier, from the records of the Assembly, expressing an opinion different from that which he, Buffet, now holds, and he ended by demanding of the Ministry whether they were going to interfere in the elections through the control of the civil service.

In parts of his speech Gambetta was intensely earnest and spoke in generalities of his love for France. He was very eloquent and his most eloquent passages were exciting, in that he spoke at the very top of his voice and gesticulated in a manner that would be absurd for any but a Frenchman, making movements with his fingers, hands, arms, and whole body so fast that it was hard to follow them, and he spoke no less rapidly. It was not the controlled, well-regulated indignation which seems all the more powerful for being a little repressed; but he let his feelings go away with him entirely at times so that we seemed to see all there was of them. There was nothing held in reserve. He was always able to control himself after these outbursts. As to his gestures, his whole arms revolved like the sails of a windmill.

Monsieur Buffet, the Premier, got up and answered this speech. He spoke of the advantages of the "scrutin d'arrondissement" in a plain, logical way and said what he had to say slowly and distinctly, with few gestures and little excitement. He did not answer, so I observed, the question of interference by the Government at the elections through its civil service employees.

One man who next tried to speak found the noise so great that he gave up before he had gone far and descended, but when at the bottom of the steps, regretted having stopped, and for some moments was undecided whether to go back and mount the tribune again or not, and at last gave it up altogether.

At another time a member desired to speak out of turn and tried to mount the tribune. The President called for the "sufferance of the house," or what I suppose we would call "unanimous consent," but that was lost. However, the man, who was in a great temper, went on speaking to those about him, for two minutes nearly, from the steps of the tribune, and when made to step down from them, kept on talking for some time afterwards from the floor. I heard Monsieur Buffet speak a second time. He was again listened to with respect and attention.

The angry and passionate remarks were not confined to the Left, but some of the Legitimists and Imperialists were equally out of order, though the Left was the most noisy. In one of the wrangles I thought a man's coat would be torn off his back, but the material was too strong to yield. The good speeches were always clapped by the favoring party. The *séance* broke up a few minutes past seven, after a division of the house.

Saturday, November 27
CALLED again on Monsieur Marmier and found him at home. We talked together for some time, about twenty minutes, and almost all the conversation was in French. His little, fiery, black dog has become quite friendly to me now. He rarely makes friends and is very jealous, in great contrast to his dear, kind master.

At home we had a nearly dinner, quarter after six, for Monsieur Laya had had a box at the Théâtre Français given him by the management, on account of his father, the celebrated play-writer. There were four places and they were kind enough to make me the fourth of the party. The plays were "Marcel," which we missed, "Philosophe sans le Savoir," by Sédaine, and "Bataille des Dames," by Scribi and Legouvé.

Got acted in the last scene. He is the most celebrated actor in the theatre by general consent, and yet in the "Demi-Monde" the other day he took an inferior, stiff, and stupid part. His part to-night was totally different, being rather comic. The two pieces were very good, both interesting and clean. Madame Brohan acted one part admirably, but though a famous actress she was rather too stout for the part. In one of the plays in the Comédie Française there was a young actress, tall, slender, taking a minor part, that of a servant who had become interested in the young man of the house to a greater extent than she realized. Her expression of emotion without a single gesture, when she heard of his engagement to be married, was some of the best acting I have ever seen. She is the most promising of the young actresses, they say, and her name is Sarah Bernhardt.

Sunday, November 28
AT ten-thirty heard the Archbishop of Paris preach in St. Philippe a special sermon to young men. The Archbishop was rather infirm, though not very old, and had a very earnest manner. He had shown great courage in the Commune. He sat down while preaching, only standing for the benediction. His sermon was interesting, but on no one train of thought. There were too many ideas to leave any one decided impression.

About five in the afternoon called on the Vicomte de Pérusse and his family, who receive Sundays. They live in the Faubourg St. Germain, 74 rue de l'Université, on what we should call the third story of the apartments, but which the French called "au second," or even "au premier," by counting the first story as the "sous sol" and the second as the "entre sol." To get to the parlor, which was comfortable, cozy, and well furnished, it was necessary to pass through the diningroom; an inconvenience not uncommon, especially in the old part of Paris. A pleasant call of about three quarters of an hour. The father and mother of Madame de Pérusse were there; both are very intelligent. The father knows a good deal about America, although he has never visited it. He and his wife had been great favorites at the court of Napoleon III. In the evening I dined with Mrs. Healey and family.

Monday, November 29

IN the evening the Layas took me to see the "Duc Job," a play written by Monsieur Laya's father, Jean Louis Laya (1761–1833), and acted at the Français. The Layas had a nice box given them. We arrived in the middle of "Philberte," a curtain-raiser by Angier. The plot of the "Duc Job" is interesting and simple. The success of the piece (and it was successful, for it gained the author $40,000 and even now draws large houses) lay very much in the sentiment and in the wit and nicety of language. The elder Laya wrote some plays with a democratic tendency and for a while had to keep in hiding, under Charles X and Louis Philippe, but the public demand for his plays and presence was such that the authorities had to allow his reappearance and the presentation of his plays. In the "Duc Job," Got was the principal actor.

Wednesday, December 1

IN the evening went to the theatre again in a box given to the Layas. The second box to the right held the secretary in chief of the Bank of France, and among others a marquise of the best society and who was known to the Layas.

Once, while the curtain was down, all the house was startled by hearing loud and angry voices from the orchestra chairs, which were answered by similar cries from the upper, the fourth gallery. They told me that they were very like the disturbances in theatres just before a revolution. The noise was not made by boys, but by men, some of them past middle life, some even gray-haired. The noise continued for some time and was allowed to die out of itself, its authors not even being spoken to by the police. The theatre was the Chatelet and the play a very exciting drama with guns fired off, prisoners tortured, horses running about the stage, and numerous assassinations committed. I think it was called the "Moulin."

Friday, December 3
SENT some roses to Monsieur Marmier as I learned it was his fête day; the day of his patron saint Xavier.

In the evening went to the opera and saw "Don Juan" with the following wonderful cast:

Doña Anna	Mlle. Kraus
Doña Elvire	Mme. Gueymard
Zerline	Mme. Carvalho [the best singer in France]
Don Juan	Faure [the greatest baritone in France, if not in Europe]
Leporello	Gailhard
Don Ottavio	Vergnet
Mazetto	Caron

It was the greatest opera of the season. The ball scene in the second act exceeded not only anything I had ever seen, but anything I had ever imagined, in the beauty of the halls, in the richness and harmony of costumes, and of the whole taken all together. This *tout ensemble* of coloring is a thing never lost sight of by the French. There were no inharmonious dresses brought near together.

Sunday, December 5
MONSIEUR MARMIER called. He said that he was disobeying his physician, who advised his staying at home on account of a cold, but that he wanted to thank me for the flowers I had sent him. I was very glad I sent them, for he was touched by the attention. He is, I

fear, often lonely, for he has no family and no near relatives in Paris. He certainly has been most kind and devoted to me, of course on Longfellow's account, but I think his warm heart has taken me in too.

Tuesday, December 7
WENT to Monsieur Marmier's by appointment. He had offered to go with me to buy some books. Before going he gave me another of his publications called the "Voyage du Nord." It was an early edition, now out of print, and as not many like it were published, it is, or may become, rare. He also gave me, to read on the train, a paper edition of Shakespeare's "Henry VIII" in French. When about to dress, his little dog brought his things, disappearing into another room in search of them and then laying them one by one at his master's feet, who rewarded his little pet with some sugar, a kindly smile and pleasant words, which latter were not lost even on the dog.

In walking the streets Marmier took my arm until his hand was so cold that he had to put it in his pocket. We had some difficulty in finding the books I wanted, for some new editions were coming out soon and the booksellers had sold off almost all the old ones. Marmier advised me to go to Egypt directly from Marseilles. He said December was the best month in Egypt. While talking to me about the pyramids, he stopped in the street and lifted up his foot to illustrate climbing the high steps. At another time he kicked out to show how the donkeys did it. He is so very simple and friendly! As I left him at the entrance to the Academy I felt I should rarely meet a man just like him, so gentle, so kindly, and so true.

Called on Madame Mohl. She did not remember who

I was at first, but when I reminded her, she was very kind and pleasant. She is a small, absent-minded woman, very intent on what interests her and oblivious of everything else. Her husband had been very ill and had lost his brother, so I had not seen them for some time. She regretted that she had not been able to offer me more society. Called on the Vicomte de Pérusse, but all were out, so I left my P.P.C.'s.

In the evening called on Monsieur Laugel, where were Mrs. Dicey, Mr. Henry James, the author, and some others; among them was a young American who had recently graduated at Cambridge, England. There was no noteworthy conversation notwithstanding James, except that a French officer said that soldiers in battle often have compunction about firing upon an enemy, and gave some instances to prove his case. The idea was entirely new to me, though I could understand they might have that feeling until they had been fired upon once and some of their number had been shot. Then I should imagine that they would retaliate with fury, which, however, is not inconsistent with what he stated, for he instanced the opening of fire and not the returning of it. I learned that the Laugels had called on Monsieur Mohl just after I had.

Wednesday, December 8
I FOUND that I had delivered a letter of introduction to the wrong Vicomte de Chabrol, who, on his return from Italy two days ago, wrote me a kind note explaining the mistake, enclosing the letter, and offering to be of any service to me. The letter was for his cousin, whose name was not in the Paris directory because he lives in Versailles. I wrote a note to the Paris Vicomte de Chabrol thanking him for his kindness, but saying I was on the

point of leaving Paris and could not avail myself of his friendly offers. By this mistake I lost the chance of seeing a man for whom my father had no little admiration and who had been a guest at my father's in Cambridge, Massachusetts. He doubtless would have entertained me and given me a chance to see other interesting and distinguished Frenchmen.

The Vicomtesse de Pérusse at dinner. She was bright and cheerful as usual. She gave a rather bad account of French society in general.

Monsieur Laya told us a story about the Duc de Praslin. He said that on the day of the news of the death of the Duc de Praslin, which opportunely occurred in prison just a few days before the Duke was to have been hanged or guillotined for the murder of his wife, he, Laya, was passing by the prison and mentioned to the coachman the news. In the ensuing conversation with the driver, the driver said that he and several of his associates were in a tavern near by playing cards about two in the morning, when they heard wheels, and on going noiselessly out, saw a carriage approaching the door of the prison, from which a man came out who entered the carriage and drove off. The coachman gave a description of the man who had thus left the prison and Monsieur Laya said that it exactly suited the Duke, whom he had often seen. The coachman said that a coffin was also brought out of the same door from the prison not long after. From various answers to his cross-questioning, Monsieur Laya thought the driver had told the truth.

The Vicomtesse de Pérusse gave me a letter of introduction to her sister, Baronne Haoverman, in Naples, who, she says, will show me the best society in that city.

Among the distinguished men I saw in Paris and who called on me was Cárlos Calvo y Capdevila, a corresponding member of the Institute. We had some interesting talk on many topics of the day, not without their educational value to me.

CHAPTER XIII

ATHENS BY WAY OF THE MEDITERRANEAN —
BRITISH AMBASSADOR — THE ROYAL BALL
AND SCALING THE ACROPOLIS

FROM Paris I went to Athens by way of Lyons, Avignon, Arles, Nîmes, Marseilles, Nice, Mentone, Monte Carlo, the Cornice Road, Genoa, and Leghorn, and from the latter place by boat to Naples, Palermo, Messina, and Taormina.

Sunday, December 12
As we passed Orange on the road to Avignon, a young Frenchman told me that they played an opera in the summer of '74 in the Roman theatre, which is wonderfully preserved, and that the acoustic properties were so good that, though much larger than the modern theatres and though all out of doors, one heard perfectly well even from the most remote seats.

Wednesday, December 15. Marseilles
AT the old port the scene was a busy and interesting one. Nothing seems more lively and prosperous than men actively at work on the docks, loading and unloading merchandise on or from ships. However, grain, for example, was handled in this place in a good old-fashioned way, not with one of our new-fangled grain elevators, but taken out of the hold a sackful at a time by men, who emptied the sacks on to the wharves. From this pile baskets were filled, containing about two thirds of a bushel, with no other implements than the baskets and the hands of the men. The baskets were then

taken and emptied into sieves hung from three poles at their joint. Without going further into the details, it is enough to say that the whole process required a large number of persons to handle a small amount of grain. Their wages are low, but how could they be otherwise; for if all the extra value put into the handling of that wheat had to be divided among forty instead of among six, let us say, as in America, how could each of the forty be as well paid or capital receive as much as in our country? This is an illustration of how we can afford to pay higher wages without increased cost of production.

Thursday, December 16
STILL at Marseilles. Took a row with an old boatman about the harbor. I found it hard to understand him, for he spoke provincial French and used many nautical terms, but one thing he made quite plain to me, and that was that he and his fellow-countrymen were all saving money and putting it into government bonds so that the French might be able some day to whip the Germans. The feeling over the defeat is still very bitter.

Saturday, December 18
AT last I am walking on the celebrated Cornice Road from Nice to Mentone, which I have so often pictured to myself, and the reality is not disappointing. I was never before so high above and yet in sight of the sea. The horizon does not seem to keep its old low level, but rises with one until the sea seems like a great mountain opposite. It is no wonder that the Athenians looking from their hills said that the ships ἀναβαίνουσι, — go up, — as they saw them sail off towards the lofty horizon. The blue of the Mediterranean exceeded anything I have ever seen in variety, harmony, and delicacy of

color. The blue was not so dark or deep a blue as I have seen at times at Manchester, on the north shore of Massachusetts Bay, but it was far less hard and cold.

Before I had gone far clouds began to come up and the shadows cast on mountain, shore, and sea were wonderful and bewildering. I saw some clouds which were below the level between my eyes and the horizon. The water had so many different shades and the line of the horizon in that direction so cut off by these clouds that it gave the effect of making the whole sea seem like clouds itself.

The heights above were also grand and the grandeur was not in the least diminished by an occasional misty cloud pouring down between the heights, dimming the top of the mountain so close and so steep that it appeared to go up and up and never to end, but merely to be lost to sight in infinity.

Sunday, December 19

WHILE at Mentone I called on Sir William Heathcote of Hursley Park, England, who is here for the winter with his family. He has been ill, I was sorry to learn, and came to the Riviera to recuperate. He said he was better, but he did not look to me strong, not as strong as Lady Heathcote, nor as well as when last September he was so kind to me.

Monday, December 20

WHEN in Paris Miss Hammond (afterwards Mrs. Dr. William Appleton of Boston) had asked me to risk twenty francs for her on the roulette table at Monaco. Accordingly, I took four five-franc pieces and put them one after another on the table, choosing the double zero. The first and second and third were lost, but to my delight, at the fourth upturned the double zero, and quite a pile of gold was pushed toward me. The double zero turns up but seldom, but when it does, the winnings are large. An old, withered lady, dressed in black, started to grab this pile with harpy-like fingers, but the croupier apparently knew her, was on the watch, and declared that the money was mine. I then felt the true gambler's spirit come over me; I was trembling with excitement. My first impulse was to risk more, but I was determined to stop right then and there, so I put the winnings in my pocket, walked away from the table, and the next day bought with them a draft to Miss Hammond's order in Paris and enclosed it with a note of congratulation.

The name of the steamer I took at Leghorn for Athens was the *Simeto*. At Palermo, where we stopped for several days, the brigandage was so prevalent and so close to the city that we were not allowed to go to the celebrated church and monastery at Monreale, only a few miles distant.

Saturday, January 1, 1876

AT Messina for the beginning of the year, which I celebrated by a trip to one of the seven most beautiful places in the world, Taormina. Messina is a commercial and rather uninteresting city. It had been almost totally destroyed in 1783 by earthquake and had since been rebuilt. The streets of Taormina, excepting one broad one running through the middle of the town, were very narrow, several only four or five feet wide. There were no carriages about, not even mule carts (none of the pretty, brightly painted Sicilian carriages that came in later, after a road was built).

While we were in the celebrated Greco-Roman theatre the sun went down to the right of Ætna and lighted with a pink tinge the smoke which was slowly pouring up from the top into the sky above. The mountain was covered with snow. It made, with the blue sea to the left and some intermediate flat land, a marvelous picture, framed between arches of the old ruins, with flowers, grass, and weeds growing on the top and in the crevices, altogether a scene so glorious as to make one's pulses beat with joy. After dinner we went down by another path and as we looked back, we saw in the moonlight the Norman battlements on the southern cliff of the town.

On leaving Messina we sailed round the southern end of Greece. A Frenchman aboard, who came from Nice and had stayed in Greece for over a year, said the Greeks were very poor, proud, dirty, and ignorant, that every Grecian man confidently expected to be Prime Minister some day, and could talk for hours on politics, but always on personal politics. The officials, he said, always robbed and a man was thought stupid and *bête* if, when in office, from Prime Minister downward, he did not make the most of his opportunities (perhaps no worse than some of President Grant's Cabinet who were later convicted). He said the elections were not fair — that many were kept from voting by the military. He said he had traveled in the interior and seen the battle-fields. It made me quite sad when he said of Thebes that there was "absolument rien, rien, rien — rien." I could not help thinking of the "Antigone" and "Œdipus Tyrannus," and of how not a trace was left of the city where lived the persons of those great tragedies. A Belgian aboard told me that the work on all the railways in Turkey was done by other than Turks. He said the Herzegovinians were strong and industrious, but very haughty and hard to rule except by kindness.

Wednesday, January 5

WE arrived at the port of Piræus during the night and in the dark had passed the island of Salamis. There was much delay in getting my baggage through the custom-house. I had nothing dutiable and had so declared and was ready to have trunks opened and examined. It was evident from their actions that the custom-house officers were looking for bribes. Never had I bribed a government official and I did not want to begin, though I was told by some of my fellow-passengers and by the officers of the ship that the Athenian custom employees had no salaries and lived wholly on tips and bribes. This seemed so incredible that I could hardly believe it, but I was assured from various sources, including a Travelers' Agency, that this was true.

Drove to Athens along the ancient road from the port of Piræus, now well macadamized but minus the old walls. Not even a ruin or trace of them was to be seen aboveground. Here I am at last in Athens! How one sides with this city in all her past history! I felt very blue to think that the stupid Spartans had ever pulled down the long walls and ruined the great city of poets, philosophers, and artists, and when at last I got sight of the Acropolis and the Temple of Theseus I felt that I had been repaid for all the study of Grecian history and the Greek classics and, too, for all the troubles of the long journey, even were this all that I should see of Greece. It seems to me that there is far more romantic feeling about Athens than about Rome. The history of Athens is more brilliant, more startling, more wonderful. The Romans were matter of fact and military and administrative. Strangely enough, students generally side with the enemies of Rome, beginning with the Second Punic War. Who does not wish that Hannibal could have conquered? Then, too, Athens is older and was never so corrupt as Rome. There has been no mediæval history and no mediæval buildings have been erected over the old sites. This is where Socrates walked, where Demosthenes spoke, where Æschylus and Thucydides and perhaps Homer, where Plato, Aristotle, and Sophocles thought and wrote, and where Xenophon was born, and lastly and most of all where St. Paul boldly preached Christ and the resurrection of the dead, "to the Greeks foolishness." What courage it must have taken to say all this in the presence of the most refined, the most cultivated, the most philosophical, the most critical, and the most scornful audience in the world! I felt a strange yearning for the past, a sadness mingled with delight as I drove along.

Much less has been done here than in Rome in the way of excavations, but, on the other hand, the ancient monuments are not so deeply buried and those on the heights or near the tops are practically uncovered.

Thursday, January 6
To-day is Christmas according to the old calendar followed by the Greek Church. On this public holiday I walked round the base of the Acropolis until I came suddenly upon a cutting into the side of the hill with steps or seats. I approached nearer and was at once convinced that I was at the Theatre of Dionysus. It was almost like discovering it for one's self. Being Christmas there were no guides and at all times in Athens the monuments are free. I was there absolutely alone; no bars to keep me out, not even a drachma to pay. There I stayed two hours and a half, making out the plan of the theatre and copying or reading inscriptions. The old marble seats of the priests in the front row were still

there, though the rest of the marble, for the most part, had been burned to make lime, as have been the arms, legs, and heads of many statues. This is the unfortunate fate of many an interesting monument in Athens, and it seems all the more absurd when one considers that there are marble and limestone quarries of unlimited extent everywhere about. It merely saved cutting the stone from the quarry to use some statue, column, frieze, or bas-relief.

It is interesting to note that the seat of Dionysus or Bacchus, to use the Latin name, is in the centre with Zeus on the right and Apollo on the left as one faces the stage. The place had a special charm to me as being the very spot where were acted the plays I have read in college. This spot is mentioned in history and in the oration "De Corona" of Demosthenes, and also by Æschines. I remembered Professor Goodwin told us at Harvard that there was no reason to doubt that these marble seats were the old ones used in the fourth century B.C., so I sat in the seat with the old priest and with the envoys of Philip I of Macedon and perhaps where Socrates sat when chosen *epistates*.

I went into the Russian church and heard the Christmas services. These were all choral and very solemn. There was no organ or other musical instrument. The bass had a superb voice. He took B flat and possibly A natural below the low C and held it long, with a full, rich, rumbling sound like the soft pedal notes of an organ, vibrating after the other voices died out at the end of the responses. This is the first time I have ever heard any note sung below D that did not seem strained and unpleasant. To be sure, this chorister had the advantage of singing in a small building of splendid acoustic properties.

While among the ruins of the Temple of Zeus there passed a Greek funeral. I saw coming toward me the procession headed by priests in long white robes, plain or trimmed with red and gold, wearing tall black hats with a rim at the top. In front of the priests were carried two banners and two lights and in front of these was a man carrying something blue and white, long and narrow. As they neared I found it was the lid of the casket or coffin, covered with blue and spangled with silver stars and lined with white. Behind the priests was a singer, chanting from a book, and behind him was the body carried on a flat bier by six men. The body was so arranged as to be seen from all sides.

This procession coming from the outskirts of the town, passing the grand old ruins and slowly winding its way across the Ilissus, and through the narrow road bordered with cypress-trees leading to the distant burial-ground, and the solemn chanting becoming more and more indistinct and carried away by the wind and then heard faintly again and then more faintly still, seemed to be an emblem of the ancient times, as they came and went. The sadness of the poor mourners on their Christmas Day blended fittingly with that strange sad yearning for the heroes of the past that hung about me still.

Friday, January 7
CALLED on Mr. and Mrs. Wyndham, English Secretary of Legation, whom I had met at the British Embassy at Paris, and found Madame at home. I left Tenterden's letter of introduction to the Honorable William Stuart, C.B., the English Minister to Greece. He is a son of Lord Blantyre. On returning to the hotel I found the card of General Read, United States Minister to

Athens, and a card of invitation to dine to-morrow with the Wyndhams.

Sunday, January 9
ENGLISH church in the morning. We had a good sermon from Sullivan, the headmaster of Winchester School. In the afternoon strolled about and heard in the Place de la Concorde the King's band playing opera airs. Most of the men, except the foreigners, wore the picturesque Greek costume with a thickly plaited skirt called "fustanella." Almost all the women wore Paris fashions and the Maid of Athens was seen no more in public and even her costume was not to be found excepting among a few of the poorer class. However, there may be more women who hold to the old costume than one sees, for they are kept very much at home and do not go abroad to be seen as in the west of Europe.

Met King George out walking. He is young and has a graceful figure. Dined in the evening with the Wyndhams at Hotel New York. After dinner came in the Reverend G. B. d'Arcy with the Reverend Mr. Sullivan, headmaster of Winchester School, and three boys who were "doing" Greece with him during the holidays. Very pleasant evening. Sullivan uncommonly bright and entertaining. Received an invitation to dine with Mr. Stuart, the British Minister, on the 12th.

Wednesday, January 12
THE day before New Year's according to old style. The streets were crowded with people all dressed in their best. The cathedral was decorated with flags and the shops filled with toys, fancy articles, and sweets. I noticed that on this gala day most of the men had doffed their strictly Greek dress, which I fear will soon

pass out entirely except in the country districts. The streets were very noisy, each person in them vying with the others to make the most disturbance possible. Middle-aged and otherwise sensible-looking men were blowing whistles of various kinds, some trilling, some changing their notes, and others on the same note, but shrill all of them. I saw various kinds of rattles, like watchmen's, and one youth of about seventeen looked very proud in the possession of one of these rattles nearly two feet long. I walked about the antiquities as usual in the afternoon. Fortunately, most of them were away from the noise and dirt of the city.

In the evening at half-past seven dined with the Honorable William Stuart, the English Minister and Envoy Extraordinary. Here I met Mr. and Mrs. Wyndham, and a young Englishman, one of the delightful sort, and General and Mrs. Read. The latter were very kind. General Read believed in President Grant most thoroughly and considered him the equal of General Washington. He said that President Grant as early as the fall of '73 told him that our debt must be paid in coin honestly, and not in written promises. This is interesting as it has sometimes been said that Grant was only converted to that view later. Stuart, a Trinity College, Cambridge, graduate, has been in the diplomatic service in Rio de Janeiro, in Naples before the united Italy, in Washington, U.S.A., during part of the Civil War, in Constantinople, St. Petersburg, and Argentina before coming to Athens. He represents one of those diplomatic careers we do not have in the United States, beginning as Secretary of Legation and working his way up by distinguished service. He also acted in some capacity in the conference on American treaties in London in 1871. He talked of his experiences in the United States, where he arrived just after the settlement of the *Trent* Affair.

Mrs. Stuart at table said she was glad to hear that the bitter feeling against England was dying out in America. Good feeling was then sure to come, "for there had," said she, "never been the slightest prejudice on the part of England." No one assented to this remark, not even Mr. Stuart.

After dinner they played a game of cards, in which I joined. There were some counters used and when the game was finished I had, with a beginner's luck, won a good many of these counters. To my astonishment and mortification I found people pulling money out of their pockets and turning it over to me. I had thought we were playing merely for the game; indeed, had I lost anything like what I then found I had gained, I should not have had enough to pay the gambling debt, but should have had to give an I.O.U. I hesitated as to what to do. The Stuarts and their guests were very good people and gambling on a moderate scale in games of cards is not uncommon in England, even among church people. I decided it would be better courtesy to accept the situation. The following day I sent some very fine flowers to Mrs. Stuart, who had been one of the chief losers.

Drove back from this dinner with General and Mrs. Read and spent an hour talking in their pleasant rooms in the Hotel Grande Bretagne. As I came out I found a bright moon, just past the full, and as this was the first clear evening we had had for some time, though late I walked round the boulevard, stopping and sitting in the seats of the old Theatre of Dionysus. I longed to go up on the Acropolis, but at night a written permission is necessary and that can be obtained only during the daytime from the public authorities. I went to the entrance and tried to persuade the two Greek officers to allow me to come in, explaining that I was a stranger from America, that I had failed to get the pass as the weather was so cloudy in the afternoon, and that this was my last chance in all probability for a clear night, and I hinted at giving them any suitable fee to cover any responsibility they might undertake in granting me the permission. Each officer eyed the other in such a way as to make me think that either alone would have accepted such a fee, but each was afraid of the other. "How happy could I be with either, were t' other dear charmer away."

Walking back from the Propylæa or entrance gate to the Acropolis, I turned sharp to the left and followed along under the wall on a narrow ledge, then climbed a steep embankment and stood on the narrow path at its summit. From there I looked up at the perpendicular walls. I happened to notice that above my head the wall was a few feet lower than in most places and that there were several large crevices between the huge square blocks of stone. I became impressed with the fact that this was my last opportunity of seeing the Parthenon by moonlight. The next evening was to be the King's ball and the evening after the moon would rise too late and be in its third quarter. Then, too, I wondered if it were not really possible for the Persians to have scaled the walls about 490 B.C., as traditional history states — a fact much doubted by many commentators. Perhaps the professors were not good climbers themselves. The cool, bracing air of the evening after the heated rooms, the romance of the hour and place made me feel bold and reckless, so without further thought up I began to climb with my long ulster, patent-leather shoes, dress suit, and opera hat on. I had got up about nine or ten feet when my hand touched a loose stone. It gave me a sudden start. I had now gone high enough to prove that it was possible to scale such a wall and I stopped to consider about getting down again. But on looking under me I could not see, in the uncertain light, where to put my foot to descend. The ledge or path from which I had mounted was very narrow, not over a foot or two broad; just outside of that was a steep slope as steep as the débris from excavations would lie, and below that a precipitous wall probably of the Odeum of Atticus with large blocks of broken marbles at the bottom. To drop from this height on to so narrow a ledge would have meant certain death. Then I began to realize what a rash thing I had undertaken. What if I should fall and be instantly killed, or, if I had a breath left in my mangled body, what reason could I give for being in such a place, or suppose if I kept on climbing up I should be discovered in the act!

I heard distant bugles, perhaps from the palace guard, but all was quiet above and below. There was nothing for it, then, but to continue my upward progress. I had only to get my feet about where my hands were now, then I could nearly reach the lowest part of the breach in the wall. I felt each stone to be sure it was firm before trusting myself to it. My fingers were becoming a little tired and torn. Stopping and listening at each step, at last I got my head on a level with the opening, which I found was just even with the ground at that place.

One of the top stones I found loose. Then moving sideways and getting hold of the inside of the wall at the left of the breach, I lifted myself up, getting first my knee and then my foot on the ground and ran for several paces away from the wall, feeling as if I were pursued by a demon who would drag me back and hurl me down.

At last, calmed by my sure footing on level ground, I walked among that forest of white marbles, mounted the winding stairs to the top of the Parthenon and there had the most magnificent view conceivable — the Ægean Sea sparkling in the moonlight, the distant islands, the near city, and the ancient monuments about me. The moonlight made the hills of Attica look nearer than they really were, while the Caryatides, or Maidens in pure white marble supporting the porch of the Erectheum, seemed alive, but sadly, calmly, and proudly looking on a time of heroes, philosophers, artists, and poets, and, disdaining an era of mechanics, practical science, business, and filthy lucre, stood awaiting the return of the Golden Age.

Perhaps an hour, perhaps thirty minutes of luxurious revel in romance; then I had to settle the question, in common with the rats, how to get out of my trap. Then, to my surprise, I saw three men enter, one of them about my height with a long overcoat and tall hat very like mine. The other two were short and had low-crowned derbies. Sitting in the shadow of some columns, I watched them and waited until they had been just about long enough to make their return probable. I did not dare to wait longer for fear they might actually start to leave. Then, at the selected moment I walked straight and boldly to the entrance gate, planning if there were any question from the keepers, who could not speak English, to make as though my supposed friends were following me. I got to the gate and found the keepers and coachman in a hut near by warming themselves beside a fire. I pulled my opera hat well over my eyes and bowed as I passed. One of the keepers unlocked the gate, while the coachman stayed behind to put on his coat and relight his pipe. The keeper looked over my shoulder to see the other two, but I did not quail or waver. I passed slowly and with dignity and walked calmly away and smiled to think how puzzled the man would be to settle in his mind how it was possible for him to have let out four men when he had let in but three. Perhaps one of the three was put in jail to languish there till the representative of his country should see the Secretary of State for Greece and get him released. If that was not the outcome, at least the keepers from then on believed in ghosts. After walking and then half running rapidly away and fearing I should be called back and myself thrust into an Athenian prison, I spent a short time on Mars Hill, far enough away to be safe, and then went back to my hotel, passing some marble pillars of the old market-place.

Thursday, January 13
DANCED in the Queen's set at quadrille at the Royal Ball in the evening. Meanwhile I found at breakfast the young Englishman I had met the evening before at the Stuarts'. He belonged to the diplomatic service at Constantinople and had come to Athens in the Embassy's steam yacht. He was bound for Piræus, the port of Athens, and asked me aboard. I accepted and when on the yacht met the ship's doctor who thought it necessary to drink some rum and water to counteract the effects of the sherry he had been imbibing. He showed much concern lest some one should forget to carry the brandy to the Royal Ball in the evening. This doctor expressed a supreme contempt for the American navy, where they drank only water, as he thought, though I

believe there is no prohibition against the American officers having liquor at their own expense.

It was very pleasant to see the English sailors looking so clean and trig in comparison with the dirty Sicilians, hardly deserving the name of sailors, who were on the Italian steamer by which I came to Greece. I saw some cannon of modern invention. They were breech-loaders and could be charged very quickly. The King and Queen went to the Cathedral in full style in the morning and stayed there some fifteen minutes.

In the evening I went to the Grand Ball. This is given by the King once a year. About eight hundred guests were there. I had the honor to dance one quadrille in the same set with the royal couple and I was put opposite the Queen whose hand I took in the ladies' chain, and grand right and left. She is handsome, attractive, and well favored, and was smiling and gracious to me throughout. She sat down between the figures. I was asked by the manager to dance in this set. Who suggested me to him I do not know. While it may have been Mr. Stuart or General Read, Mr. and Mrs. Stuart were in mourning and were not at the ball and General Read told me that he had got me the invitation to the ball, but said nothing about my dancing with the Queen. Was it possible the suggestion came from a higher source? Most probably, I thought, some one had given out and the manager took me as an unplaced foreigner to fill the gap.

The King took Mrs. Read into supper. At supper many of the men ate with their hats on. There were no napkins and some of the finest-looking ladies wiped their mouths on the edge of the tablecloth. There were virtually several courses, but no clean plates, so cold meat, salad, jelly, and fruit were eaten with the same knife and fork and off the same dish. The King and his select party of about twenty had a special supper by themselves, where they were probably better served.

Many of the Greeks drank champagne as if they had had none since the last annual ball. They did not mind drinking from glasses already used. All the military and naval officers and diplomats were in full uniform. There were no Greek costumes among the women, but all Parisian, and very few among the men.

After supper was a cotillon which was very well managed. The two figures were simple and such as were well known to me at home. Both were figures where you were led to your new partner by chance. The dance was a waltz. During the evening I once saw some one, probably an American, who reversed for a short time. In general, however, all danced round and round in the same direction, moving in a large circle. In beginning to dance the man puts his right arm round his partner's waist and they both begin to walk and almost run in a straight line for five or six yards and then revolve very fast. This method of dancing has the advantage of making the figures short, for even when accustomed to it, one cannot revolve long in this fashion without becoming dizzy.

The Queen wore a handsome and expensive wine-colored overskirt above a lavender underskirt and a crown richly set in diamonds, but her dress did not become her. The King danced very well. He is King George I and brother of the Princess of Wales (now Dowager Queen Alexandra of England). The Queen is Olga Constantinovna, a Grand Duchess of the Imperial House of Russia. (George I was assassinated in 1913 and was succeeded by Constantine with his German wife.)

QUEEN OLGA OF GREECE AND PRINCESS MARIE

A GREEK SUNSET

Friday, January 14
MADE afternoon calls on Mr. d'Arcy, the Wyndhams, and the Stuarts, and in the evening on the Reads, where I lingered for three pleasant hours, at least pleasant to me and I hope not wearisome to them.

Saturday, January 15
WALKED with Mr. Cross, an Englishman I met at the Embassy, to the Bay of Eleusis and back, a tramp of sixteen miles.

Wednesday, January 19
I MET the King out walking. He had on a stiff-crowned, tall hat and brown kid gloves. His companion, a middle-aged man, had on white kid gloves, though walking on a lonely and dusty road. We bowed as we passed and the King seemed to recognize me, probably as a dancer in a set with himself and the Queen at the Royal Ball six days before, though I would wager he could n't for the life of him either tell my name or whether I were English or American.

Thursday, January 20
As I turned to walk home from a tramp toward Charvati the sun was beginning to set amid great profusion of separate clouds. As I was winding round a gradual bend in the road, with a hill on my right hiding the sun, I came upon a drove of ten or a dozen donkeys heavily laden with fagots. These were ahead of me, so the sun was shining among them while I was in shadow. The effect was strikingly picturesque. The animals, with their irregular-shaped burdens, were darkly marked against the violet hills beyond while the clouds of dust stirred up by their feet were richly tinted with orange.

As I gradually rounded the curve in the road under the base of the hill, I saw before me the "city of the violet crown," till at last the sun burst full upon me, shining through the columns of the Parthenon, and then, while I was looking, only too quickly sank behind the Acropolis, leaving the ground about me in shadow; then looking back I saw its rays suddenly lighting up snow-topped Hymettus and in a moment after the whole of the cloud above. This sunset, whether superior to any other I have seen before or not, was certainly rendered thrilling by the Acropolis and the snow on the classic mountains, and warmed me with the associations of the place. Whether there may be in the Alpine sunsets combinations of color more gorgeous still than this, I do not know, but there is no place in the world that has for me the background of history, literature, and art to set off the wonderful effects of nature that are here.

The more I see of this country, the more I am impressed with its smallness. I think it is Goethe who spoke of "a great country with a small area." From the Acropolis of Athens one can see into Argolis. Marathon is but twenty-two miles away by a winding road. The amount of arable land of the valleys of Attica even a Highland Scotchman might despise, and as I was walking along, musing on the wonderful history of Greece, I was more forcibly struck than ever by the great contrast between the small size and barrenness of the country on the one hand, and on the other hand the great power and influence of the Greeks upon the world. Why is it that at Harvard, Oxford, Cambridge, and, in fact, in every university in Europe the history of this little place should be carefully taught, often to the neglect of that of larger and richer countries in Europe? It seems to show more plainly than anything else the great superiority of the intellect and soul over mere materialism. I wish some of our politicians at home, who talk of the "vast extent and boundless resources" of our country, could be made to feel this. It is quality and not quantity that counts.

Saturday, January 22
I BADE good-bye to the Acropolis, the Pnyx, Mars Hill, and the Theatre of Dionysus. As I said *au revoir* to Greece, I thought with sadness how the jealousies and extreme states' rights doctrines kept the ancient Greeks from combining into one large and powerful nation. No state was then willing to part with one jot of its sovereignty for the benefit of the whole, itself included. The Athenians had to meet the whole Persian force at Marathon with only a few troops from the town of Platæa to aid them, while at Thermopylæ the Lacedæmonians had only a handful of Thebans and Thespians to assist. The internal wars, too, between these states still further weakened Greece so that it was easy for Philip of Macedon to take advantage of the jealousies of these belittled nations, to prevent united action against his encroachments.

Traveling into the interior was practically prohibited because the Government would not allow any excursion even to Marathon or Corinth or to any part of the Peloponnesus without a strong armed guard. Only a little over five years ago an Englishman by the name of Vyner and his friends were carried off by brigands within thirteen miles of Athens on the road toward Marathon.

Lord Byron's prophetic dream "that Greece might still be free" has come to pass, but what will she make of her freedom? That remains to be seen. The states once kept apart are now united into one nation and local jealousies have ended. On the whole, I do not think the Greeks are so dishonest or worthless as commonly stated. When the Turks were repudiating some of their bonds, the phrase was current, "Le Turc est devenu Grec." But I think that is unfair. While in politics they are corrupt, in ordinary business transactions they are pretty honest and keep their word as far as I can judge from all I hear and see.

I was sorry to read to-day in the "Times" of the 11th the news of the death of Lord Amberley, the eldest son of Lord and Lady Russell who were so kind to me while in England.

Sunday, January 23

IN the afternoon, before sailing, called on General and Mrs. Read. Mrs. Read said that the Grecians were very inhospitable. This was caused, she thought, partly by their poverty. Her painting master has charge of the drawing in all the schools and he says "there is not a particle of talent for drawing among the modern Greeks." Think of this for the country of Phidias!

I left for Egypt in the evening in one of the new steamers, named the *Behera*, with which the Khedive is trying to build up a merchant marine for his country. On this vessel the third-class passengers all slept on deck, the women in a kind of tent by themselves aft of the first-class smoking-cabin, while the others were kept forward. A temporary fence was put up and a guard set to watch. The third-class passengers were mostly Turks and Arabs with a few Greeks; many of the two former were pilgrims. During the passage the vessel rolled very badly for the size of the waves. Her cargo was placed too high because it was more convenient to have it near the top for loading and unloading. Before we lost sight of the poetic island of Naxos, where Theseus left his faithful Ariadne, the rolling became horrible. Directly above my stateroom were some donkeys or mules on the deck, and as my berth was an upper one and the decks a good conductor of sound, I was all night long reminded of the presence of these poor struggling animals. The vessel would roll over to starboard and those on the port would be struggling to prevent being hung by their halters. The vessel would lie over for a long time nearly on its side as if she would never right herself again, it seemed to me; then suddenly would turn with a great rush as far the other way; and then the poor donkeys would all begin backing to prevent their heads being knocked into the bulwarks. I went on deck to see what could be done, but there were no appliances at hand to better conditions for these suffering creatures.

At other times when the vessel was pitching I would hear the stamping begin in the distance and then come nearer and nearer as the mules tumbled upon one another like a row of card houses, until at last a kick close to my head sounded as if the feet were coming through the boards. The stamping would be followed by a little silence, then would come again the slipping of feet and trying to get hold of the deck again. After this another silence, sometimes lasting for five seconds, and I would try to get to sleep before the whole process was repeated, but vain were my attempts till the early hours of morning. We stopped at Rhodes, but only for a short time during the night and leaving about three in the morning. Think of it! Rhodes! The Colossus of Rhodes has disappeared.

CHAPTER XIV

EGYPT — THE ENGLISH EMBASSY — GENERAL-IN-CHIEF — EGYPTIAN INJUSTICE

Wednesday, January 26

PREPARATIONS went on for landing at Alexandria. The deck was swabbed up for the first time since leaving Athens. On other days it had just been swept a little in the neighborhood of the first- and second-class passengers' seats only. The log had been thrown over regularly during the voyage.

The sailors were mostly Arabians and more dirty than the Sicilians of my last steamer. They had a great lack of physical force and energy. They had twice very nearly let go of the log and they only worked with a will for a moment or two when it was absolutely necessary. Perhaps they were all seasick; they acted as if they were. Usually they took hold with only one hand in pulling on the ropes and they sang a refrain in a low undertone in answer to a call from one of them on a higher key. The effect was strange. It was not a loud, stirring call like that of sailors on the North Atlantic, but soft and quiet as if they were murmuring to themselves or saying an evening hymn to Allah. Seventeen of them took part in hauling in the little dingey astern on leaving the Piræus, and the whole lot took about five times as long as it would have taken two American or British sailors to do the same job. "What," said I to myself, "would happen in case of an accident and an attempt to launch the large lifeboats?"

Before reaching port the women's tent was taken down and disclosed a harem with its mistress. The faces of the women were pretty with large eyes and pink-and-white complexions, but they had either no expression whatsoever or a silly one. They were much amused at seeing men and some of them most boldly winked at us. They probably never had had such a chance for a little flirtation before and never would again.

The journey of four and a half hours from Alexandria to Cairo was a succession of delights and I was in high spirits. The morning lights on the perfectly calm water in the pools and rivers of the Delta, reflecting palm-trees, huge water birds, and every cloud in the sky; the fresh, juicy-looking clover; long cotton fields looking like huge flakes of snow fallen upon a brown soil; the mouse-colored Egyptian cattle with crooked, flattened horns; long rows of solemn camels; and not least of all the small mud villages looking like muskrat huts placed among palm-trees, only they had their entrances above instead of under the waterline; the fine, manly, dark-colored natives; the graceful water-carriers with their long, dark blue cloaks, and the endless fields stretching off without fences to the horizon; the cities with their mosques, palaces, and huts, a sight of the distant brown, red, and yellow hills of the desert, and before reaching Cairo a glimpse of the great pyramids reflected in the river — all seen when in such good spirits and with a light heart were thrilling indeed. I felt as happy as a king, or sultan I suppose I should say here.

Went to the Hôtel du Nil. The approach was through a long, narrow street, too narrow for carriages, leading off the Muski, where we left the omnibus and put the trunk on the back of a carrier. I began to think there must have been some mistake and that he was leading me off into an obscure quarter to rob me, but soon the hotel was reached and proved to be both pretty and cozy. It is built round a garden about one quarter of an acre with seats, summer houses, palm-trees, and shrubs.

After lunch I took a donkey and a boy who ran on behind whipping the donkey and directing me where to go, headed for the bankers Todd, Müller et Cie., who were down the darkest, dirtiest alley I ever saw. When the boy told me to get off at a stone gateway leading into an unlighted passage without any sign, I thought he was mad, but he was n't; he turned out to be right.

I delivered letters of introduction to General Stanton, the British Consul-General, and to General Charles Pomeroy Stone, a West Point officer who is now commander-in-chief of the Khedive's forces in Egypt and has charge of the chief engineering works, especially those connected with the great dams and reservoirs to increase the flow of the Nile during the low season.

Friday, January 28
SPENT the day seeing the usual guide-book sights, and in the evening dined informally with General Stone and his wife. He explained the military, engineering, and commercial problems of the country most interestingly, and we also talked of common friends at home.

Saturday, January 29
I LIKE the native Egyptian men. They have good figures, manly bearing, fine heads, straight and well-shaped noses, and are industrious. They strike one as far superior to the Italians of southern Italy and are more useful men than the modern Greeks; less posing and more simplicity. General Stone said they make the best soldiers he has ever seen, for they bear great fatigue, are energetic, subordinate, and intelligent. In speaking

with them one forgets the color as Desdemona did Othello's.

After lunch went on donkey to the Citadel to meet General Stone by appointment. He showed me about a little, but then, having some business appointments, handed me over to Major Hall, an American, formerly an officer in the Confederate States' army. Major Hall spoke with great warmth of General Stone's ability and high character.

With him I visited the soldiers' boys' school. Every soldier and officer in the Egyptian army has a right to send his son to this school from the ages of six to sixteen. It is a day school. There he is taught reading, writing, arithmetic, geography, a little geometry, English, and French, and there he is clothed and given one meal a day. There are now twelve hundred such boys. They are bright, neat lads. I heard several classes of them recite, and read. This is all General Stone's idea, which the Khedive has allowed him to carry out. In another year General Stone hopes that all the soldiers' children, not living near enough to come and go every day, are to be housed as well as fed.

I saw the printing office of the War Department. They made their own type. For printing in Arabic, which is the language of the country except of the court, which is Persian, there are 256 different letters to be used.

I saw the "Volunteer Corps." This is made up of boys and men over sixteen. They drill, live and dress like soldiers and study courses between the primary and the upper military schools. The most promising of these become, if they choose, candidates for the Egyptian West Point.

Major Hall, being a Southerner, puts the position as

held by the Southern Confederates in this way: they were neither wrong nor mistaken during the Civil War, but now that the question is settled, again to try to secede would be treason.

While I did not agree as to right of secession, I made no reply, not caring to enter into discussion with a gallant foe over a now dead issue.

After dinner had a call from Mr. C. Inman Barnard, who is out here as secretary to General Stone, a gentlemanly, friendly, handsome and agreeable fellow.

As illustrating the value of ancient history, the other day an inscription four thousand years old was made use of as the only source of information as to the position of the wells in Upper Egypt, where is the present military expedition. It is rather odd to have to refer so far back, one hundred years before Abraham, for practical information necessary to the movements of the army of to-day.

Sunday, January 30

AFTER church called with Barnard on General Stone, who told me there are about 140,000 Egyptian children in schools not counting the military establishments. This is out of a population of a little over 5,000,000. General Stone gave Barnard a holiday for to-morrow that he might go with me and see the pyramids. Dined this evening with Barnard.

Monday, January 31

EARLY breakfast. Left hotel at eight o'clock calling for Barnard on the way. Beautiful morning. We passed some of the numerous palaces of the Khedive. What is very curious is that the Khedive builds his new palaces very near his old ones. He must be building them with an idea of giving employment, like Mill's illustration of breaking panes of glass to keep the glaziers busy. The approach to the pyramids is now over a straight carriage road, bordered with trees. I was not disappointed even on first sight, as many are said to be, for the pyramids seemed colossal from the most distant view to the nearest.

Went up to the top and inside the King's and Queen's chambers. It was very annoying not to be left alone. The natives were chattering, quarreling, and trying to prove that we could not mount the pyramids without their assistance, and, with attempts at pushing and trying to get rid of them, it took away much of the pleasure and romance. When inside the chambers, which are only reached by a long, low tunnel through which we had to crouch and almost crawl, a crowd of these fellows came about us and began shouting for baksheesh, gesticulating and evidently trying to frighten us. We kept, however, placid, smiling countenances and did not yield a penny.

One of the best-looking of these Arabs took our side and quieted the others. He was a fine, strong fellow, with beautiful, well-shaped muscles. After coming out I tried some feats of strength with him. He is said to be the strongest man hereabouts. He looked far stronger than I, but I found my grip was stronger than his. In trying to bend each other's arms we came out about even. We put up the same size stone, though he may have done it a little better than I, and he held out a stone horizontally longer than I could. I outjumped him on running long jump by about three feet, though he was barefooted and I had on thick shoes, both of us jumping on the sand. He works his farm every morning and lifts people up and down the pyramids every day, so he is in better training than I. It was strange to have such friendly, almost fellow-college-student dealings with this Arab so far from my home and so separated by race and education.

Mr. Piazzi Smyth has some theories that the Great Pyramid is an observatory as the opening points to the North Star, and that the sarcophagi are units of measurement, cubic, square, and linear; but as all the pyramids in Egypt, and there are many of them, are in burying grounds and have sarcophagi of varying size and some of them with mummies found inside and with inscriptions relating to the dead, Smyth's theories seemed to us absurd. Back in time for dinner.

Tuesday, February 1
A SIX-THIRTY o'clock breakfast. Left the hotel soon after seven and rode, I on one donkey and the donkey boy on the other, carrying luncheon and crossing the river to the railway station at Gizeh on our way south to Sakkarah. I had engaged the donkey boy on the understanding that he could speak English. "Oh, yes," he said, "I speak English." I asked him about one of the palaces. "Is that the palace of X. Pasha?" "Oh, yes," said he. Then later I asked, "That must have been after all the palace of Y. Pasha." "Oh, yes," said he. "Then why did you say it was the palace of X. Pasha?" "Oh, yes," said he. "Then," said I, "you were a humbug." "Oh, yes." "And you lied about that palace?" "Oh, yes," he answered. However, I found he knew a few French words, and what with gestures, French, signs, and pointing we got on pretty well.

Sakkarah is the necropolis of ancient Memphis. At Gizeh, just across the river, we put the donkeys aboard the train and left at eight for the first station to the south, Bedrashen. We passed through large groves or almost forests planted by the Government. So many trees have been planted by the Khedive that it is thought here they make the climate more variable. At Bedrashen we got on our donkeys again and skirted the mud village. We met great numbers of peasants going to market, as it was market-day at Gizeh. The dress of the women was very graceful. It consisted of one loose tunic coming down to the ankles and buttoning round the neck, but opening in a narrow slit over the breast. There was a cover to the head of the same color, a dark blue, nearly black, coming down to the eyes. The dresses, as they were walking against the wind, shaped themselves to the figures and fluttered off behind. The erect, slender form, the bright eyes, long lashes, smooth complexion, and shining teeth were combined very artistically.

We saw near Mitrahenny a colossal statue which, though having lost its cap and all below its ankles, was still about thirty feet long. It was made of one piece of stone and was lying in an excavation at an odd angle, in about one half foot of water. Parts were still beautifully polished. It had on its breast an amulet like the Urim and Thummim of the Hebrews as described in Leviticus. This gave me pause. How much of the divine order to Moses about the priests' garbs may have been but recurring visions of what he saw in Egypt? was the question. The statue had a scroll in its hand with a name. We then climbed up the edge of the desert from the low river bottom, passing many excavations of tombs which had yielded a harvest of mummies, but the excavations had all been filled with sand again.

After visiting the Great Sakkarah Pyramid, we returned, the boy and I riding all the way home on our donkeys. Going through a village which I believe was Abookirr, crowds of angry men followed us, waving sticks over and near our heads, shouting and pressing against our donkeys. I kept the same placid, smiling self-assurance of face that had worked so well inside the pyramids and unconcernedly moved safely along. When we got out of the village the best explanation that I could get from the donkey boy was that some Englishmen had got into trouble in the village not long ago such as had aroused hostility to foreigners in general.

Between this village and Gizeh we were riding over a mere donkey path in among sand hills when suddenly there appeared a very well and expensively dressed Arab woman who was extraordinarily beautiful, young and plump, carrying a baby. She wore a necklace of gold coins which came down to her breast, and had gold earrings. She had none of the dust of the desert, and was as neat as if just stepping out of a house in, let us say, Chestnut Street, Boston. She had very handsome eyes. She was no darker than a Spaniard, and seemed to be of a superior class to any of the common women I had seen about Egypt. She came close to us and begged for money. I gave her a few sous and she still kept on for quite a distance. I rather imagined that it was a trap set by some wily Arabs who were hiding behind the hillocks, but there was no house or even mud hut in sight.

After reaching the hotel in the end of the afternoon I met the Reverend M. Warwick, one of the Cowley Fathers at Oxford, on his way to India. We had several long talks, mostly on philosophy, politics, and religion. He remembered seeing my father at Oxford.

Had a call to-day from Major-General Stanton, English Consul-General.

Thursday, February 3
IN the afternoon returned General Stanton's call, but he was out, and later in the day got a note of invitation from him to dine on Saturday, the 5th.

Saturday, February 5
IN the evening dined with General Stanton at the British Embassy. He has the title of consul-general instead of ambassador in deference to the Sultan of Turkey, who is the nominal ruler of Egypt. As a matter of fact the Khedive, Ismail Pasha, is practically independent excepting that he pays a tribute of about $2,500,000 a year, I believe it is, and, that being paid, rules as he pleases and can even float Egyptian bonds without the approval of the Sultan. General Stanton had recently come into great prominence in connection with the purchase by the British Government of the Khedive's 176,000 shares of the Suez Canal. This was the great *coup* of the Disraeli Government which saved it from the mediocrity into which it had fallen in the last two years. The purchase was made in the end of last November and Stanton was the go-between in this delicate transaction. (Some years later it transpired that neither Stanton nor Earl Derby nor Disraeli, the Prime Minister, deserved much credit for the idea. The news that the Khedive was planning to sell his shares to the French was discovered by Mr. Frederick Greenwood, editor of the "Pall Mall Gazette." He took the news to Lord Derby, who would not believe it, giving as his reason that Stanton had never spoken of it and would have done so if the shares were being sold. Inquiry was made, however, through Stanton, who found out that the rumor was true. At first neither Derby nor Disraeli took any interest in the subject, but at last they were strongly

urged by Greenwood and some influential members of Parliament and adopted the scheme which so redounded to their glory.)

At dinner were Mr. and Mrs. Stevenson, two young English lords, and the secretary to Mr. Cave. Mr. Stevenson told me he was at the head of Lloyd's Insurance in London, and that with them the decisions of our Judge Joseph Story on insurance were considered better than any of the English decisions. Indeed, Judge Story's decisions about partnerships as well as insurance were adopted as English law, though when first made they were contrary to it.

This was one of the rather formal, dull occasions, with no bright conversation, no humor or wit, no secrets told, no topics discussed, though I was pleased to see Stanton, who is a faithful diplomatic public servant in a high and important position.

Sunday, February 6

IN the afternoon called on the Stantons and Stones. Mrs. Stone said she had visited the Khedive's harem, that the women were handsome, that there was much done to amuse them, but not much to instruct, though a few of them were fairly intelligent.

After dinner, or about eight-thirty in the evening, Barnard and I started off on a donkey each with a donkey boy behind, to spend the night at the pyramids. As we were entertained by an Arab for breakfast, and got some idea of Egyptian justice or rather injustice, and had an exciting night, I give the details of this trip. We carried two blankets each and had on thick clothing. We rode through Cairo at a slow trot, crossed the Nile by the new iron bridge, and skirting the village of Gizeh, struck across the low plain between the river and

THE PYRAMIDS AT NIGHT

the desert. There was a mist over this fertile land and we could not see far horizontally, but above, the sky was blue, a few stars were shining clearly, and a clear-cut, brilliant moon followed us along almost directly overhead. Neither of us spoke. A jackal crossed the road, howling, whining, or barking all the time. Suddenly we began to make out the pyramids through the mist. They loomed up enormously, and again we saw their reflection in the water of the canal on the left of the road. I thought of the inscription on the tomb of Tih which lets us know that the Egyptians called their houses "hostelries," but their tombs their "eternal dwelling-places." It seems sad that, with all the care these builders took, their bodies should have been carried away so long ago that even in the ninth century the desecration was forgotten and no one then even knew where the opening was. But sadder than all is it that now every rude and thoughtless traveler may enter and disturb and drive away, by laughs and jests, by candles and magnesium lights, the spirit that haunts the chambers. The poor homeless ghost! But the body is not, like some of its fellows, to be preserved in a museum to be measured, weighed, stared at or jested about, but yet, though saved this misery, how vain was the hope of an "eternal home" in "houses built with hands"!

We hoped at that hour of the night to be preserved from the troublesome Arabs, but unfortunately some had been following a carriage on its return to Cairo and saw us and insisted upon staying in our immediate neighborhood.

On the desert heights the air was clear and warmer than below, and about eleven o'clock we lay down to sleep, wrapped in our blankets, and a few Arabs who wished to "guard us" crouched near by, in the very shadow of the Sphinx. Before lying down the Arabs had asked us to shoot at a jackal. I suspected that it was a trick to see if we were armed, but we replied that we did not care to kill a harmless animal. Whenever awake I heard the dogs in the neighboring village barking. I noticed the blueness of the Egyptian sky at this late hour of night. I remembered having seen a picture in the Paris Louvre or Luxembourg — I forget which — giving an Egyptian night scene with the sky blue. It seemed unnatural then, but now I see that the artist was true to Nature's night sky in Egypt.

We slept well in the sweet desert air and on the soft sand. Waking up, however, about four o'clock in the morning, when the moon had set and morning twilight had not yet come, I saw an Arab slowly stealing toward Barnard and carefully lifting the corner of the blanket till he had uncovered the coat pocket. From his actions he seemed to be in search of money. I then spoke sharply to the Arab and waked up Barnard. The Arab pretended that he had only been "tucking" Barnard in. After that we sat watch and watch the rest of the night. Strange to say, we were very much bitten by fleas. What they can find to sustain life on in this barren sand, I do not know. However, I am satisfied that the nourishment there cannot be very abundant, for they all had voracious appetites.

Monday, February 7
THE moon had set behind a few light clouds. Toward six it was my watch and I was trying to make out the features of the Sphinx. Suddenly I saw it lighted up by the first rays of the morning twilight that came with the quickness of a flash. We climbed the Great Pyramid, getting to the top a half-hour before the sun rose. We

BREAKFAST WITH AN ARAB

saw the gray and pink tints and then the beautiful warm colors which, later still, faded into "the common light of day."

We came down and breakfasted in the house, or rather hut, of one of the Arabs. He seemed much pleased that we accepted his invitation. We found on crawling on our hands and knees into his one-story stone and mud plaster hut that a carpet was spread before us. It was woven in long strips of black and red and was thick and strong. We made some pretense at trying to take off our shoes, but our host would not allow that. At the door we met his wife, who shook hands with us and then kissed her own hand, put it to her head and bowed. We were immediately in the principal room. Our host told us his house was not finished. The roof was only cornstalks laid over palm-tree poles and not woven. It keeps off the sun, while rain they never have. The cooking was done out of doors. Mahomet, our host, invited in some friends and showed us his two sons while his wife was getting breakfast ready. We sat down on the carpets with crossed legs, for there were no chairs.

Mahomet said he was going to send his oldest son, Solomon, to school and then make him a soldier. None of these Arabs can read, not even the chief. We asked after Mahajob, the strong man who had befriended us before, and for Sardi, a bright little boy of about fourteen. They told us that Sardi's sister had died since we had been there. However, both Sardi and Mahajob came in to see us. Breakfast was soon brought in in a shallow basket. We had boiled ducks' eggs with salt and pepper, goat's milk, some Arabian bread, rather coarse and made with the bran in round, flat loaves, and some white, saltless butter or buttery cheese. We were supplied with about four times as much as we could eat, but we relished the food we took. Black and very good coffee was brought in to us and poured from a silver coffee-pot into pretty little china cups. Such refinement seemed strange to see in a mud hut. But our host explained that they had to build small houses so as to appear poorer than they were, as under the pretense of back taxes the chief would take anything of value he could lay hands on.

An Egyptian buffalo or ox kept looking in at the door as we were eating. The dogs were numerous and barked a great deal. They lived on the tops of the houses and came down only for foraging excursions.

Our host was very polite and attentive to our words and wants, and we gave him a present of money, which he readily accepted. He urged us not to pay the chiefs the usual two-shilling charge at the top of the pyramid. He said it was an imposition they had no right to place on us, and he wanted us not to pay, saying he would go to Cairo with us and see General Stanton and the Khedive about it, and got quite excited. However, we did pay the two shillings and hoped our friend got into no difficulty from the sheikh or chief, who is judge, jury, and jailer, and from whose decisions there is no appeal for a poor man. The sheikhs are quite independent of the people, for they are selected for life. General Stone confirmed this and said that the Egyptian courts were corrupt and the decisions usually obtained by bribery, and that there was no justice at all for the lower classes. These had to protect themselves as best they could by hiding their money and valuable chattels. (This is a great contrast to the present absolute justice in the courts in Egypt under the British occupation.)

CHAPTER XV

ROME (VIA NAPLES) — AMERICAN AND ENGLISH
AMBASSADORS

Tuesday, February 8

TOOK the steamer *Ebre* of the Messagerie Line for Naples. On board I saw a good deal of the Reverend C. Haggard, of England, and a little of Mr. Ashbury, the former owner of the yacht *Cambria* which beat the American schooner on the great race across the ocean.

Saturday, February 12

NAPLES did not prove very hospitable.

Passed the volcano Stromboli, which was long in sight, rising straight out of the water. About eight in the evening we passed the island of Capri. Vesuvius was under a heavy cloud. While coming to anchor, the moon rose behind Vesuvius so that we saw it below the smoke which rested horizontally, stretching toward the south and above the mountain. When the moon was behind the cloud the effect was beautiful, indeed. On coming into Naples it seemed like turning toward home and, with the cold, snow-touched wind in my face, while alone on the upper deck, I burst out singing, "Oh, Carry Me Back to Old Virginny."

I secured a good *pension* on the Chiaia, the best part of Naples, for ten francs a day, all included. There was a cheaper one for eight. At Naples I saw the usual sights, climbed Vesuvius which was in partial eruption, visited Pompeii, Capri, Baiæ, Virgil's tomb, where I quoted line after line of hexameters, and made other expeditions. I met, too, many pleasant English and Americans, but there was little out of the way to mention excepting that I called on Baron Haoverman, who lived at the Castel Nuovo, a brother-in-law of the Vicomtesse de Pérusse, to whom she had given me a cordial letter of introduction. He was out and in five days returned the call and we had a pleasant talk, but he gave no other recognition of the letter and never even took me inside of his house. They told me many of the Neapolitan nobility were both poor and proud. They could not afford to entertain, and it was only by painful deprivation at home that they could keep a carriage and horses for outside show, a thing which they felt essential for their station in life. Not only the nobles but the people generally seem to be poor. There are no industries giving employment, no saved-up capital with which to start business. The hotels are run mostly by Swiss, and the other common business of selling tortoise-shell articles, corals, etc., to strangers is of rather a parasitic kind, and over all is the reign of terror from the secret societies.

Tuesday, February 22
TO-DAY I passed King Victor Emmanuel and the Queen, each in a separate carriage, on their way toward Naples.

I cannot leave Naples without paying a tribute to it. There is the beautiful blue water of the bay with Capri and Sorrento in the distance, sometimes purple and sometimes azure, Vesuvius smoking at the left and a background of hills with villas, churches, monasteries and vineyards, altogether a scene of rich harmonies of color and form that will linger in the mind among its sweetest visions. Every little cab has its horse decorated with spangles and colored tassels. The sharp cracking of the whips, the men and boys sunning themselves in picturesque attitudes as if taking part in an opera, and the women strolling about with their pretty headdresses and aprons, give altogether an air of ease, gayety, and careless happiness which pervades the place.

Saturday, February 26
LEFT Naples for Rome. For the first eight days or so devoted myself almost wholly to seeing the wonderful sights in this ancient city, not delivering my letters or seeing English or American friends, as, when once in the maelstrom of society in Rome, one has hardly time for anything else.

Monday, March 6
DELIVERED letters of introduction to George P. Marsh, the American Minister, from my father and to Sir Augustus Paget, the English Ambassador, from Lord Tenterden. I am paying eight francs a day for my *pension*, including wine and everything but candles.

Saturday, March 11
SUDDENLY cleared up at half-past eleven at night. Donned thick overcoat and scarf and strolled down the Corso and stopped at Trajan's Forum for a few moments. While on the Via Alessandrina I saw two hearses on their nightly duties, and as they crossed each other the drivers gave a lively whistle of recognition. One of the hearses stopped in front of me, so I stepped aside in the shadow of a wall and waited to see what would follow. A man got off the box next the driver and entered the house close by. The door was immediately opened for him. Not long after I heard a shaking of a cloth, and on glancing overhead I saw a black pall drawn quickly back from the window, just under the eaves. Soon

after a man and woman walked up to the hearse, not coming from the house, but from a cross-street.

Then the door of the house opened again and the man who had gone up appeared carrying a long white pine box with a large black cross painted on the top. The stranger who had come up with a lady on his arm helped to put this box in the hearse, where it made the sixth with five others like itself. Each coffin had a crayon number hastily written on one end. The stranger who had come up seemed to be known by the man at the hearse. The only other person attending to what was going on put his or her head out of the upper window, from which the pall had been shaken. The hearse was quickly shut, the man mounted beside the driver, and off they went, dead and living, at a brisk trot, the four lanterns at the corners of the hearse marking its way down the street until it turned off, and the lady and gentleman who had mysteriously appeared from a cross-street disappeared quite as mysteriously. There was no prayer and no priest. Perhaps the body was merely being carried to a dead house to await a funeral or perhaps it was the body of a stranger. The Italians' fear of death and contagion is so great that it is said they dispose of a stranger in a few hours after death and with little or no ceremony.

Walked on in the moonlight, passed the Basilica of Constantine with its ponderous arches, which gave the model of those of St. Peter's, and under the Arch of Titus, with the bas-relief, including the seven-branched candlestick, borne in his triumph from Jerusalem. The moon was one day past the full and there was an occasional cloud passing under it. Shadows below the arches of the Colosseum were dark and gloomy, but the inside of that great amphitheatre was flooded with light.

There were two parties wandering in and out, each with its torch flickering and looking to me more like spirits coming back to find something lost centuries ago.

I wandered next through the Forum and back under the Capitoline Hill, past the Arch of Septimus Severus, through the Via Bonella, and got to bed soon after two.

Sunday, March 12
WENT to the American church and to the second service in the English church. In the evening I dined with Mrs. Dorr, of Boston, "very informally" as by invitation. Miss Trollope, a niece of Anthony Trollope, and Baroness Hoffmann, *née* Lily Ward, were the guests.

Tuesday, March 14
AT eight o'clock I dined with Sir Augustus Paget, K.C.B., the British Ambassador. Lady Paget is a German, Countess Hohenthal, and is very handsome and agreeable. She has two young children and is lady of honor to the Crown Princess of Prussia. At table were Mr. Wurts, the American Secretary of Legation, Colonel Dalton and daughter, a young Mr. Wilson, Lady Paget's niece, and the German secretary. Strawberries for dinner! Sir Augustus said that the Italian Parliament trifle with their work, that they do not take up serious questions, and that they broke up or tried to break up the Ministry out of mere spite or petty jealousy, and the result is that no one who is capable is willing to take the responsibility of the Government. Paget is about fifty-three years of age and his wife thirty-seven. He has had a long and honorable career in the diplomatic service, having been in Paris, Athens, Egypt, The Hague, Lisbon, Saxony, Sweden, Norway, and Denmark. He was the grandson of the Earl of

Westmoreland. (Later Sir Augustus was transferred as Ambassador to Austria and died in 1896.)

There was some little talk of the question of precedence. It appears that a claim had been made — I could not make out by whom, perhaps it was a wholly theoretical question — that an imperial princess should go ahead of the daughter of the Queen on the ground that "emperor" was a higher title than that of "king." Instance was made of the Duchess of Edinburgh. The Duke of Edinburgh is the second son of Queen Victoria and married about two years ago Her Imperial Highness, the Grand Duchess Marie Alexándrovna, only daughter of the Emperor of Russia. I did n't understand that there has been any actual dispute, but the question was an interesting one and might become important.

Wednesday, March 15

IMMEDIATELY after lunch went to the Italian Parliament. We had very good seats in the gallery and from there could see the whole house. The members sit in armchairs which are all arranged in semi-circular rows, the rows being raised as they recede from the centre as in a theatre. Before each member is a little folding desk which discloses an inkstand, three or four small perpendicular pigeon-holes for papers, and makes a comfortable-sized writing-table when unfolded. Beneath this is a small cupboard for holding blank paper. There are in all seats for about 480 or 490 members. Before the front row of seats is a large, curved table for the Opposition bench. The Government Cabinet members sit at a long table under a raised platform on which are, first, the voting urns, then the passage for the members to pass when depositing their votes, and above that

THE ITALIAN PARLIAMENT

the Speaker's (to use the American term) or President's chair. Between the Opposition and Government benches is a flat space with a small table at which shorthand reporters sit and take down all that is said.

When we came in the members were voting. There were three urns and each member was given or got for himself three slips of paper, one green, one red, and the third white, and wrote something on them and then deposited one in each of the urns, marked with the corresponding colors, the green paper into the green urn, etc. As they passed in front of the President, before voting, the name of each member was marked off the list. The man keeping this list seemed to be a member, for he voted himself. There was a small attendance only. At 3 P.M., two hours after the nominal opening, there were but 105 members present. There is no rostrum as in France, but each member speaks from his place and gets the floor, as with us and in England, by attracting the President's eye. Members do not wear their hats as in England nor was there any crying out, but all was quiet and orderly — a perfection of an assembly in outward appearance.

At half-past five went to Mr. Wurts's reception. His rooms were very tasteful, and many diplomats and distinguished strangers in Rome were present.

Friday, March 17
AFTER lunch I went to Mrs. W. W. Story's reception, where I was introduced to Mrs. Terry, the remarried widow of Crawford, the sculptor, and mother of my St. Paul's schoolmate, Marion Crawford (who later became celebrated as an author), and also a young English lady named Miss Bailey. During the evening I went to Mrs. George P. Marsh's reception for for-

eigners, hoping especially to see some interesting Italians, but got put off on some English young ladies for most of the evening. They were hard to entertain. Their short, crisp "Yes" and "No" were like so many stumbling-blocks to conversation. Mrs. Marsh, the wife of George P. Marsh, the American Minister, is a dignified, gracious, accomplished, and fine representative of the best sort of American lady.

Sunday, March 19
CALLED on Lady Paget, who received Sunday afternoon. A number of people present, coming in and going out, making their formal calls, but giving very little opportunity for any interesting or prolonged conversation.

Saturday, March 25
TO-DAY is the day of the consecration of the first Protestant church building within the walls of Rome. It is the Episcopal Church of America. I arrived at ten-forty-five, and to my surprise everything was in order and looking nicely, where only a day or two before all was confusion, dust, and rubbish. Great bare places on the walls, to be filled up with marbles eventually, had been covered with tapestry, flowers had been put around, and carpets laid down, and all was orderly and church-like.

The service was interesting, of course, and the singing good and effective. The sermon, by our American Bishop Littlejohn, was very long and doctrinal and contained some talk of the advantages of national divisions of the Church, prophesying separations of it in the English possessions of India, Africa, and Canada, in the same way that the American Episcopal Church had separated from the English after the Revolution. All

CALL ON GEORGE P. MARSH 245

this must, of course, have been very pleasant and acceptable to the English, who formed a large part of the congregation. Some of them contributed to the church and there were three English bishops and several British clergymen officiating. The sermon was eloquent in passages, and had it been shorter, more people might have been left to put something into the offertory when the sermon was over. The second service ended at half-past two, making three and a half hours of continuous attention, or inattention I fear from natural fatigue of mind.

Sunday, March 26

WENT to the service in the new Episcopal church. The sermon to-day was by the Bishop of Peterboro, England. He is said to be the most eloquent preacher, if not person, in Great Britain. The sermon was extemporaneous, but there was never the least fear of a pause or misuse of a word. It was a logical, connected discourse, very thoughtful and solid, and waxing eloquent in places. The words were always well chosen, showing careful scholarship and doubtless frequent practice in writing.

Called on Mr. Marsh, our American Minister. He said he was ashamed to see me on account of the action of the United States Senate Committee. My father had been nominated by General Grant as Minister to Great Britain and the Senate Committee had reported against confirmation. Marsh said that it was a greater disgrace to the country than Belknap's actions for which he was being indicted. Belknap was a member of Grant's Cabinet. His actions, Marsh said, were those of one man while this was the deliberate action of several. He hoped that if my father was not confirmed he would be made President of the United States. He said that Van Buren was nominated President just after being rejected by the Senate for the same office and to the same country.

Mr. Arthur Dexter, who was present, told me that he had just got a letter from General McClellan advising him not to go back to a country whose Senate Committee reported against the confirmation of such a man as Mr. Dana, but rather to stay in Europe for the rest of his days and disclaim America altogether. Marsh thought that this was a question of senatorial courtesy. President Grant, contrary to the usual custom, nominated my father without consulting the leading Senators of his party, who had other plans for filling the mission to the Court of St. James, including a whole set of changes, one of which was getting Don Cameron, of Pennsylvania, into the United States Senate.

I called on Lady Paget later in the afternoon to bid her good-bye. She was fortunately in and I was graciously received by the handsome and cheerful ambassadress. We had a chat on various topics, none of great importance, but all very agreeable. I came away with the impression of having had a delightful call.

In this account of my visit in Rome I have not only omitted almost all of my sight-seeing, but very many delightful social events with English and American friends and acquaintances, where the experience was not different from that of the usual social life in that delightful city.

CHAPTER XVI
ENGLAND AGAIN VIA TURIN AND PARIS

LEFT Rome for Florence, Venice, Milan, and Turin. At Turin I saw Professor Danna and Count Sclopis.

Monday, April 24. Turin.
RECEIVED a letter from our Minister in Rome, George P. Marsh, with an introduction to Professor Danna, *avvocato* of Turin and also a professor at the University. To the University I drove to get Professor Danna's address and then left my card and letter to him at his house. He lived *au quatrième* next to the top story in some nice apartments in the Piazza Maria Teresa. The stairway belonging to the whole building was rather old and the stone steps were not as clean as might be, but that is not uncommon in Europe where the stairs correspond almost to the streets with us.

After dinner Professor Danna called on me. He is a tall, wiry, fine-looking man, with gray hair. He is earnest, enthusiastic, optimistic, and kindly. There was a little confusion at first because he said there was another Richard Dana traveling in Europe who had left a letter on him, but on learning that I was my father's son, he was much pleased. He said that Count Sclopis had expressed a wish to see me if I were the son of the man who had written the notes to Wheaton's International Law. Count Sclopis was one of the judges in the Geneva Arbitration Case between the United States and Great Britain that decided on the *Alabama* claims. Professor Danna promised to call for me next morning to take me to see the University, the town, and Count Sclopis.

Tuesday, April 25
LUNCHED at one of the cafés with Professor Danna and we then went to the University, where we heard a lecture on "The Influence of the Discovery of America on European History and Political Economy." There were about two hundred persons present including a number of ladies. Professor Danna introduced me to several people, one of whom, General ——, tried to present me after the *séance* to the grandson of Lafayette, who had sat opposite us but who went off too soon.

After a cup of coffee in a neighboring café, Professor Danna took me to see Count Sclopis. The Count lives *au premier* above some shops, and the general staircase was narrow and dark, but the rooms were large and comfortable and servants in livery were in attendance. The Count appeared glad to see me and shook me warmly by the hand. He is nearly eighty years old and has a large frame. His hair is not yet gray, and he is still capable of work, but he shows some signs of age. I stayed there about half an hour. He asked me about my travels, about William M. Evarts and Charles Francis Adams, Sr., and sent a message of regards by me to Lord Selborne. In the course of the conversation he spoke of my father's notes on Wheaton's International Law. He wanted to know how many editions of them there had been, but I could not tell him. He spoke highly of them and said that they had been of great assistance to him. He wished me to send his compliments to my father when I wrote. He saw me to the door and shook hands with me three times in all.

The Italians I have met to-day — and this is, with

the exception of the "Baron" at Naples, the first time I have met any eminent ones on intimate terms — seemed warm-hearted, kindly, and simple; something deeper than mere good manners. An Englishman in Florence who knew many told me that he found them on long acquaintance to be sincere, faithful, and friendly. The Count was seated in a comfortable library, furnished in a cozy English or American style.

Professor Danna had not yet asked me to his house. He apologized, however, for not taking me there to lunch.

Wednesday, April 26
AT quarter past seven in the morning Professor Danna and I started out again. He is an early riser. We walked across the river, which was swollen with recent rains, and ascended the hill called "Il Monte dei Capuccini" and had a partial view of the Alps. The sun was shining brightly, but there was a thick haze which prevented our seeing much of them. The view which I did get, however, fired me with enthusiasm for next summer's trip in Switzerland. At about nine Professor Danna left me, inviting me to come to his house in the afternoon. During our morning walk Professor Danna asked if we had any American literature besides translations from other languages. I tried to give him some adequate idea of our enormous literature and of the excellence of some of our best works.

I let him know that a considerable amount of classical reading was required to enter our universities. This was new to him. I also had an opportunity to talk on metaphysics and philosophy of which I availed myself, and I think I gave him some idea of the sort of work we do in college. He was fundamentally wrong on American religious thought, and he could hardly understand how such difference of opinions between the various sects could exist with such perfect toleration as we have.

In talking about our country I soon saw that he had the idea that our last war, the Civil War, was between North and South America; that South America encouraged slavery, and that the United States, which included most of North America, waged war against South America to break up the system and free the slaves. He thought it was so strange that North America should want to be joined to South America in one republic when they were so naturally separated by the Gulf of Mexico, with only the narrow Isthmus of Panama to connect. Carefully and as politely as I was able I explained his mistake and gave him the best idea I could, in so short a time, of the size of America and the total independence of the United States from the rest of the American continent, north or south. This ignorance was on the part of a professor in one of the most celebrated universities in Italy. He is known as a literary man, has intimate relations with the leading men of the north of Italy, attends lectures on the influence of the discovery of America on European history, for example, and reads Italian newspapers every day.

He thought that the American family of Dana, though the name was spelt differently, was descended from the Italian, which is really a Piedmontese family. He suggested that several of the Piedmontese in the last great religious persecution had left the country and that they had gone to America. Unfortunately for his theory; that persecution and emigration was after the first Dana had arrived and settled in the British colonies in Cambridge, Massachusetts. (It is pretty well settled that the "original" Richard Dana came, about 1640, from England, where there were families of the name of Dana at that time.)

Visited picture galleries, and after lunch went to Professor Danna's apartment. I saw his family, a wife and four daughters. They were all cordial and pleasant. There is a superb view of the Alps from the window. We saw, I think, Monte Rosa.

> "How faintly-flushed, how phantom fair
> Was Monte Rosa, hanging there."

We drank healths in Italian wine with the family and exchanged compliments. I took a great fancy to Mrs. Danna, with her quiet, good breeding, pleasant manners, and motherly ways with her children. I stayed only three quarters of an hour and then went with Professor Danna to see a collection of armor in the Royal Palace. It was the best of the kind I had seen anywhere.

Professor Danna has just about the position I always supposed. The family is eminently respectable and respected, not noble or even very prominent, but a family of gentlemen; men of education, including professors and clergymen, for many generations back. In Turin, where they measure their salutes by the regard for the man saluted, Professor Danna receives a low bow except from the titled families. They, too, show respect, making a kindly if not profound bow and a slight lift of the hat.

Thursday, April 27
LEFT for Paris by the new Mont Cenis tunnel.

Friday, April 28
IN Paris the leaves are well out, especially the horse-chestnuts, though the nights are chilly. I went to the Layas' who had a room reserved for me.

Sunday, April 30
IN the evening Signor Franceschi, a great Italian singer and singing master, perhaps the best in Paris for men's voices, called and sang for us. He did this with great ease and there was nothing forced about his method. He sang, too, with great delicacy of expression. He coaches many of the leading grand opera soloists.

Tuesday, May 9
IN the evening was the second of the receptions at the Layas'. Many of the old friends, with the addition of the handsome and attractive Countess V—— who was here the week before. She is French by birth and married a Russian count of good family, but what we would consider bad morals. He, the Layas told me, was fascinating, but no sooner was he married to this beautiful woman than he began to carry on with others; not that they were more beautiful than his wife, for such would be hard to find, but from mere love of excitement in intrigue and conquest. When he came to Paris he wanted from his French teacher only words for making love, paying compliments, and the like. The Countess has two pretty and attractive children, a boy and a girl about seven and eight, and she is still young, about twenty-five or six. She is a younger cousin of Mademoiselle Laya. She takes this conduct of her husband somewhat as a matter of course and hopes he will come back to her before long. He assumes the rôle of Don Juan and glories in it. That is his ideal and his career in life.

Thursday, May 11
VISITED the French National Library and one of the librarians, a friend of the Layas, took me about.

THE FRENCH NATIONAL LIBRARY

When one is uncertain of the name of the book wanted, considerable difficulty arises from the fact that there is no complete catalogue. The librarian acknowledged the inconvenience, but said it was difficult to remedy. They had been working for years on a catalogue and had only got a short way down the alphabet, and by the time it was anywhere near completion, it would have to be wholly revised on account of new books. I told him of the card system in the Boston Public Library where there were nearly as many books as in the French National. He professed to know of the system, but thought it would be "clumsy."

When a reader has finished a book, he takes it back to the desk, and if he takes out no more he has a duplicate paper given him with *rendu* stamped on it. This has to be given the door-keeper before he is allowed to pass out.

The *magasin*, where are the books oftenest used, was so badly ventilated, the librarian told me, that in the upper part of it the books were being injured by the heat. I was shown shelves devoted to American literature. Cooper's novels were conspicuous and Marryat appeared there, an Englishman, though it is true he was in America for some time and wrote one or two works there. There were no private rooms in the library for special workers, but behind the clerk's desk there were tables where some fifteen or twenty could be accommodated and could work; not with less noise, however, for there was a good deal of it from the clerks' passing back and forth, but at least apart from the multitude.

The whole library was a curious illustration of ingenuity and inconvenience combined. There were all sorts of little railroads, electric bells, small elevators for books, several speaking-tubes, and a double glass slide so arranged that one end or the other was always kept shut so as to avoid drafts, yet the reading-room was so cold that at this season, when there were no fires, the clerks and librarians had to keep on their overcoats. From lack of a catalogue the public was put to great inconvenience. The principal railway was never used, it being found much easier to carry the books for the short distance than to go through the loading and unloading.

The whole afternoon I spent in the annual Paris Salon, where there were over three thousand pictures. The collection, I thought, was very creditable, indeed, though lacking in great masterpieces. Even Doré's "Entrance into Jerusalem" was not so very wonderful. The painting appeared to be too flat. There was not enough difference in the color of the near and of the distant greens. There was no air or atmosphere in the picture, values were lost sight of, and effects of distance were produced by perspective or strong contrasts of light and shadow. However, the life and expression in the figures were very striking and the whole subject well conceived; in short, I thought it better drawn than colored. There was a superabundance of paintings of nude women in various postures. There were also some portraits of celebrated *demi-monde* women.

Sunday, May 14

AT dinner was the sweet Countess V—— again, at the Layas'. I bade every one good-bye on retiring, as I was to start off early the next morning. Madame Laya, who has been almost as kind to me as a mother, was very much affected at my going away. She is a brave, good woman, now pretty old and infirm. She has had a great deal of suffering in her life.

A FRENCH COURT

Left Paris for London by way of Rouen, Havre, and Southampton. At Rouen went to the Court of Appeals in the early afternoon and heard a sentence of imprisonment for two years and the beginning of a new suit and the swearing-in of the jury. When I saw a sentence for two years' imprisonment quietly given by the judge, as if it were a matter of course, the look of despair on the condemned's face, and the guards marching him off, and at the same time had not heard the case myself, it seemed almost cruel. The judges were dressed in red and the *avocats* had long black gowns with large square white ties hanging from the neck. The jury were sworn in one by one instead of all together as with us.

On the train from Rouen to Havre I rode with a nice English gentleman and lady of very quiet manners and dress and much dignity and I saw them again on the steamer.

Tuesday, May 16
PASSED the Isle of Wight early in the morning and Cowes by half-past five. We saw the Solent on our left and got into Southampton after breakfast. Again I happened to ride in the carriage with the same English people as from Rouen to Havre. We fell into conversation and I found the gentleman very intelligent on American politics. Suddenly he asked me, not having the slightest idea of my name, but knowing I was an American, whether I thought there was any chance of Dana's being elected President of the United States. I happened to have in my hand a pamphlet by my father which he had recently mailed me entitled "Aliens and Alien Enemies" on a branch of international law. I suddenly had a fit of shyness. I thought it would be so strange to tell them I was the son of the very man they

were talking of. Of course I had my visiting cards, this pamphlet, and letters addressed to me for confirmation, but I never told who I was. (Ever afterwards I wished I had plucked up courage and made myself known to these cultivated and agreeable people.)

After the Continent, the houses in the suburbs of London struck me as dirtier, smaller, and uglier than ever and in London itself the usual dwelling-houses low. The public buildings, however, looked well. The wind was east, blowing from the "City," and the air had that peculiar London odor, a mixture of malt and bituminous coal smoke. The air was soft and soothing. Went to Mrs. Brooks's where I had secured lodgings. Met an American named Horsfall, a friend of Henry F. Wild's, who is engaged to one of my sisters. He invited me on a party to see the great Derby races on my return from Oxford and Cambridge.

CHAPTER XVII
OXFORD AND CAMBRIDGE

Thursday, May 18

ARRIVED in Oxford in the early afternoon. I entered by the road from the station. Had I known how ugly that part of the town was I should have got out at the station before Oxford and entered by the Magdalen Bridge. Coming in as I did by the station and freight yards with goods trains about, I was a little disappointed, not finding it at first sight as romantic as I had expected.

The students do not wear tall silk hats even exceptionally, but either the soft cap, or round hat of dark stiff felt, or a straw hat with the ribbon of their college crew or cricket club. They carry canes in clear weather and umbrellas in wet. They dress like, though perhaps rather better than, Harvard students and have the same general air. The cap and gown are not now required in the afternoon and, of course, are not worn when not exacted by the rules. I met many fellows with their flannel suits for boating or cricket, with soft, round cloth caps, of different colors, having small visors. White flannel trousers are always worn in the exercise suits. A dark blue coat is the most common, with the arms of the college over the left pocket. Magdalen men wear a bright scarlet coat. I called on Edmund M. Parker (later Bishop of New Hampshire) at Keble College and found him in, just putting on his flannel boating suit or "flannels" as it is called, to run with his crew. It is the second day of the bumping races.

The Keble College dormitory rooms are small in

comparison with most of those in Harvard. They are, however, for only one man each instead of for two. Each study has a bedroom attached. The entries are as dreary and dirty as those in Hollis, or Stoughton, or Gray's at Harvard. We went down to the boats by the broad walk with its overarching trees and the meadows at one side.

I saw the river and barges for the first time. The barges, which are moored along the bank, look very like the saloons of small river steamers. They are flat boats with a top not unlike a horse-car, only larger, with rows of windows close together. One end of each is fitted up as a reading-room with chairs, tables, daily and sporting papers, writing-materials, and furnishings more or less luxurious according to the taste and wealth of the various colleges. Keble is the only college without a barge. It hires some rooms on the opposite bank and further up the river.

The smallest and poorest barge is that of Brasenose, which bumped University last night and is now head of the river and was the college of "Tom Brown" at Oxford. The other end of each barge is an ordinary dressing-room, generally with hand-basins, but never baths, for the use of members. The dressing accommodations are rather small. Each barge has its college flag flying, and the University barge for the use of the 'Varsity crew and officers of the O.U.B.C. has the flags of all the colleges hung from one mast in the order of the boats as they stand on the river, and also has a band of music. There were many ladies, mostly young, with gay dresses, bright cheeks, and sparkling eyes, on the top of their favorite college barges or along the banks, making a brilliant and lively scene.

We crossed the river to get to the towpath by means

of a little "punt" poled by a water-man who expects a penny unless you are a subscriber to Sadler, the boat-builder. The river here is about two hundred feet broad, while in most places it is not more than one hundred. We went down with the crowd of students and I had pointed out to me the "Gut," the "Lay Bridges," and other classical spots. We stayed above the "Gut" and waited for the boats.

It was the second division that was rowing. Each college at Oxford has a boat club and nearly every club sends an eight-oar crew to row and maintain its position on the river. There are twenty-one eight-oar crews racing this year, and as the course is short, they are for convenience divided into two divisions. The races are rowed in the following manner: The crews are moored along the bank one hundred and fifty feet apart and start off at the signal of the gun firing. They row upstream against the current for about one and a third miles. If a crew catches up with one in front and succeeds in touching the boat ahead with their oars or prow, the crew thus catching up is said to have made a "bump." The races are continued for eight days and each crew having made a bump is placed on the following day above the crew it has tagged. The second division rows first and the boat at its head rows last in the first division an hour and a half afterwards. Each year the crews are placed in the order they were at the end of the bumping races the year before, and if any college should fail to send a crew, it has to begin at the bottom of the line the next year and work its way up, if it can.

We had not long to wait, but at exactly twenty-five minutes past five the five-minute gun was fired and at twenty-nine past, the one-minute gun, and at half-past, the starting gun. The latter is fired at the exact time for which the races are appointed. If a boat is not in position and ready, it loses its place. There is no delay on account of rough weather on that narrow river, and so certain is one of promptness that there is no time wasted and people make their arrangements to dine, take tea, or study in the hour and a half between the two divisions. Soon we heard a distant roar and saw the crowds of fellows in their flannels running along the towpath below the "Gut" and could just catch glimpses of the jerseys of the crews swinging backward and forward in regular time. The men running on the bank divided themselves into clusters, cheering the boats of their respective colleges. I ran along with the crews the last part of the way. Their rowing was in general not unlike ours, only that in Harvard as a rule none but the University crews carry out the correct principles so well in actual practice. The men were not stronger or larger than members of our ordinary class crews, if I except two or three crews in the first division.

Between the races of the divisions Green, a friend of Parker, put my name down at the Oxford Union and showed me their library, reading- and debating-rooms. The entrance to the Union was not prepossessing. It was through an alley, but the building was pretty, built of red and black bricks, and was well arranged. The debating-room was fitted up very like the House of Commons in Parliament. Around the gallery, in which, alone, strangers were admitted during debates, were cases of books, which gave a look of richness to the room and served as library at the same time. There was a large, comfortable writing-room in which were numerous tables well supplied for the writers' needs, including sealing wax.

All letters of members are stamped without charge. The stamps are supplied at the expense of the club. They find that the system works very well and is certainly a great convenience. After a hurried dinner at the hotel, went down to see the first division row. The rowing in the first division was naturally better than in the second. Some men rowed very finely. The crews had been practicing only three weeks on account of the lateness of the Easter vacation this year, and so none of them were perfectly "in swing together." It was only surprising to see that there was as much rhythm where the men were so little used to each other's motions. It showed what good coaching could do.

The advantages for coaching at Oxford are excellent. There is a towpath about eight feet broad close to the river for twenty miles or more up and down, and so narrow is the river that a shout can easily be heard across. The coach for the University crew follows it on horseback, and day after day they never row out of his sight.

After these last races, which took place at seven, I went to the Oxford Union to hear the debate. The question proposed was "That the present constitution of the House of Lords is totally unsatisfactory." The meeting began with some club business about buying books for the library and certain proposed extensions in the way of building. There was a good deal of calling out, "Hear, Hear," as in the House of Commons. One rather nervous fellow, beginning to speak on a simple matter of buying certain books, was so embarrassed that when several fellows called, "Speak out, don't be afraid," he abandoned his attempt. Upon that the librarian arose and requested that the House might be quiet enough to allow the member to proceed, for he did not wish any suggestion to be lost or any criticism shunned through the disorder of members.

The debate on the main question of the day began with a very long radical speech, not well spoken and badly thought out, with several exaggerations and glittering generalities. There were more radical speeches than conservative, and yet there was a large conservative majority in the House. At last one conservative member got up and gave a very good speech in manner and style, at least, wholly superior to any that had gone before. He said, in substance, Why does not every conservative member jump to his feet to defend his cause against such attacks? Why do they show so much apathy? Do they feel that they are defeated? No. They feel that these questions have been put to the country and have been answered. They feel that the House of Lords does not need vindication from such attacks. That was the general outline of his speech, perhaps too strongly on one side, but well arranged and effective. It brought down a storm of applause. The speaker was a graduate and a "fellow."

There was considerable noise at the back of the room, where a number of young men were playing tricks on one another, calling out and laughing. Two requests from the president had no effect, and then he got up and said that he would be very sorry to go to such an extremity as to use a prerogative only once employed before in the history of the Union, namely, to adjourn the meeting on account of noise, but that if it was not more quiet he should be obliged to do so. Then he spoke of the disrespect to the visitors (the gallery was filled with ladies and gentlemen) and hoped he would have nothing further to do on his part, but that the noise would stop of itself. The House was quiet in a moment. I counted some two hundred and fifty members on the floor at one time. I think the number must have risen to about three hundred later. I left about half-past ten while the meeting was still in session.

Friday, May 19
SPENT the morning in writing letters at the Oxford Union, of which I had in due form been given the "privileges." On returning to the hotel I found a card from Professor Burrows, of All Souls, asking me to meet him at his college lecture about two o'clock, which I did after lunch. His lecture was a review and criticism of the ideas regarding the history of the seventeenth century, and especially on Clarendon, very interesting to me as I took a course on that period at Harvard. He presented me to his nephew, F. R. Burrows, a high rank scholar, who invited me to breakfast with him to meet the president and secretary of the Oxford Union to-morrow morning. In the lecture-room I also met Mrs. and Miss Burrows, who arranged to have me at lunch to-morrow. After the lecture Professor Burrows showed me about his college a little. In the main room was a rare picture of Jeremy Taylor, said to be the most authentic in existence. There was a poor one of my friend Sir William Heathcote, who is a fellow of All Souls. Professor Burrows showed me the new reredos in the chapel made on the remains of the old one recently discovered, and, oh, the beautiful flowers, smooth lawns, and grand trees all about, to say nothing of the satisfying architecture!

Charles P. Parker (later professor at Harvard) called and asked me to lunch at Cowley, where he is staying with the Cowley Fathers, on Sunday. Some of these young men need to be taken in hand and made to speak without stammering. They exaggerate in themselves the faults of Father Benson, the head of that order, in that respect.

Went down the river to see the second division row. Keble made a bump. I met Louis Dyer, my beloved classmate at Harvard, at the hotel. He invited me to dine with him at the Hall in Balliol and said he would make arrangements to have me live in college and was very kind in every way. He has a perfect genius for friendship and his quiet humor and devotion to others has made him very popular, I am told, all over Oxford. (He was afterwards lecturer at Oxford and held many other distinguished positions. He died as a result of a bicycle accident in 1908. See the very interesting notice of him by William T. Piper in the Ninth Report of the Harvard Class of 1874, 1909, pages 34–37.) We went down together to the river to see the first division row. They pointed out to me some of the University oarsmen now rowing in different crews. They were very fine fellows, but none larger or better oarsmen than Daniel C. Bacon or Wendell Goodwin, my fellow members of the Harvard University crew.

As I was walking through the street, I was thinking how little the men looked like our idea of Englishmen, when I saw one coming toward me and I said, "Here at last is the very picture of one" — bushy side whiskers, pantaloons with a pattern of enormous checks, a single eyeglass, a carefully studied squint, and a nonchalant air. On coming nearer it turned out to be Waldo Story, the elder, the son of W. W. Story, the American sculptor whom I had met in Rome. He invited me to dine with him to-morrow in Christ Church College.

Balliol Hall, in which I dined with Dyer, is not a particularly fine one. It has several pictures, but plain walls. We dined at the strangers' table, where we had a good dinner, better than the ordinary one, and afterwards had dessert in Dyer's room, and there I met Lockhart, grandnephew of Sir Walter Scott, a Mr. Standish, and others. We passed the evening pleasantly with music and talking. I was the only non-smoker. We all sipped sherry and a large three-handled mug of claret "cup" was passed round as is the custom. Balliol, Dyer's college, ranks high in scholarship, doubtless the highest of any at Oxford. Its entrance examinations are severe.

Saturday, May 20

WENT to breakfast with F. R. Burrows, of Trinity. On my way there I heard a great noise over the gateway, and on meeting Burrows a few moments afterwards below, he told me he had gone up into the room over the gate to await me, and that some fellows had locked him in. He made a great row to attract the porter's attention, who let him out. He then threw the shoes of those who had locked him in over on the Balliol College green. I found in Burrows's room Milman, president of the Oxford Union, and two others. We had to wait about an hour and a half for the secretary of the Oxford Union, who had overslept himself. We stayed talking till half-past ten, when all but Burrows had to go off. Milman told me that when one has been "up" for a couple of years and has the general reputation of a "reader," he can "cut" as many lectures as he pleases and a large number of prayers without being called to task. He said that he had not attended a lecture for a long time, and also that after a certain point it was waste of time for a hard reader working for honors to attend lectures.

They said that the system of gates was only a question of money up to twelve o'clock at night, and that after that hour one could be out several times, especially if he was not a freshman, without serious trouble. On the whole they thought the gating system good. It appears that the proctors keep several professional runners, called "bulldogs," to chase and catch any students seen breaking the rules. After the others had gone Burrows took me to Trinity Chapel and then to see the celebrated Lime Walk and Christ Church Cathedral. In reading a Latin quotation, I made a false quantity by a slip of the tongue, and instead of immediately correcting it, I looked to see whether Burrows had noticed it, but I could not make out whether he did not notice it or was too polite to make any remark or even lift an eyebrow.

We walked across the Magdalen Bridge and looked at the Tower and fortunately a cart and horse came down the opposite bank. The horse leaned down to drink and made altogether a perfect setting for a picture. I am now much more in the spirit of Oxford and begin to feel its fascinating influence. Like Niagara Falls it grows on one slowly. It requires several days to enjoy it fully. We visited Magdalen Chapel and cloisters and looked down Addison's Walk. Words fail me to express the charm and beauty of these places.

The proctors at Oxford hold altogether an inferior position to those at Harvard. At Oxford they are nothing but a police force. They wander about the streets day and night and are obliged to look into billiard rooms, hotels, and bars, and have the right to search any house in town with only ten minutes' notice, by virtue of an old provision in the charter of Oxford. They are despised by the best students and detested by the rest and get no respect from the professors or tutors. With us a proctor is usually a recent graduate who is given a room in a college hall, has to maintain reasonable order and quiet, but is not obliged to go round the town spying on the students.

I lunched with Professor Burrows, who lives at 9 Northam Road, in a pretty brick house. He and Mrs. Burrows were very kind. He had unfortunately to hurry off before lunch was over, but asked me to breakfast to-morrow morning and to go to church afterwards.

I met Dyer by appointment soon after. He had procured a room for me in Balliol. Its occupant had gone to London "to bury a grandmother." Its back windows face on the Martyrs' Memorial. It is on the second story and the stairs are just past the Tower, on turning to the right after entering the gate of Balliol close to the Martyrs' Memorial. We visited New College Hall and cloisters. This name shows the antiquity of Oxford. New College was founded one hundred years before the discovery of America. We stayed for the afternoon services at New College Chapel and heard probably the best choir in Oxford sing "I waited for the Lord."

We saw the races from University College barge. Then Burrows presented me to Boit, the admiral of the O.U.B.C., who was very cordial. I dined in Trinity Hall with Douglas Robinson of St. Paul's School, Concord, New Hampshire. He was a nephew of J. C. Tinné, captain and largest man of the Oxford four that beat our Harvard four in the Putney to Mortlake race in 1869. Some of the English newspapers had tried to make out that the race was not close, though Oxford only beat Harvard by six seconds, a much closer finish than in the average race between Oxford and Cambridge, but Robinson told me that his uncle said that it was a very hard race to the end; that Oxford had expected to pass us much sooner than she did, that toward the end we began creeping up, and they had to row every ounce that was in them to keep the lead.

Later I went to the elder Story's room and had dessert, as it is called, or wine. There I met a son of Matthew Arnold, to whom I took quite a fancy. We had some "Derby" talk, some college stories and singing and piano-playing. Arnold played with much feeling and enthusiasm, but not in a finished style. The dining-hall of Trinity is very fine, with dark, old oak carving and paneling and a superb entrance. I returned to my room in Balliol, which I found ready for me, and had to ring at the archway as the gate was shut.

Sunday, May 21
BREAKFASTED with the Burrows family. Professor Burrows said that Lord Lyttelton was going too far in university reform. He said there were some old fellowships and special endowments which were perfectly useless and might well be changed, but that Lord Lyttelton wished to go much farther and to have, for example, money given for maintaining choirs used for new buildings or establishing new fellowships and, in fact, wished to be allowed to change special endowments from one purpose to another as if they were unrestricted funds. He said that now with the conservative turn in politics he thought these plans would not be carried out. We went to hear the Bampton lecture by the Bishop of Derry.

I had an appointment to see Edward Moss, the stroke and captain of the Oxford University crew, in his room in Brasenose after church. When I got there he had gone, but his friend who made the appointment

LUNCHEON WITH THE COWLEY FATHERS

said that Moss had mistaken the hour and was off holding the "Derby" lottery for the great horse-race. To think that such things are going on on Sunday in quiet, religious Oxford and that, too, before most of the chapels were over! I was out at that hour because the Bampton sermon began earlier than any of the others.

I walked out to Cowley and lunched with the Fathers. I saw Father Benson, Father Ritchie, Charles P. Parker, and others. It struck me that the conversation was in general rather weak and that there was a good deal of rather trifling talk, not on higher spiritual things or necessary business or on literature or philosophy, but on the clergy and their personal peculiarities and small details of church matters. In fact, there was a great deal of "shop" talk. In a conversation about the thirty-nine articles, it turned out that one or two who were at least deacons had rather vague notions about what was necessary to believe; whether it was not enough to have believed their general spirit or most of them; and yet these were men who had testified to their belief in these articles. Father Benson and Charles Parker were rather more serious and refrained from joining in the personalities.

They all dined at a semi-circular table. The dining-room walls were bare and the Brethren sat on wooden benches. After grace and during the helping, verses were read from the Bible by one of the acolytes. The dinner consisted of meat, potatoes, turnip tops, and rhubarb pie with heavy crust, and badly brewed beer. The idea of plain food was good, but this dinner was unwholesome, badly served, badly cooked, and the surroundings had a mediæval want of cleanliness. A little of the Jewish or Mohammedan idea of water connected with worship would do the Brethren no harm. After thanksgiving for the repast we went to the chapel in the story above, Father Benson mounting the steps two at a time and yet with an air so grave and dressed in so long a cloak that the effect was really comical.

We went through a service in the chapel from a special book, but I soon lost the place and all was confusion, for the reading was so mumbled that I could not follow what was said. A few minutes of quiet were given to all on our knees. When Father Benson enters a room the conversation stops and all rise and are evidently not at their ease. When they address him they are unnatural and become slightly confused. He is a king and not a brother among them. Charles Parker and I took a walk up one of the neighboring hills and had a superb view of Oxford, one that is quite noted, he told me.

I walked back in time for the afternoon service at Magdalen College; pronounced here "Maudlin." The singing was very fine; the anthem was the "Wilderness." A little boy sang up to high A with soft, pleasing quality. I dined with Jupp, of Magdalen, at Magdalen Hall. Jupp has some sort of fellowship in mathematics and a good fellow he is too. Young Burrows introduced me to him. I drank beer out of an old beer mug made in 1698. There is very little silver older than that in Oxford, as it was almost all used up in the revolution in 1649. We went to Jupp's room for dessert. It is a corner room, overlooking the Magdalen Bridge, and is in one of the towers of the college. The air was delightfully soft and balmy and all was still outside except for the singing of the nightingales and the soft chiming of distant bells. We sat a long time in the old window seats, talking in low tones. The captain of the Christ Church Cricket Club, the president of the Magdalen Boat Club, the cockswain of the Magdalen eight, Burrows, and myself made up the party. We listened to the old Tom ringing at nine o'clock. They told college stories, and from them I learned much of the inner life of Oxford, on the whole rather creditable.

Walking home with Burrows, he began to hurry and said a proctor was following him and that he had not on a gown and cap, which were required in the evening. When we came to the corner of a street he bade me a hurried good-bye and ran rapidly off at full speed. He is a sprinter and a half-mile runner and doubtless got safely away. To have obeyed the rules he should have carried his cap and gown into Magdalen Chapel, which was not necessary for him to do in the afternoon, or else have gone way back to Trinity between the service and dinner at Magdalen. I met many students without caps and gowns; I should think nearly one third were without them, and yet if they see a proctor or "bulldog" they have to run for dear life.

Monday, May 22
A "COLD" or ordinary breakfast — that is, nothing brought from the buttery — with Dyer. We had, however, toast and tea hot, and Dyer made some hot scrambled eggs at the open fire, and we were as cozy as cottagers and happy as kings. The younger Story, Julian (who afterwards married Emma Eames, the opera singer), invited me to breakfast, but I had an engagement at that time. The engagement was to meet Edward Moss at Brasenose in his room. When I arrived he was out. From there I went down to the boat-houses and had a talk with Salter about his system of letting boats. Fast pleasure boats were the most popular. Lunched with Waldo Burnett at Keble. E. M. Parker was there, and after lunch Viner, who is on the Keble

boat, came in. From his account the Keble crew were more limited in their diet than we were in '72, '73, and '74; about as strict as we were in the freshman crew in '71. It was raining for the first time since I have been in Oxford this afternoon, but cleared off in time for the races. In the second division there was a close and exciting race between Trinity and Lincoln. Trinity just succeeded in making the bump only a few feet before it would have been too late, as Lincoln was close to the finish.

A four-oar row down the river had been arranged for me. Jupp and Darbyshire, the nephew of the celebrated late University stroke oar of that name, went with us. We left our boat under one of the long bridges and walked to the start of the first division. The boats were kept in position by long poles held by water-men from the shore and also by a cord held by the cockswain. The Oriel crew had been bumped every night for several nights running, and the men were thoroughly demoralized. They tried to appear calm, but they were evidently very nervous. They lose their heads as soon as they start and have not once got through the "Gut" before being bumped, so that Hall, their cockswain, the famous one who steered the Oxford four against Harvard in '69 and almost won the race for Oxford in '70 by sheer good steering, had no chance to show his powers.

Dined at Balliol Hall. After dinner Arnold, Smith, McMillan, and others came to Dyer's room. McMillan gave a rendering of "Hamlet" after the style of Irving. Very well done. He also acted a small piece called "The French Schoolmaster." It was in broken English and very touching. Its point lay in its human pathos and the fine sense of honor in the Frenchman. When it was over, H——, a rather conceited fellow, assuming great innocence asked, "Where is the point?" His remark fell very flat, for it struck all as extremely rude.

Tuesday, May 23
I BREAKFASTED at Christ Church with Douglas Robinson, of St. Paul's School (Concord, New Hampshire), and we had Russell also who had been there, so there was a good deal of old school-day talk. (Douglas Robinson afterwards married Theodore Roosevelt's sister; he died in 1918.) We visited the Christ Church kitchen and the old Tom and saw Dr. Johnson's desk at Pembroke College, the Oxford gymnasium, and the Martyrs' Iron Cross. The gymnasium is not free. There are always persons present to watch the exercising and control the amount and kind of work done by each man. Prizes are given every year. The gymnasium is not generally popular. Outdoor work is preferred by most of the men. The English climate is wonderfully adapted for exercising and even forces it. Seldom is the weather cold enough to keep one indoors, and yet it is usually chilly enough to be uncomfortable if one sits still in the open air.

Stopped in at Richard P. Arnold's room, which is directly under mine, and he played charmingly for me. He offered to give me a letter to a great friend of his at Cambridge, where I am going next.

I lunched with Professor Burrows and went off with him to the Convocation. The subject of discussion that created the most interest was the question of removing the botanical gardens. It had been the idea of Dr. Ackland, who unfortunately was away, to have all the scientific departments together, his reason being that science is a unit and ought to be studied as such. The answer was that the present ground was richer and better suited for the botanical gardens than the proposed plot. There was some other question of rent also, and some did not see why having the buildings together made the teaching any more unified. Professor Palmer, brother of Lord Selborne, was there and spoke very much to the point. Burrows told me that it was said of Professor Palmer that he should have been the lawyer and Lord Chancellor and that Sir Roundell Palmer, now Lord Selborne, the professor and the clergyman. The Vice-Chancellor of Oxford presided. All present wore gowns, some of them of a pattern six hundred years old.

Two proctors were present who called "Silence" in a severe voice, stood when the Vice-Chancellor spoke, and collected the "placets" and "non-placets." Professor Price, the mathematician, spoke a good deal. Professor Smith got very excited over the idea of having iron spikes on the walls of the botanical gardens. He thought it a great cruelty. What right had they to risk life in that way? Suppose some one should try to climb over and get caught? This was brought in somewhat out of order and *mal à propos*. A hint to that effect only made the professor more disquieted about the spikes. He was restless and uneasy for the rest of the meeting. Dean Lightfoot is Vice-Chancellor.

After Convocation I went through Magdalen Walk and Addison's Walk and then to tea at Dr. Talbot's, the warden of Keble College. (He was afterwards made Bishop of Winchester.) There I met Warden and Mrs. Talbot and Miss Gladstone, the daughter of the "Grand Old Man." Mrs. Talbot is sister of Lady Frederick Cavendish. It was very kind of them to ask me, for they were in mourning for Mrs. Talbot's father, the late Lord Lyttelton. I spent a very delightful hour there. Mrs. Talbot is very pretty, jolly, and bright. They spoke with regret about my father's not coming to England as Minister, as, in fact, almost every one does.

Went out rowing in a four-oar tub with sliding seats. The president of the Magdalen Boat Club went out with us. They made me row stroke. I was sorry that I was not in better condition, for I saw that I was committing faults which I rarely did at home, merely from being out of "swing" and "wind." I felt, too, that they were criticizing me all the way. They told me that if I could wait a few days more, when the races were over, they would get up some nice crews to row with me, but that now almost every good oarsman was in one or the other of the twenty-one college eights. I dined with Standish and Dyer in Standish's room. While on the river-bank I passed by and had pointed out to me the bow of this year's 'Varsity crew walking past. He was not quite so tall as Tucker Daland, who rowed port bow in the Harvard crew of '73, and not so squarely built. He looked like a plucky fellow.

Wednesday, May 24
At half-past eight I breakfasted in Dyer's room with the Balliol crew. They were a fine set of men, all good students, for no one can enter or keep in Balliol without being one. They were all tall and manly and had a healthy color in their cheeks. Their breakfast, which was of course a training one as the crew had one more day of racing, consisted of tea, dry toast, butter, bread, mutton chops, dropped eggs, beefsteak, plain lettuce, and artichokes, and they ended up with orange marmalade, of which they partook an abundance. They said almost all the Oxford crews used it. The Balliol crew does not take oatmeal porridge as do most of the

others at Oxford. I found that one of the crew had been in Fayal last winter and there met my dear classmate and old friend, Howard Lombard. They became cronies and mutual admirers at once. Some five of us sat on and talked together till half-past ten.

Bought a set of examination papers. Dyer took me to the Taylorian library and gallery. In the gallery was a fine collection of Turner's pictures and the best in the world of Raphael's original drawings. There were also some things of Michael Angelo. I lunched with Richard Arnold in his rooms at Balliol. He had there two cousins, one a Mrs. Humphry Ward who played very well on the piano. We had some songs, too: "O, Hush Thee, My Babie," by Sullivan; "Softly Blow, Ye Breezes," by Elvy, and some of Schubert's. Many puzzles were asked like this one, for example: if six cats kill six rats in six minutes, how many cats will it take to kill one hundred rats in fifty minutes? Mrs. Ward was also at the Talbots' yesterday. (This was six years before Mrs. Ward had published anything of note and twelve years before her famous "Robert Elsmere" came out. As I was revising these journals for publication I wrote Mrs. Ward to find whether it were she, her sister, or her cousin that sang the songs, and what had become of him. Weeks passed without any reply, and on March 24, 1920, I learned the reason for all the silence. The papers of that evening announced her death, after a serious illness.)

Went to Bishop Mylne's rooms at three o'clock by appointment. The Bishop looked tired and thin; not, I fear, in a state of vigor to begin life in an unhealthy climate. He had just been appointed Bishop to Bombay. He was one of our clergymen of the Advent Church in Boston, a wholesome-minded, devout, and delightful man and a convincing and inspiring preacher. He took me over the chapel of Keble, at which college he was staying. A representation of Christ above the chancel with a huge sword proceeding out of his mouth, intended to represent the sword of the Spirit, did not seem to me in good taste. It was absurdly realistic. It gives cause for ridicule rather than devotion. The mosaics were superb. There was, however, very little harmony, taking them all together, and so numerous were the little designs, mostly good in themselves, and so closely were they put together that there was no general impression whatsoever, as in some of the harmonies of mosaics, for example, in the cathedral at Palermo. The shape of the building did not seem to me good either; it was that of a tall, rectangular barn.

I walked down High Street with Bishop Mylne at racing speed. He has so much to do that he walks *ventre à terre* all the time. He was on his way to see a student from Keble who is dangerously ill. Bishop Mylne told me that he made use of every moment when awake; for example, he sometimes coaches the crews, having been a celebrated oarsman in his college eight, and while waiting for the crew at the college barge he would write letters. He seems more American in this "hurry up" than English. He may have been touched by "the whip of the sky" while in our Boston.

Went to the Bodleian Library and Divinity Hall. It rained intermittently in torrents for about two hours. I saw the medal won by Hampden, with the following lines on it:

> "Against my King I do not fight,
> But for my King and Kingdom's right."

What a splendid sentiment!

I also saw the first Latin and first English Bibles ever printed, the manuscript of Burns's "To a Louse," an autograph of Archbishop Laud, Laud's resignation of the chancellorship written from the Tower, letters of Henrietta Maria to Charles I before their marriage, and the lantern found in Guy Fawkes's hand when trying to blow up Parliament. These were perhaps the most striking things I noticed among hundreds of others.

They told me the story of the last librarian who had made a new catalogue, complete for every book but the one nearest him, which he was sitting on all the time.

Law enforcement here is peculiar. In case a student at Oxford gets into any legal difficulty, instead of being tried in a police or public court, he is tried in a room at the entrance of the Convocation Hall before the Vice-Chancellor of the University.

I dined with William Henry Russell, of Oriel, a former St. Paul's School boy, as I have already stated, in his room. He lives out of college, which is rather exceptional. He explained to me the system of living out. Students can only live out in those houses licensed by the authorities of the University. The owner of the house has to lock his outside door before ten o'clock and keep an accurate list of the number of times a boarder comes in after ten and the exact hour he returns. In case the owner omits to do this, his license is taken away. Any successful collusion between the houseowner and students is almost impossible, as students are occasionally watched by proctors, and then, too, a man's name is often taken down when leaving a room not his own after ten o'clock and if there is not a corresponding entry at his lodging the omission is quickly discovered.

Met again Douglas Robinson.

Thursday, May 25

I WENT to the early communion service at Keble at seven and a half and after that breakfasted with Bishop Mylne and the warden, professors, and tutors of Keble. Father Benson came in late. I came in with Bishop Mylne and he wished me to sit next the warden in the seat of honor. I protested and the warden very rightly did not allow it, but made the Bishop, who is now no longer directly connected with the college and is in the position of a guest, take it himself. After breakfast I went to see Canon Bright whom I have missed so far, and who had asked me to breakfast with him to-day, hoping to see him, but the servant told me he had just gone out to service. I then started back to Keble to hear Bishop Mylne preach his last sermon at Oxford before leaving for Bombay. He had especially asked me to come and hear him. On the way I met the Chancellor preceded by three squire beadles dressed in red and carrying enormous maces, marching along with a great deal of the pomp of this wicked world. Two students, half dressed, as he was walking by, put their heads out of their bedroom windows and said: "Hollo, this must be some saint's day." It was, in fact, Ascension Day.

At Keble I found the chapel door locked and a service going on inside. I made several attempts to open the door, causing sufficient noise to attract the attention of the door-keeper. I made three trials, each a little louder than the other. I should much have preferred to give up the task, but I wished my friend to know that I had cared to come and hear him. After the third attempt, with a slight shake of the door, I heard several feet advancing from inside and the door being unfastened. Then, when I was let in, I found that two proctors in full costume had descended from their seats and were looking very anxious as if they expected to hear that the building was on fire or that some one was leaving this life. Nor was that all. There were at least thirty pairs of eyes looking at me. I thanked the proctors, made them a bow, walked by and took my seat in as quiet, dignified, and matter-of-fact way as I could. I noticed that as they shut the doors the least sound reverberated along the stone mosaic floor and walls of the chapel, whose main fault as a chapel was its too abundant echoes. So I had the pleasant assurance that every one in the building had heard my gentle "tapping at the door." All the students wore white surplices during service. The sermon was good, both earnest and intellectual.

Lunched with Dicey. We visited the Ashmolean Museum, where I saw, among other things, the jewel which is authentically the one worn by Alfred the Great in his crown. We saw also the sword given by Pope Leo X to Henry VIII as "Defender of the Faith."

Rowed down the river in a four-oar through Iffley Lock, as far as the Swan Inn, if I recollect the name aright, where we got out and pitched quoits. The great jumper Glazebrook rowed with us. Two years ago he made the highest amateur running jump on record. His jump has recently been beaten by another Oxford man named Brooks, who broke professional records and all, jumping in a match six feet, two and one half inches. Glazebrook gave me some useful hints about running jumping.

In the evening dined in Balliol Hall with Dyer and later went to the Balliol eight wine, that is, a jollification given in honor of the Balliol crew, which had made three bumps this year and holds a good place on the river, so there was a lot of enthusiasm and the place crowded. The college authorities gave up one of the reception or lecture halls for it. Every member of the crew, cockswain included, was toasted separately. The toasts were drunk mostly in champagne. The answers to the toasts were not particularly bright and witty, but were manly, good-natured, and modest. They had no little singing, usually calling for a song as well as a speech, and all joined in after each toast with the refrain "For He is a Jolly Good Fellow." They took me in as one of themselves and called on me for a Harvard song. They knew I was a Harvard 'Varsity stroke oar and captain and had followed their crews every day I had rooms in Balliol. I was puzzled for a moment what to choose. "Fair Harvard" is dull, and most of those we used to sing were more distinctive of negro minstrels than of Harvard. At last I bethought me of "The Lone Fish Ball," which was generously applauded. As an encore I gave "Louisiana Lowlands," which did not take as well. They then toasted the United States and asked me to respond. I said in general that it is now the centennial of the disturbance between the two countries, but that such kindness as I had received here at Oxford, and indeed all over England, and from them in particular, was of a kind, if extended to others also, to make firm friends of the two nations, which have a common language, common literature, common laws, common customs and liberties, and a high sense of national character and responsibility. What these two might do as co-workers for the peace and well-being of the rest of the world was almost incalculable. These few words apparently pleased them, as they were followed up with "For He is a Jolly Good Fellow." Was this not "just awfully nice" of them? They had the good sense to break up the meeting before things began to drag. There was a good deal of drinking, but no one seemed more affected than to be slightly talkative. There was, however, more drinking afterwards in some of the private rooms. (As I look over my notes and cards received at Oxford, I see I have had more invitations and calls from faculty and students than I have mentioned. They simply showered me with acts of kindness.)

I had long known of the Oxford-Cambridge system of examinations and the better feeling and greater friendliness that is supposed to exist on that account between the students and the faculty.

With us in America the instructor is the examiner. He is the man who may cut off the student from his degree, condition him, or lose him a high mark. In an English university, on the other hand, examinations are set by committees of the university while the college instructor, be he tutor or professor, is the friend of the student who is helping him to pass an examination set by others. With us to be on familiar terms with the instructor is supposed by fellow-students to be bidding for lenient marks and not to be good form. How is it in Oxford? I find all the restraint is removed and all I had been told is true as to the good relations and helpful, stimulating intimacy between teacher and taught, and those Oxford men who had previously been at Harvard, and whom I met, believed that the difference is due almost wholly to the system of examinations.

I cannot close the account of my delightful visit at Oxford without speaking of the easy hospitality, manliness, freedom from care, even happy-go-lucky character of the men. They were much more blithe, jovial, and lightly merry than our Harvard students, who take both play and pleasure more seriously. The Oxford men, too, bore defeat good-naturedly. Oxford on a bright day in May during the bumping races, with all the young lady visitors and its spring verdure, is at its best. The hawthorns, both red and white, the chestnut-trees in bloom, the lilacs, and a profusion of flowers and flowering shrubs, the silken lawns, the many meadows, the winding blue river, the gray or red spires or towers seen through masses of dense foliage, and the odor of new-mown grass, and sweet flowers, formed the setting of these days for the triumph of youth and beauty and simple pleasure "almost unalloyed."

Friday, May 26
IN the morning I left for a visit at Cambridge University by way of London, having had a most satisfactory, instructive, and delightful visit at Oxford. I felt almost as if I had been a student there. They certainly made me seem like one of themselves in all social and friendly relations. At Cambridge all the hotels were chock full, as it was the evening of the grand ball. I had made no arrangements in advance, so could not go. They gave me rooms outside and I took my meals at the hotel. Delivered my letters and on coming back from a stroll I found an invitation to breakfast with Herbert Leaf, the friend of Richard Arnold.

Cambridge does certainly seem dull and plain after Oxford. The young men appear a little less well-bred. I saw a number sitting on a fence and scrutinizing some young ladies passing by, a thing which I never saw either at Oxford or Harvard, though it is a common enough practice at a certain other New England college.

Saturday, May 27

BREAKFASTED with Leaf at Trinity. I met there three or four very charming fellows, among others William Bradford, of New Orleans, a recent graduate, and Francis H. Mellor. During this breakfast Leaf and Bradford kindly put me in the way of seeing pretty much all that was going on. We adjourned to Bradford's room where I met Francis Peabody, of Salem, Massachusetts, who is also a student at Trinity. He and Bradford both rowed in the first Trinity eight in the recent bumping races and their crew stood second on the river. Peabody was on the winning "trial eight" and missed a seat on the University crew on account of a temporary illness. Bradford took me to see a cricket match between the Cambridge eleven and the Surrey Club. The match was rather uninteresting as Cambridge had it pretty much all its own way. Leaf was batting part of the time I was there. The fielding of the Surrey Club was bad enough to rank them third rate in baseball. The batting and bowling, however, were good.

There was a running-track made of rolled ashes round the cricket ground. This was a new idea. We passed the racket-court, skating-rink, dissecting-rooms, and physical and chemical laboratories on our way back. Lunched with Bradford and then we went rowing together in a pair-oar tub down to the first lock, Baitsbite's. Lovely day, and a good time.

The boat-houses in Cambridge are more like ours at Harvard, built of wood or stone and on the river-bank. They are all, but that of the first Trinity, very plain, ugly buildings and there are no pretty trees nor shrubs by the river, nor barges as at Oxford. Many of the toilet and sewage arrangements in these beautiful colleges are of a strictly mediæval character. The river is not fit for swimming, and woe to both bright blazers and white trousers in case of an upset. Took a drive with Bradford and Peabody in a cab to Girton and back, leaving Peabody to return later. I saw the new buildings for the young ladies' college there. I dined with Bradford at Trinity, who has been quite devoted to me. Bless his heart, for he is a dear, kind, warm-hearted Southerner! The guests were Gibbs, whose father is governor of the Bank of England, Lehmann, Penrose, and Gridley, an Eton fellow. Peabody dropped in later — a jolly crowd and a jolly time!

Sunday, May 28
BREAKFASTED late with Frank Peabody, where I met a number of men, Haddon, Lehmann, Penrose, Alexander, Corbatt, Jameson, and Rodwald, all bright, cheerful, and hospitable. In the middle of the day dined with Mr. A. Marshall, a professor at St. John's College. I had a letter to him from President Eliot. Dined at the dons' table in high style on a dais and had some rare old wine for which their cellar is noted. Some of the dons were agreeable and many no doubt very learned, but they did not converse particularly well and some of them certainly were not refined in their table manners. We adjourned to the Convocation room for coffee.

I got Mr. Marshall talking on the labor question, which he has particularly studied in the United States. He said that after most careful examination he did not find that our laborers were paid much, if any, more than the English, when one deducts the difference between paper, in which the Americans are paid, and gold, which the Englishman gets, and also the difference in the cost of living. That is, based on real wages, there was but very little difference. It seemed rather a startling statement. He made most of his studies two years ago before the cost of labor had declined very much and he seems to have worked diligently and impartially.

We went to afternoon chapel. All the students of this college, St. John's, have to attend service twice a day and wear surplices. The anthem, "Who is the King of Glory?" by Handel, was superbly sung. Quite thrilling.

I dined with Mellor, son of Justice Sir John Mellor, in the hall of Trinity College. The hall is the best in Cambridge and better than any I saw at Oxford. I went to his room afterwards and about nine we adjourned to the room of Professor Gibbons, who was musical. There we had lots of singing and playing, all of the most classical style. There I met Mr. Rawlins, to whom Mr. James Russell Lowell gave me a letter and who was so kind to me last summer on many occasions. Mellor took me to walk through "the Backs" and along Fortification Walk to hear the nightingales sing. We heard but one, which sang but for a few moments. That song, however, was delicious, only tantalizing, as it stopped so soon. Fortunately, I had heard some of these noted birds early this morning about four or five o'clock, and also at Oxford. "The Backs" are to me one of the most beautiful things in Cambridge and quite superior to any one thing in Oxford. As everybody knows, it is a river that goes on the back side of some of the handsomest of the colleges with steep, wooded, and bushy banks and lovely walks that invite one to sit and stroll and muse, while the odor of flowers, the brilliant coloring from the deep, almost black greens to the bright red and white flowering shrubs and the emerald green grass, give altogether something which I have never seen anywhere else.

Monday, May 29
BREAKFASTED with Bradford and then met Mitchell, number five of the winning 'Varsity of this year. He is unusually bright and would be a fine scholar as well as rowing man with a little more application, I am told. I was rather disappointed in not finding the 'Varsity oarsmen larger men. Mitchell, who is quite a noted oar, is no taller than I and no broader, though perhaps a little thicker-set, and not nearly as large and strong as either Bacon or Goodwin, to say nothing of Taylor on the Harvard crew in 1874, which was the heaviest on which I rowed. Indeed, I was the next to the lightest man on the University that year. After breakfast we visited the Corpus Christi College court with its notedly thick ivy, St. Peter's or Peterhouse Chapel, the oldest college in Cambridge, with its very fine stained-glass windows of the modern school, though for my part I rather like the ancient better, and the Fitzwilliam Museum all in the Grecian style, with its gorgeous marble hall and fine collection of Turner's pictures and casts from the best statuary in the world. The museum is open to the public on Wednesday and slippers are kept on hand for the rustics to wear so they will not injure the finely polished stone mosaic floors with their hobnails.

Went over the Cavendish chemical and physical laboratory, named after the Duke of Devonshire who has endowed it handsomely. Mr. Garnett, to whom Mr. Marshall gave me a note, took me over. All the nails and other work usually of iron were made of copper near the magnetic and electric departments and every room is furnished with stands for tables entirely independent of the floors. The supports for these stands rest on solid beams running directly up from the foundations. In this way, walking about the building does not disturb the most careful and delicate experiment. Much of the apparatus has not yet arrived, but all that has is of the very highest order.

Lunched with my classmate William T. Piper, of Harvard, who is taking post-graduate work at this English university, and there met Frank Peabody again and a Mr. Thornton, a son of the English Minister to America, Sir Edward Thornton. Peabody told me he is going to practice law in America, probably in Boston.

I went to the Pitt Club at two-thirty and down the river at four. The Pitt Club is not political and is not an eating or drinking club, but intended simply to furnish a place to write and read that is more select than the Union, which latter is virtually open to all who wish to belong.

On the river I rowed in a four-oar with Close, an old 'Varsity oar who coached this year's successful crew on the Thames. He stroked our boat. Penrose, stroke of Trinity, was behind him, and Bradford behind me. Penrose and Close are on the four-oar going to Philadelphia from Trinity College for the great regatta at the Centennial Exhibition. Their stroke is somewhat longer than that rowed at Oxford, just the reverse of the state of affairs a few years ago. They do not snatch so quickly from the water, which is becoming a great fault at Oxford. It is very well to correct that fault, but I think the Cambridge men are overdoing the correction, reaching too far forward and going too far back. It is proved to absolute demonstration, that going back be-

DINNER WITH R. C. LEHMANN

yond a certain point is wasted motion, requiring great effort in the recovery. The Trinity pair-oars were out practicing for the championship of the college. Trinity has six hundred undergraduate members in all, so its races are quite good. They got coaching all the way. Had a good shower bath after our row.

The Trinity boat-house has hand basins and shower baths, two large dressing-rooms and a reading-room, but no lockers, strange to say. I dined with R. C. Lehmann, of Trinity, who has very handsome rooms, with rich, old furniture, dark hangings, and all in good taste. The dinner was rather too elaborate, I thought, for college. It was a regular London one, with all its courses, servants, wines, flowers, and fruits. Sturgis, son of Russell Sturgis, of London, Frank Peabody, Foster (who afterward married Lehmann's sister), Ward, Gibbs, Denman, Bradford, Grey, Cole, and three or four others were there. I sang some songs to the guitar. They particularly liked "Louisiana Lowlands" and made me repeat it in Sturgis's room, where we adjourned for tea, and delicious tea it was too! J. P. Penrose came in later and sang a good deal. He has a fine voice and sang with sentiment. He is very popular and being Irish takes his popularity well. During the singing a proctor's servant appeared and handed Sturgis a printed notice as to the rules of the music hours, it being then past the time allowed. The fellows did not mind it at all. I left soon, for fear they were keeping it up on my account. Grey is six feet seven inches tall and is the best pianist and organist in Cambridge. (Rudolph Chambers Lehmann, who gave the dinner, was afterwards an editor of London "Punch," of the "Daily News," a member of Parliament, and for two years coach of the Harvard University crew. Though he failed to win a race for Harvard against Yale, he did much to improve the good feeling and to better the athletic relations between those two colleges.)

Tuesday, May 30
BREAKFASTED with Bradford, who had a "chap" there named James Bradford Mann, who is on the Philadelphia four, and I went to several of the colleges and then to King's Chapel and up on the roof. The view from there was perhaps the most thoroughly English that I have yet seen. The roundness and fullness of the trees, the brightness of the grass, the narrow, winding river, the rolling country with hedgerows by the roads, gave an impression of softness and peace not found in Italy, France, Egypt, Greece, or New England. The chapel itself was grand and the arches upon arches of the stone roof up so high and affording each other common support excited wonder, surprise, and admiration. It seemed to draw the spirit upward and should, if architecture could do so, raise one above everything that is sordid and low.

I lunched with Professor Henry Sidgwick. His wife is a bluestocking, really a great mathematician. She is generally quiet, is pale, very agreeable in conversation when she talks, and extremely ladylike in her manners. I wonder whether her genius interferes with her housekeeping? (She was made principal of Newnham College in 1892. Her brother is the Rt. Hon. A. J. Balfour, who in 1876 was but beginning his parliamentary career.)

I went to the rooms of a fellow of King's whom I met at lunch and strolled down with him to the boats. I measured some of the fittings of the eights used in the last races. They were not well placed. Many of the rowlocks were too high and too near the seats, measured horizontally and to the middle of the boat. This was not only my individual opinion, as different from our measurements at Harvard, but they were different from those of the Cambridge University crew. I went down as cockswain to a pair-oar tub, with the remaining two of the Trinity four that is going to America. They were not large fellows, only one of the four is taller than I. Penrose, Close, and I did running high jumps for beers. Close beat me and I beat Penrose. They said I really jumped higher than Close, but did not know how to get over the bar in the right way. Perhaps that was just their manner of being pleasant, but very likely they were right as I had never had any coaching for high jumping.

To-day they rowed the Trinity pair-oar races. Frank Peabody and his partner, Mann, easily won against Lehmann and Hicks. The river was too narrow for even two boats to row abreast, so the boats went in a straight line, the second pair enough behind not to be affected by the wash of the first. They were started by the firing of a pistol. They rowed to stakes up the river placed at a distance apart exactly equal to that between the boats at starting. A man was placed at each stake with a loaded pistol and fired it off as soon as the boat passed which was to finish at his stake, and the first pistol that went off showed which boat had won. Stop-watches were also carried by men running or on horseback alongside of each boat, and so the time was kept. A professional water-man ran beside each boat and gave the bow directions for steering during the race. The pair-oars are now rowed without cockswains and are steered by rudders worked by the bow oar, with an arrangement by which his feet can regulate long copper tiller wires. Left for London directly after dinner.

Dined again with Bradford, where I met Penrose, Peabody, Jameson, Riston, and Mann, another of the so-called "American" or "Philadelphia" four. I gave them an idea of the heat in Philadelphia and told them of some differences in our diet and training for our summer climate. Altogether we had another cozy, charming party and no mosquitoes, though the weather was warm. The longer I have stayed in Cambridge the more I appreciate some of its special features. The Cavendish laboratories are the beginning of scientific education in the big English universities. There is none at present at Oxford and it is only just starting at Cambridge. "The Backs" here are more beautiful than any one thing at Oxford. Trinity Hall is finer than any one hall at Oxford, and one chapel here is perhaps superior also; yet, on the whole, Oxford far surpasses Cambridge in general beauty and dignity. The wonderful bright-colored coats worn by the men of the crews and cricket elevens, which they call "blazers," are most striking. They seem to an American as too vivid in color, with wonderful contrasts in the way of stripes. I bought as a souvenir the dark blue coat, white trousers, and scarf at Oxford worn by the University crew men.

The habit at Oxford and Cambridge of breakfasting in each other's rooms instead of in hall and the dining in hall instead of at small dining-clubs, as is so much the fashion among the well-to-do at Harvard, tends to a great deal of sociability and perhaps has much to do with the freedom of hospitality which is so remarkable in English society; that is, hospitality among themselves and to any one who is properly introduced. At Cambridge the bumping races were over. They had had their great ball and the young ladies had mostly gone when I arrived, and the men were settling down in preparation for future examinations and the long vacation, and I did not have the advantage of living in one of the colleges as at Oxford, nor did I have as many letters of introduction. Still, my time was very agreeably filled and I saw the University to better advantage than do most strangers.

CHAPTER XVIII
FIRST OF LONDON REVISITED

Wednesday, May 31

TO-DAY went to see the great Derby horse-race. I started off from the corner of Regent Street and Piccadilly on the top of a four-horse drag which my friend J. Horsfall had engaged. In the party were some ten German friends of his and all were bound in a merry mood for the Derby races. We had an experienced driver, good and even handsome horses, a manservant, and plenty of lunch inside the coach. Before we had got fairly out of London and about ten o'clock in the forenoon the roads toward Epsom were well filled with carriages and foot passengers, all tending one way. Every sort of trap was put into use — small donkey carts, vegetable wagons, tip-carts, express wagons, omnibuses, hansom cabs, and in fact everything from a pair of bare feet up to a landau with four horses.

The day was not particularly hot, yet people were constantly quenching their thirst with beer at every inn and hotel on the roadside. All along we saw negro minstrels, some of them of the rudest sort, generally three men with a banjo, a set of bones, and a tambourine. Sometimes the company would consist of but one man who would sing, make faces, tell stories, pass round the hat, and say "Thank you, Sar," to those who put nothing in. Before we got a quarter of the way, we saw some parties who had unhitched their horses and had already begun their lunch. I wondered if they ever saw the race-course even from a distance that day. There were parties, no nearer their destination, who were overcome with the "fresh air and sandwiches" and had gone to sleep under a hedge or in some cases right out on the roadside. There seemed to be an innumerable supply of policemen all along the road. There were always one or two in sight. Large numbers of pea-shooters were sold along the way, so that one's eyes were in jeopardy both going and coming. They also sold what seemed to me the most stupid contrivance for squirting water. It was nothing but a painter's tube for oil paints filled with water instead of colors. While they were about it they might have got something which would squirt water better and not be used up in one second. However, these were uncomfortable and annoying enough as it was, so we had reason to be thankful that they were not more effective. After we left the limits of London the road was no longer watered and the air was extremely dusty.

About twelve o'clock we arrived at the race-course, had the coach driven into the two-guinea enclosure, and got close to the line right opposite the grandstand, so that we had the best place possible. Driving down our driver spared his horses at the beginning, many a trap passing us. Before our fine animals got tired or hot he watered them a little, occasionally stopping for a moment; but before we arrived at the race-course we had passed everything that had gone by us and a good many more that had started ahead of us, and our horses were fresh and brisk.

Once established in the enclosure we got off the drag and walked about. The crowd was nowhere very dense, being spread over a large area. It was a rough, dirty, and boisterous set. There were wild Indians painted in all sorts of colors, with rows of feathers on their hats, who did second-rate feats of strength and agility; there were hand organs with monkeys; negro minstrel troops of all sizes and qualities; there were Scottish bagpipes and Scotch dancing-girls; there were acrobats and jugglers and whole families of "phenomena," and each set collected a crowd about itself, the crowd sometimes more interesting than the performers. There were quantities of betters or book-makers with their assistants, their stands, and their strange costumes. One pair, for example, wore tall white hats, blue cravats, and long checked overcoats coming down to their feet; another couple were dressed in long white cloaks, with large red crosses, looking, with their backs turned, like Catholic priests at high mass. They all had some peculiar costume, and, what is strange, there was not a single face among some two hundred or more of these book-makers or professional betters that I saw, who did not look as calm, sober, gentle, and honest as could be; in fact, seen in another costume and another place they would pass for quiet, country Methodist parsons. Until the race-horses appeared just before the great race itself, the betting was carried on most quietly. Only as the horses started did it become noisy.

The chief amusement of the crowd, while waiting, seemed to be, above all, the game of Aunt Sally, which has now somewhat improved. Instead of uselessly knocking the pipe out of the mouth of a figure dressed to represent Aunt Sally, they threw clubs at cocoanuts placed on sticks about four feet high and six feet apart. If a cocoanut was hit, it belonged to the lucky shooter. Hitting the support and so knocking down the nut did not count. A halfpenny or a farthing a throw was the price. It seemed very easy to hit these cocoanuts, so every one tried, but in reality it was hard and so those running these games made no little profit.

THE GREAT RACE

Several races of more or less interest came off, all on time, and then we had lunch with champagne, various kinds of sandwiches, cold chicken, *pâté de foie gras*, and what not. During lunch crowds of dirty ragamuffins crawled under the carriage to get what was thrown away. Every now and then we would be called on to "sit still for a moment" and the next minute a man would appear with a tintype of the coach and party. We had twenty of these taken of us.

At last the bell rang for the great race of the day. The track was cleared and out came the horses and riders, going slowly up the course, and then faster back to the start, to "get up the blood." We had not long to wait before we heard from the other side a roar of shouting and could indistinctly make out, round the corner to our right and over the heads of the standing crowds, some bright colors, yellow, red, and blue, flashing past. Then we saw the horses turn Tattenham Corner and come straight for us. We were unable, till they got nearly opposite, to tell which was ahead. All about us the excitement was intense. One could feel it in the air. I took the opportunity to glance at the grandstand opposite and the crowd below. Every hat was off, every neck strained, and every head turned in the same direction. It was a sea of faces and eyes. In a moment the horses were in front of us and then past, first one and then another having the lead, but the favorite hopelessly behind. The great event of the day was over. A good view of the race, for about eight seconds at most and much less for many, had brought that great crowd of hundreds of thousands out of London and from all parts of England. There followed soon after an unimportant race, the last one of the day, and then all started for home.

Such confusion and such noise, dust, dirt, and row! Lunch was strewed about, horses were frisking, and a good half the drivers were more or less drunk. Our driver, fortunately, was in good condition. The road was so crowded that we hardly went off a walk for about five miles and we had frequent blocks when the whole procession came to a standstill. The scenes along the road were discouraging enough for any one who believes in the essential good of human nature and would quickly put to rout any theory of the self-development and improvement of unassisted, unrestrained, free human action. The amount of drunkenness was beyond belief. Dignified and quiet-looking old men would be drinking to the health of passers-by; young men would be drinking out of the bottles. The pea-shooters were livelier than ever, and before we got home small stones were used in place of peas. Water, and even beer, was thrown from one carriage to another, and so were little bags of some white powder, which would break on hitting one's clothes and make one look like a miller. A party of young men in a handsome barouche began to amuse themselves by shooting peas at an old woman by the roadside. She took up stones, and on their continuing, she let fly right into the carriage, and why the sharp-cornered stones used for macadamizing the road did not break any skulls, none of us could tell. They very much damaged the varnish on the handsome equipage. Our coachman got ahead by taking a side road, and, having used the horses well, they were fresh, and once out of the thickest of the crowd we passed everything and got back to our rendezvous at about half-past ten in the evening, all having had "a very nice time, thank you." One of our own party was overcome from imbibing too much and had to be put below.

Another, who was in pretty bad condition, made friends with a street-walker along the side of the road and insisted upon her getting up on the coach and sitting beside him. I felt thoroughly ashamed of my company and only trusted I was not recognized by any of my good English friends. Altogether it was about as disgusting and discouraging an experience as I have ever had.

Thursday, June 1
DINED with John Westlake, Esquire, Queen's Counsel, and Doctor of Civil Laws at Oxford. (Later was made Professor of International Law at Cambridge and a judge of the Hague Court of International Arbitration.) There I met several barristers. A good deal of friendly interest in American politics was developed. I explained the bad influences of the present civil service and patronage system and how, through it, we created political machines which manipulate the caucuses, primaries, and conventions in favor of those who put them in office, so that no longer does our Government represent the wishes of the people, but rather the wishes of a ring of unscrupulous politicians, the office-holders working for the "ins" and those wanting their places working night and day for the "outs." We go through the form of voting, as the Roman citizens so long did under the Empire for their consuls, but, just as they voted for candidates named by the Emperor, so we vote only for those whom the political party machines nominate.

The Royal Titles Bill passed in April and the declaration of Queen Victoria as Empress of India a month ago came up for discussion. The usual reason given for the change of title was to impress the inhabitants of

India, where "empress" seemed a higher title than "queen." Whether it would not at the same time settle any question of precedence in England itself as between a royal and an imperial princess was considered as at least a probable consequence of, if not a motive for, the change.

Friday, June 2

CALLED on Mr. Rawlins at Lincoln's Inn, New Court. I find that many of the British barristers have a way of looking at the law, not as a system intended to bring about the best justice possible and to be developed for that purpose, but merely as a bundle of traditions with no concern as to the reason for their existence other than that they are what they are. That is a very convenient state of mind for an active, practicing young barrister, but I am inclined to think that only those men will become great as judges or leading lawyers in the realm who are seeking to develop a wise and helpful jurisprudence fitted to the needs of the people.

Spent the afternoon in the South Kensington Museum, mostly in examining the scientific apparatus. There was so much to see that one had to choose between merely looking over everything just to get an idea of the size and variety of the whole or else to examine a small part carefully.

I dined with Mr. Albert Rutson at the Devonshire Club. Mr. Rutson had taken the trouble to look me up, saying that my father had been kind to him when he was in Boston during his travels in the "States." He is not well. At the dinner were Mr. Charles Parker, Professor Gurney, somebody named Rice from India, and others. After dinner I went to hear Albani sing in "I Puritani." I was delighted with Albani's voice, charm of manner, and good looks. The cabman who drove me home was somewhat drunk and demanded extra pay, telling me when halfway home that he would not go on without this extra amount. I told him to go ahead or I should call a policeman. When at the door of my lodgings he insisted on extra money. I gave him the full fare and a little more for *pourboire* and then unlocked the door and walked in. He followed me into the house, slipping past the door before I could shut it. I then, as they say in law, *posui manus molliter*, and ejected him from the house. I had the suspicion from hearing a heavy thud that he fell on the sidewalk, but in a moment he was up again, banging and knocking on the door and threatening all sorts of things. However, having a clear conscience and knowing I had a right to defend my castle, and that I had used no unnecessary force under the circumstances, I quietly went to bed and to sleep.

Saturday, June 3
LUNCHED in Piccadilly on pickled salmon, bread and butter, and a half a pint of stout for 1*s*. 4*d*.; a pretty cheap lunch and not bad. I visited the British Museum, where I saw the rest of Athens that Lord Elgin had taken away and which I had not seen in Greece, and a good deal also from Egypt and Syria. The Theseus is badly injured, but still has dignity and repose. I called on Professor Gurney and Mr. Westlake and found them out; on Signor Franceschi, who was in. I walked home through the park, where I saw all the world and some of my world, too, out driving and riding. I dined at St. James's restaurant with music during the meal. They had a wonderful dinner for the price, namely, soup, fish, an entrée, joint, pudding,

tarts, ice cream, and fruit for 3s. 6d. I spent the evening talking with a dear old man with fine curly gray hair, Mr. Jonathan Amory, of Boston, who was lodging in the same house with me. He gave me an interesting account of his meeting Louis Napoleon and Charles X. He was trying to perfect an invention on a smoke-consuming patent of his for use in locomotives. Theoretically it is good, but whether it will work out in practice is another matter.

Whit Sunday, June 4
WENT to All Saints', Margaret Street, in the afternoon. Read Pascal till time for dinner. I dined informally with Joe Horsfall and his brother. Talked over our Derby experiences and saw some of the sights of London.

Monday, June 5
BEING Whit Monday all the banks and shops were shut and no work was done. On going up Regent Street at about eleven o'clock in the forenoon, I passed two well-dressed, rather good-looking girls, both drunk. They were talking very loudly, kissing and embracing each other. The police never put a stop to such things in London, day or night, unless the drunkenness gets so noisy as to be a breach of the peace and a public disturbance. With us in America drunkenness in public places is a misdemeanor and it is the duty of the police to arrest. I called on Mrs. Dr. Julius Pollock, whom I found in, and Lord Tenterden, who was out. Went to hear Albani, this time in "Lohengrin," and her beautiful voice grew on me the more I heard it.

Tuesday, June 6
LEFT at ten-fifty for Windsor to see Eton College on the day of the annual celebration. How I remember

June 6 as the great Eton day, when reading of the public schools of Great Britain in my days at St. Paul's, and here I now am on the very day and at the very school! It rained as the train drew out, in the quiet, noiseless way the English railway carriages move, but it cleared up before arriving. At the station were a large number of boys to meet their friends. The small boys wore white vests and short black jackets, with black neckties and turnover collars. The older ones wore long surtouts, with black vests and white neckties. They all, young and old, wore the tall silk hats of the Eton lads, which were to-day well brushed and new, and most of the boys had flowers in their button-holes. I met a Mr. Rawlins, one of the masters at Eton, brother of the one I had known, who had given me a letter to him. He took me to hear the speaking, which had already begun. The speaking was confined to the sixth form — the highest class, and considering the small number from which the speakers were chosen, it was quite good. There were several dialogues, funny pieces, serious speeches, bits of poetry, and parts of plays acted out. A French dialogue by Molière was particularly well done. A piece by J. R. Lowell — spelled on the programme with one l — was given, but not well. There was a lot of enthusiastic applause among the boys and their friends.

Lunched with Rawlins, the master, and some of his pals. After lunch his brother, my old friend the barrister, turned up and took me under his charge. He had arranged to have me invited to the grand lunch and to sit at the head table, but I had come too late for him to find me.

We then walked to the cricket field. It was the most lovely bit of ground, perfectly level, of well-rolled and closely cut turf, thick and green, and it was surrounded on all sides but one with grand old trees, the foliage growing down to the very ground. Ladies in pretty, bright costumes were walking about and under the trees; the Royal Band from Windsor was playing delightfully, and in perfect tune, which is not always true of the bands in England outside the most noted ones. I was presented to the headmaster of Eton. He is a great rowing authority, and we agreed that the English eights, or racing boats, were built without enough "floor" fore and aft. I was also presented to Mr. Chitty, who was stroke oar for a year or two of the Oxford 'Varsity crew and also a double first, and is now a successful barrister (afterwards an eminent judge) and always umpires in the great boat-race between the university crews of Cambridge and Oxford.

He said that whatever improvements they may have made since his day in boats, oars, and style — they had introduced the sliding seats — they did at least one thing worse and that was the coaching. Nowadays a coach, says he, thinks he is not doing his duty unless he is constantly calling out to his men and correcting them for some fault or other. The oarsmen get confused and irritated and then do not pay any attention. I do not know that that applies in America to any particular generation. In fact, coaching from outside the boat itself has been rather new at Harvard, but most of our coaches do call out and even swear at the men far too much. I coached the 1875 crew till just before the race and they beat Yale, and I found it was much better to talk calmly, explain fully, and have private talks with the men, merely giving a word of reminder when they were actually rowing, and that no shouting or swearing is the least bit necessary or does any good.

Took tea with the headmaster and afterwards at a Mrs. ——'s, where I met Professor Gurney. On account of a dinner engagement in London I had to leave before the great procession of boats and the fireworks, but I saw some of the boys in their boating uniform. The cockswains were dressed in full admiral's toggery, and all wore gaudy uniforms varying according to the crew they represented.

Drove back in open carriage to London with Professor Gurney and dined with Mrs. Julius Pollock, where I met Lord Tenterden, Mr. and Mrs. Rowcliffe, another Mr. and Mrs. Pollock, the Reverend Mr. H. R. Haweis, a distinguished and rather free-thinking clergyman, Mrs. Haweis and four or five others. The death of the Sultan of Turkey was discussed. Lord Tenterden said he thought the Sultan committed suicide. In general, in England, people laugh at the idea. Tenterden said it was a great mistake to think that the Sultan was nothing more than a pleasure-seeker. He was a man of ambition. He prided himself on being the only absolute monarch in the whole of Europe, unless the Czar of Russia was to be excepted, and his word was law. Tenterden said that in all the conferences with the various English ambassadors, the Sultan had been reported as a man of determination, good sense, and strong will. He had force of character enough to travel all over Europe, and he was the only Sultan, it must be remembered, that had ever done so. Then, too, he was a man of strong passions and one who had not been taught to control them. From his high position, then, this ambitious monarch suddenly found himself deprived of all power and not even allowed the dignity of carrying side arms, a thing much thought of by the Turks. So great a change for the worse with a man of hotter blood than our Westerners, and with no chance ever to regain his power — what would be more natural than suicide with him? Of course, when one considers that this was the opinion of the head of the Foreign Office at a critical moment in European affairs, it ought to have great weight, and he would not have said so much, I believe, on this subject unless it was really his strong conviction.

The ladies sang after dinner. Lord Tenterden and I walked away together, he leaving me at the corner of Jermyn and St. James's Streets, and we talked a little of our last summer's experiences; all in his cheery, jovial, and bright way, though he had some cause for being depressed, as his wife was seriously ill and their marriage had been a love affair. On returning to my room I found a kind note from the Honorable Dudley Fortescue, asking me to dine.

Wednesday, June 7
DELIVERED some letters of introduction in the afternoon and dined at Simpson's celebrated restaurant.

Thursday, June 8
BY appointment Mrs. H. Rowcliffe called for me with her sister, Mrs. Pollock, in her carriage for a drive in the park. We got out of the carriage and walked up and down the broad path. We met Lord Tenterden and several other friends. There was a great scarcity of pretty young ladies on horseback, or rather the young ladies on horseback were few of them pretty. Perhaps the present costume is not particularly becoming. They all ride side-saddle, with long skirts and tall silk hats. At half-past one I went by invitation to Mr. Russell Sturgis's box at Drury Lane to Buckstone's benefit.

Sturgis is one of the senior partners of Baring Brothers, the great bankers. This benefit was the great theatrical performance of the year and I was extremely lucky to see it, for all the seats had been taken long before and I could not buy one for love or money.

All the best actors in London took parts in the play, "The School for Scandal." Irving took the part of Joseph Surface, Miss Neilson, of Lady Teazle, etc. Irving was rather stiff and formal and seemed unable to descend from Hamlet and Macbeth. The play was not over till five, and then Buckstone made a long speech in answer to a complimentary and by no means short poem spoken by a popular actress. He began by explaining why the Prince of Wales could not come to the performance, but had regretted, etc.; how the Duke of Connaught had been present during the early part of the play, but had been called away. Then he told of his own life; how he began at eleven shillings a week and at the end of the first week the company broke up and he was never paid; how the actress who just recited the poem was his first love; how he was still obliged to act and not leave the stage to younger and more brilliant actors — cries of "No! No! Hear! Hear!" — but that he had seven apologies which were his seven children; how his feelings overcame him, and how many pounds, shillings, and pence had been subscribed and taken at the door.

I met in the box Mr. Sturgis and his daughter, Professor and Mrs. Gurney, and a man whose name I did not catch. Mr. Sturgis made a remark which implied that all men were bad, but some were hypocrites and some, like Joseph Surface, more honest. I think I could have shown him several of my classmates and friends who were genuinely true. I remember meeting one fellow in Paris who, because he belonged to a rich club and associated with rich friends and drank a good deal, though never to excess, I assumed to be rather loose in his morals, for he had no religious professions, but I saw a great deal of him in that tempting city and found, from his actions and from what friends said of him and the friends he chose, that he was as true to high principles as any of the best of the fellows I know. Why a man of Mr. Sturgis's character and social and banking influence should say such a thing before a young man like myself, I do not know. For some young men traveling abroad, whose principles were perhaps hanging in the balance, a remark like this might have tipped the scales for the worse.

Delivered more letters. I found Mr. Gladstone had moved from his handsome house on Carlton House Terrace, where I saw him last year, to 73 Harley Street, Cavendish Square. Gladstone very much regretted the change. The Carlton Terrace house had been his home for forty years, in which most of his children had been born, and where he had most of his great triumphs in politics and literature. He felt he must take a smaller house now that some of his children were married, for reasons of economy, but he left the old one with a pang.

From four in the afternoon to about half-past eight in the evening, the cabmen prefer taking their chances on short affairs to being engaged by the hour at 2/6. As the rate is but sixpence per mile, it shows that they get a good deal to do. They tell me that they make most off short trips of about three quarters of a mile for one shilling each. While the rate is sixpence a mile, one shilling is the minimum fare.

Friday, June 9

CALLED on the Claytons, Parkers, and Mr. Smalley, the London correspondent of the New York "Tribune." Mr. Smalley said that he thought Governor Hayes, of Ohio, was the most probable candidate for Republican nomination this summer. (This turned out to be a true prophecy and shows how well informed Smalley was.) Had a pleasant talk on politics. I thanked him for what he had done for my father in the London press at the time of his nomination as Minister to England. Got a kind letter from Lord Coleridge inviting me to two or more breakfasts with him and suggesting taking me to the courts. In the evening I dined at Dr. Pollock's and went to a musicale at a friend's, where there were many professionals and amateurs. All the music was of a very high order. While the English generally are not a musical race and many of them do not know whether a band is in tune or not, and many, both men and women, with good voices lose the pitch, yet there are in London especially some of the most highly cultivated musical people that are to be found anywhere in the world, and it was my good luck to strike one of these very sets this evening.

Saturday, June 10

LETTERS from Professor Gurney, Lord Houghton, and Mrs. Arnold, all inviting me for various occasions. I went to a matinée concert and heard Beethoven's "Kreutzer Sonata" for violin and piano splendidly played. I got a note from Mr. Russell Sturgis later in the day asking me to spend the next Sunday at his country place, but had to decline, having accepted a dinner with Lord Coleridge for that day. This evening I dined with the Honorable Dudley Fortescue. I met there his wife,

Lady Camilla Fortescue, Mr. and Mrs. Loyd — spelled with one *l* — and a Mrs. Ford. I took the latter into dinner and sat next to her. I was very glad to meet Fortescue, whom my father thought one of the most refined and intelligent men in England. He has no title beyond that of "Honorable" and is the second son of Earl Fortescue. He has for many years been a member of Parliament and has held several important offices. He is modest and most attractive. He talked delightfully and on many interesting topics, but I kept no notes of the conversation. Lady Camilla is the daughter of the Earl of Portsmouth, and is also, like her husband, a good conversationalist, speaking with intelligence, choosing appropriate words, with a delightful enunciation, and showing an interest in every subject that came up.

Sunday, June 11

ST. JAMES'S CHURCH, Jermyn Street, in the morning; a beautiful Ibsen interior. At six-thirty in the evening I dined very informally with Lord and Lady Coleridge and their daughter. After the ladies had gone out, Lord Coleridge was good enough to talk to me alone for nearly an hour. It appears that it was he who attracted the attention of the editor of the "Guardian" to an article on the English Ministry in connection with my father and had him write some correction. The English newspapers have all taken the stand of greatly regretting my father's want of confirmation, but a few of them made some error regarding the action of the Senate Committee.

Lord Coleridge spoke of his father's death. I told him how glad I now was I had seen his father and how my father had particularly wished me to meet him as the representative of the perfect type of the gentlemen of the old school, as well as a distinguished judge. I told him how I was visiting the Duke of Argyll at the only time that he, Coleridge, could arrange to have me visit him and see his father, and how pleased I now am that I had shortened my visit and not stayed on as the Duchess had kindly asked me to do.

Lord Coleridge, in speaking of his American friends, said it had been his fortune never to have met a disagreeable one. He spoke particularly highly of Horace Binney, Jr., as being one of the pleasantest men he had ever seen of *any* country.

Speaking of the House of Lords, he said that if that body would oftener put out its whole powers, say once a week, as it had done twice during the year, it would be a very great weight in the country. The debate a few weeks ago he said was better than anything he had heard during the year in the Lower House. In the Lords no one is afraid to speak out and one hears real opinions. Motions in general were more thoroughly discussed than people supposed. Because there was less form and less time taken up than in the Lower House, it did not necessarily follow, by any means, that there was less thought in the same proportion. He said that the Chancellor was not respected and obeyed in the House of Lords as the Speaker was in the Commons and that he could not absolutely maintain order; he could only suggest. This want of power might be a source of trouble in exciting times, Coleridge said.

To show the entire trust in the Speaker of the House of Commons and how he is allowed to act arbitrarily at times, Coleridge told me two stories. In one case an admiral stood up several times the same evening and several times it was quite clear that he was the first man standing. The discussion was on a university bill. Not being able to catch the Speaker's eye, he complained of it afterwards to that august officer. He was answered pretty much as follows: "Of course I did catch your eye. I saw you rise several times first, but you must be aware that you do not know anything about the university bill. Had it been a naval bill I should have had you out several times." That was said in good nature and taken pleasantly. Another speaker in Lord Coleridge's time used to say that after ten o'clock P.M. he never got anybody's eye back of the front bench. What a row would such language from the President of the French National Assembly produce!

Once when a university bill of Coleridge's was brought before the House, Disraeli said some rather cutting things, to which Coleridge replied, although he knew at the time that the reply was somewhat out of order. "Dizzy" got up and objected. The Speaker hemmed and hawed somewhat, but decided he would not interrupt. No one objected any further. Afterwards the Speaker said to him alone, "You really were out of order, Coleridge, and I shall have to stop you another time, but I let it pass then." It was pretty well understood by all that it was giving a chance for a telling hit back and no one objected. All had perfect confidence that the Speaker would keep the reply well within bounds.

Lord Coleridge said that the Duke of Wellington used to be a duelist, and on one occasion had argued that sometimes a man's words were such that he should be made to retract them or be willing to stand by them with his life. This language was rather curiously brought up against him when he was advocating the suppression of dueling in the army. The late Sir Robert Peel had fought one or more duels in his lifetime.

While in Parliament, in the Lower House, Lord Coleridge told me he once wished to quote something from Goethe, and when he came to the point, he was afraid to pronounce the name, for he was not a good German scholar, so he said, "As says a celebrated German." He told this story against himself in very good humor, and how he made it a rule to mention the name wherever possible and not to make vague allusions in his public speeches.

While talking of Greek art I happened to mention Praxiteles as in the fifth or sixth century B.C. Coleridge corrected me, but he, being for the moment doubtful, I suggested that I might possibly be right. Before, however, we had looked it up in any book of reference or history, we began to compare historical facts, and I soon saw that he was right and that I for a moment had confused the date of Praxiteles with that of Phidias.

He told me that his father, when fresh from Oxford, once corrected a Chief Justice. His father turned out to be right and the Chief Justice afterwards said, "You happen to have been right in this case, but as a rule I should advise you not to dispute a Chief Justice." Lord Coleridge said, while alone with me, that he had been very doubtful about accepting the peerage, but that Gladstone urged it very strongly on the ground that it would be a benefit to the bar in general if its leaders should become titled. It would spur them up to their best efforts. He, Coleridge, also said that the Queen had asked him no less than three times to accept.

I found that Lord Coleridge had never read Quintilian, which gave me so much help and delight in college, but that he had begun to read him lately. This omission was the more strange, as Coleridge was not only a classical scholar, but intended to follow the profession of the bar and to take up politics, and the "Institutio Oratoria" was just in the line of his training, thought, and ambitions, and as an orator would have been helpful. He has a very bright mind that acts quickly and surely and it does one good to be with him, and then, too, he is so utterly frank and has such a beaming smile and friendly manner! I only wish I could remember one half of the good things he said on this and other occasions.

Monday, June 12

BREAKFASTED with Sir Frederick Pollock, whom I met last spring. He is the son of the late celebrated Chief Baron Pollock who tried so hard, by his decisions and by refusing to allow an appeal, to let the Laird rams built for the Southern Confederacy go from the port of Liverpool in violation of England's neutrality. This branch of the family has little to do with the other branch whom I knew through Lord Tenterden. Sir Frederick and Dr. Julius are only half brothers.

Sir Frederick spoke of the general feeling of disappointment throughout England at not having my father as Minister to Great Britain from the United States. Lady Pollock, an authoress and a woman of large experience and great taste in literature and the French stage, thinks Irving has the *vrai feu sacré*. In a certain sense I agree with her and in a certain sense not. Irving has done much to elevate the stage, has his plays well prepared and all his fellow-actors well trained, but there is something artificial and stilted in his manner that always reminds one that he is acting, and in that he so differs from the great French actors. Lunched with Lord Houghton — pronounced Howton. There I met Baroness Burdett-Coutts, Dean Stanley of Westminster

Abbey, Professor and Mrs. Gurney, the two daughters and the son of Lord Houghton. I took the younger daughter down. Both daughters are pretty, and pale. At the first sitting at the table, people had arranged themselves badly, and in the subsequent changes Lord Houghton told his younger daughter to go over and sit next to me. She, being a little bashful, hesitated somewhat. I immediately got up, went over, moved out her chair, and escorted her to the place next me, and that broke the ice. Lord Houghton was well known as an author of both prose and poetry, by the name of Richard Monckton Milnes before he was made a peer.

Baroness Burdett-Coutts must be about forty years of age. The date of her birth is carefully omitted from the "Peerage," but as in 1837 she inherited a large amount of property and changed her name by adding Coutts, she was at least alive then. She is immensely wealthy, fabulously so, has founded and endowed numerous institutions for religious, benevolent, and philanthropic purposes, built model lodging-houses in Bethnal Green, and the magnificent Columbia market, the latter costing about $1,000,000. She has brilliant eyes, bright color, wore a broad-brimmed Gainsboro hat, and was very well dressed. She was bright in conversation, though more serious than witty, and was pretty much the centre of attraction at the lunch. I talked with her a good deal on sociological and philanthropic subjects.

Dean Stanley was extremely kind to me. He offered to show me over Westminster Abbey in person and gave me his card, which I was to send in, and he mentioned some hours when he would be at leisure. I accepted the card, but told him I thought it was too great an imposition on his time to show me about and thought the card would help me to see many portions of the abbey usually closed to strangers. I never availed myself of his kind offer to conduct me in person. Perhaps it was a mistake, because they say he enjoys showing the abbey, and as for myself, it would have been a great delight to spend an hour or so with a man of such high character, charming conversation, deep religious interest, and profound knowledge of the history of the abbey.

Lord Houghton was in very good spirits and bright, keen, witty, and cheerful. Usually the English lunches break up immediately after the meal is over, as do the breakfasts, because the London days are so full that it is the etiquette to leave at once after these meals are over, but in this case the conversation was so interesting that we lingered on at table for an hour or more after the coffee. The Baroness was talking to the Dean and Lord Houghton about some further plans of hers for some special philanthropic work, I do not remember just what.

Dean Stanley told us some Jews were now looking over several old Hebrew manuscripts at the abbey, among which were old accounts of money lent the Government. I walked with the Dean from Houghton's till our ways parted. Lord Houghton asked me to breakfast with him on Saturday, the 17th, but I already had another engagement for that hour and only wished I could be in two places at once, he is so delightful. On leaving the house Dean Stanley could not find his hat. I remembered seeing it upstairs, so I started up to get it for him, but he followed me three quarters of the way.

Called on Lord Tenterden, Mr. Russell Sturgis, the Honorable Dudley Fortescue, and Mrs. Pollock, and

DEAN STANLEY

left a card at the Duke of Argyll's, though I knew he was out of town for the present. I dined at St. James's Hall.

On account of the lunch at Lord Houghton's I had to decline a second pleasant invitation for a day's outing with Mr. Russell Sturgis at his beautiful place on the Thames River. I forgot to say, too, that I had to decline an invitation to spend Sunday the 11th at the Edwin Arnolds' on account of my dinner with Coleridge. The Sunday evening dinner hour at the Arnolds' I saw was fixed in the note very early, namely, at half-past five.

Tuesday, June 13

BREAKFASTED with Lord Coleridge; his son and heir Bernard being present. I was asked for quarter to nine. I arrived at five minutes of, and found them just finishing morning prayers. Lord Coleridge had expected to have for to-day the summing-up of the Albert Grant case, but just as he was about to leave his house his clerk said that this case was put off till Wednesday. Lord Coleridge was pretty certain that he had set it for to-day. The clerk hesitated and stammered, not liking to contradict "his lordship," but said that he had remembered it was Wednesday and that he feared it was so announced in the "Times." A "Times" was brought and the clerk proved to be right, though there may have been an error in fixing that date; but it settled the matter, however, for the day's proceedings.

During breakfast Lord Coleridge told several funny stories. One was of a young dandy army officer. He was asked at the opera if he did not think the prima donna, who had just been singing divinely, had done well, and he replied, "Verwy — ah — haw — easy is the word." Lord Coleridge imitated the fop with supreme contempt and with an excellent drawl, followed with hearty laughter from us all. We drove down in a four-wheeler. On the way the conversation was largely on family horses. Lord Coleridge opened the court, looking very odd in his ugly pink-and-blue caped gown. His long, curling white wig was becoming to him. There were six cases on the short list; that is, subject to immediate trial. Four were put off for various reasons, one of them being on account of the absence of the oath of physicians as to the insanity of a person; a letter the judge held not being sufficient. The barrister on the defense for the sixth case was in another court, so the judge returned to the fifth. It was a complicated case on many business transactions, with numerous letters involved, but Coleridge had tried it once at *nisi prius* and it had come up on appeal. The barrister was not very familiar with his brief. The attorney sat below and kept handing papers, written slips, and memoranda, and whispering to his barrister. But Lord Coleridge cleared the ground rapidly, remembering many of the incidents from the former trial, put the barrister at ease by refreshing his mind, and soon the case went on smoothly. Coleridge asked many questions of the witnesses, showing that he understood the case better than the barrister, and his questions very much aided in getting at the merits of the case in hand. This English practice of allowing the judge to ask questions, and also giving him power to shut out irrelevant testimony without request of counsel, helps very much to shorten the trial of jury cases; but in America, especially since the Know-Nothing movement in the fifties, we have been very averse to giving our judges the old Anglo-Saxon authority, and we thereby very much lengthen trials and give up one of the best aids to securing justice. I left the court at noontime. This was in the Court of Common Pleas, of which Coleridge is Chief Justice with a salary of $35,000 a year. Lord Coleridge told me that when he was very busy, as Attorney-General trying cases in the daytime and sitting in Parliament in the evening, he made it a rule to ride horseback every morning before breakfast, but that now that his work was easier he had given up that practice.

Wednesday, June 14
VISITED London Tower in the afternoon. Dined in the evening with Mr. Shean, Upper Phillimore Gardens, Kensington. I was ashamed to find that I was late by some fifteen minutes. The hour was set at seven-thirty. Mr. Shean is a celebrated barrister and a friend of Westlake, at whose house I met Shean and his wife. I had to decline another invitation for dinner for this same evening at the Russell Gurneys'. The Sheans were extremely kind, and I passed a delightful evening, discussing many topics of public interest in England and America. Mr. Francis Allston Channing, a cousin of mine, was expected, but did not turn up. He had very high honors in college and is a promising young member of Parliament (and was made at first a baronet and afterwards, in 1912, Lord Channing of Wellingborough).

The ladies in England, as I said before, take far more interest in politics than the ladies in America. This is perhaps more natural because it is the educated classes that rule, and their wives and daughters become naturally conversant with all that is going on; but even in the families of those Americans who are educated and also in politics, the ladies do not seem to take the same interest, at least in the large questions. This may be because there are so few of them to stimulate one another and they often do not follow their husbands to Washington, and when at Washington so much time is taken up with the concerns of petty squabbles for patronage. (Of course this is very much changed in America especially in recent years.)

Thursday, June 15

BREAKFASTED again with Lord Coleridge at his usual hour of eight-forty-five. All the servants, some ten or more in number, were present at the morning prayers. It does one good to see a man who has had more than the usual share of worldly honors and success still keeping up the religious duties and finding time for these daily family morning prayers during all the claims of a London season and his duties as a judge. Lord Coleridge has to be at the courts before ten-thirty, and the courts are half an hour's drive from his house, number 1 Sussex Square. These morning services were impressive, and as Lord Coleridge read a passage that seemed to strike him, he marked it in the margin with his pencil, just as he had done at Honiton. The reading was slow, clear, well but not over-emphasized, and reverential. The servants went out, and then we had the usual breakfast without their aid, each person passing what his or her neighbor needed and the gentlemen going to the sideboard to carve and serve the meats, etc. Lady Coleridge poured out the tea and coffee.

During breakfast Lady Portland called to see Lord Coleridge on the vivisection bill on which Lord Coleridge seemed to be somewhat non-committal. After breakfast he read me some passages from Erskine on the treatment of animals. Coleridge has deep sympathy for the animals and is in favor of preventing cruelty to them, but felt that vivisection was too valuable an aid to saving human life, health, and happiness to be given up, provided proper precautions were taken to avoid unnecessary suffering. Lord Erskine was, said Coleridge, the greatest bar orator England has ever had.

Bernard, the eldest son of Lord Coleridge, is rather quiet, but very sensible and his remarks are fitting and forceful. He is not tall like his father, who is over six feet, but is about five feet nine inches, I should judge.

I drove down to Westminster with Lord Coleridge in the four-wheeler that comes for him every morning. On the way down he spoke of the visits of Victor Emmanuel, King of Italy, to Buckingham Palace, saying that the King attended his Catholic services with the utmost regularity and conscientious scrupulosity, but that in his private morals he was so bad that he had to be spoken to and reminded that Queen Victoria and Prince Albert did not allow such actions as his in Buckingham Palace.

Lord Coleridge took me by the judges' entrance to the high court. The case under consideration was that of the *Strathclyde*, and the question was whether there was criminal jurisdiction for the British courts over a foreigner on a foreign ship which was passing within the three-mile limit of the English coast, but not within any harbor when the act complained of took place. There were fourteen judges. Cockburn, Chief Justice of the Queen's Bench, presided, with Lord Coleridge at his right. When we first came into the court-room thirteen of these judges were on an upper bench or platform with large desks in front, and one, Sir Robert Phillimore, had been put down at a lower bench on a level with the clerk of the court, but that position he did not like, and so with considerable moving he had a separate seat prepared for him on the upper row in a much more dignified position and more suitable to his attainments and rank.

I sat in the jury box close to Sir Robert, and he spoke to me several times during the day, pointing out some of the eminent counsel and in the intervals asking me what I was doing. I had nothing but a series of English hospitalities and kindnesses to report.

Judah P. Benjamin, who had been Secretary of War in the Southern Confederacy under Jefferson Davis, was chief counsel for the defense. The *Strathclyde* was a German ship and it was a German captain who was under criminal indictment. Benjamin, of course, was against the jurisdiction so as to get his client freed from trial in an English court. He opened the argument as it was on an appeal on a point of law, and during his argument he quoted from Dana's "Wheaton." Lord Cockburn said he had only Lawrence's edition and the Solicitor-General, who was arguing on the other side, said he had been unable to own Dana's, though he had tried to get it, as it was out of print.

Benjamin quoted from Bluntschli and Lord Cockburn stopped him and asked who that was. It was strange that Cockburn did not know a writer on international law of that celebrity, whom I myself knew of, though I had never made a special study of that branch of the law. Benjamin began to explain, and in order to give him his proper status, said that Bluntschli was often quoted, as His Honor would remember, at Geneva; that is, during the great *Alabama* arbitration case. His Honor then said that he had never heard him quoted before as an authority, but that it might have been done at Geneva, and ended with these words: "There were many things said there not worth attention." This remark was followed by great applause from the bar. The court was crowded with barristers. This was rather a peculiar remark from one who was the arbitrator on behalf of Great Britain in the *Alabama* case sitting with the United States and neutral arbitrators, and as one of them it was his duty, of course, to hear all that could be said on both sides, and especially was it ungracious, as the decision was unanimous against Great Britain, with the exception of Lord Cockburn, who was in a minority of one. Cockburn had shown loss of temper at the decision and refused to sign some papers or to do some other act — I forget just what it was — that would normally be required, just out of ill-will.

Such language very much confirmed Lord Coleridge's stories about Cockburn which he had told me when I visited him at Honiton last September and which he repeated in outline again to-day.

Cockburn kept constantly interrupting Benjamin and asking questions. He started with a strong prejudice in favor of jurisdiction and hardly allowed Benjamin to finish his sentences, but Benjamin was wonderfully patient and respectful and kept driving his point home, which in the main was that there was no precedent whatever for this jurisdiction; that if it had existed it must have been brought into play on one or more occasions; and that the absence of any such precedent was pretty strong evidence that the jurisdiction never existed. He also argued that the three-mile limit was established for international purposes of other sorts, such as fishing, and to stop naval fights among belligerents too dangerously near the shore.

Lunched at the Parliament bar with young Drummond. (I wonder if this was perchance Henry Drummond, the author in 1883 of "Natural Law in the

Spiritual World." He was of the right age and the only one of that name and age in England I can find any trace of. The Drummond I met was a promising young man, and we found we had some interests in common, just such as he cared for and wrote about.) Returned to court and stayed listening to the argument till the adjournment, which was at four o'clock. In the evening dined at Mrs. Rowcliffe's and there met my dear Lord Tenterden, Mrs. E. S. Rowcliffe, Dr. and Mrs. Pollock, and Mr. Charles Lanyon, son of Sir Charles Lanyon. He had been in America and was in Boston at the time of the great fire of 1872. A quotation was made from my father's notes on "Wheaton" in the course of the evening. Lanyon thought the new part of Boston in the Back Bay one of the finest things of its kind in the world unless he excepted some of the new parts of London. He thought Fifth Avenue, too, was "fine for its houses," but they were more monotonous with so many more built alike than in the Back Bay of Boston where more individuality of architecture was shown.

After dinner we all went to a dancing party at Judge Lushington's. The dancing seemed to me poor, for they never reversed. They started off dancing round and round very fast till they got dizzy. There were the two young Coleridges, sons of the Chief Justice. I danced with a young lady, some relative of my friends, and spoke of becoming dizzy from lack of reversing, to which latter I was accustomed. I had come to the dance unexpectedly, it was a sort of afterthought, and so had no kid gloves — neither had Lanyon — while most of the men wore them. In reply to my remark on the absence of reversing, my partner said, "You must have become dizzy because you did not wear gloves."

On this I asked her if I should not take her to her mother. She is said to be very bright and to think herself a great wit, and often makes cutting and impolite remarks. Lanyon took me to a small club where men gather in the evening, not the Cosmopolitan, but a less celebrated one for younger men. He was very kind and offered to make me a member of the Reform Club. Found on getting back a note from Dean Stanley asking me to breakfast with him at Westminster Abbey day after to-morrow; also a card from the Reverend and Mrs. Hugh Reginald Haweis for afternoon tea, with music and a weekly "at home."

CHAPTER XIX
LAST OF LONDON REVISITED

Friday, June 16

I BREAKFASTED again with Lord Coleridge, who took me a second time to the High Court, where I stayed till twelve. Charles Lanyon was with me. I was introduced to Benjamin, with whom I had a few words; he was very cordial and spoke of my father; and also to Cowen, a leading barrister, reporter of decisions, etc. (and afterwards a judge); also to a Mr. Wilson who was in the same box with me. In the afternoon called on various people, among them Sir Robert Phillimore, who was at home and spoke about some books he was sending my father. Called also on Lord Houghton, who was out, Professor Gurney, who was out, Lady Pollock, who was at home, and Mrs. Russell Gurney, who was also at home and who asked me to dine with them on the 28th. I left cards, too, on the Sheans. Dined at St. James's Restaurant and in the evening was taken by the Pollocks to a public concert, where was good music of the very best type. On coming back to my lodgings, found a note from Lanyon asking me to breakfast with him at the Reform Club.

Saturday, June 17

THIS was the morning for my breakfast with Dean Stanley at the deanery, Westminster, and I was promptly on hand. His wife, Lady Augusta, had died only a few months before and there was a look of deep sadness in his dear gray eyes. He and his wife were made one when they married, lived together as one, but *le bon*

RT.-HON. SIR ROBERT PHILLIMORE

Dieu, as the French call him, had not willed that they should leave this world together, so he lingers behind. It was as interesting as it was a great honor to be breakfasting in his rooms at the abbey and a rare privilege to hear his sweet mind opening itself on the deep topics that absorbed him. Though myself rather inclined to be High Church, but not ritualistic, I felt inspired with his desire to conciliate the High and Low Church factions into a wide toleration and comprehension of different points of view. Why should Christians, and especially those of the same Church, wrangle over unessential differences when there should prevail the essentials of divine love, love and respect for fellow-men, and the supremacy of morality and conscience? His hope of a higher and more pervading Christianity, whenever the unimportant differences should be lost sight of and the great things kept in mind, on which he touched, was simply superb. His face, as he spoke earnestly, was as near the face of an angel as I ever saw, and yet it was a sort of human angel; the kind of heaven where such love and goodness would prevail was far more interesting than one of winged beings and harps of gold, and how infinitely grander than some of these spiritualistic manifestations of that life with all the talk about clothing, troubles, and usual incidents of our daily life.

He said he was sorry I had not accepted his invitation to have him take me about the abbey in person, as he had meant it sincerely and it would have given him pleasure, and perhaps he might have arranged to take one or two other people at the same time.

Almost immediately after this delightful breakfast, went by train to the south end of London to spend the day with Lord Tenterden on the borders of the Thames.

There was a yacht race and we went out sailing to see it. The race was between two boats, one an American owned by Sands, and the other English owned by Mr. Clark. The water was rough and the wind fierce at times, though at others there was only a fresh breeze. We saw the best of the race, though not the finish. One of the boats lost a topmast. At one time the balloon jibs of both boats were set and that on one yacht was carried away, but another was set quickly. Returned to shore and lunched with Lord Tenterden and we fished in the early afternoon with moderate luck. Tenterden is something of an Izaak Walton in his enthusiasm for the rod and line, though the broad waters of the lower Thames in this case were not quite Walton's setting. Returned in the end of the afternoon.

On getting back to my lodgings, found a note from the secretary of the great Reform Club announcing that I had been unanimously elected an honorary member for one month. Lanyon tells me this was outside of the rules and a special compliment. These people are really too kind and flattering in their attentions. I dined at the club. I also found a pleasant note from the Duchess of Argyll asking me to an evening reception on the 25th and expressing regret that they had missed me when I called. They got back to town only a few days ago.

Sunday, June 18
To church with Mrs. Dr. Pollock and Mrs. Rowcliffe and afterwards lunched with Mrs. Rowcliffe. Immediately after lunch started for Pembroke Lodge, Richmond, where I saw Lord and Lady Russell, Lady Amberley, Rollo, and some other young men. Lady Russell very kindly asked me to stay to dinner and she

expressed sorrow that my father had not been sent as Minister to England. There is the same beautiful view from the terrace over the valley of the Thames. "*That* has remained unchanged," she said to me as she laid her hand on her daughter's shoulder. Her eldest son, Lord Amberley, had died not long before, making a great change in her life. She asked me to visit them Saturday and Sunday next. I was not able to stay to dinner, so, following afternoon tea, went back to London, where I dined with the Edmund Diceys. There I met a brother of his who commands a fleet in China and was at home on a furlough. I had also to decline a dinner with Anthony Trollope as I had accepted the Diceys' dinner first. Dicey is a clever writer, a brilliant man, well informed on all the topics of the day, and a well-known lecturer. We had much interesting talk. It is a great education to meet such men.

We adjourned to the Cosmopolitan Club. There we saw and had chats with Lord Houghton, Lord Alexander Russell, the son of the sixth Duke of Bedford, Mr. Field from America, Sir Henry Thompson, the great surgeon, Anthony Trollope, and Sir William Vernon Harcourt. The latter I only bowed to and shook hands with, for he went off only too soon. Had a little talk with Trollope, who was sorry I could not come to dine with him and again spoke pleasantly, as he did last year, of many agreeable evenings with my father and mother on the Continent. He said my father was one of the most entertaining *raconteurs* he had ever met and spoke of his wit and wide information, all which made conversation where he was present so entertaining.

Monday, June 19

CALLED on Rawlins with my classmates Wigglesworth and Sanger, to whom he was very kind and helpful. In the evening dined at Fishmongers' Hall at the invitation of Mr. Russell Gurney, who presided. I sat opposite him and next to Mr. Cyrus Field. There were many speeches, toasts, and songs, and an enormously elaborate and expensive dinner, beginning with a course of turtle soup, the most delicious I ever tasted. As we went out they gave us each an enormous box of choice sweets, London's very best. The dinner lasted from five-thirty to ten-thirty. Friendly relations between America and England were brought out in some of the addresses, and as usual at these big dinners, a touch of English politics. From the dinner I went to the Princess Theatre, where I had been invited by Lord Tenterden with Mrs. Pollock and a few others in his party. Irving was acting in the "Bells" and "Stratagem." I was too late to see the "Bells" which was one of his favorite pieces, but the "Stratagem" I enjoyed very much. Irving, to make himself appear young, rises on the balls of his feet, but does this more than any youth in real life, so produces an air of affectation in walking. His phrasing was excellent, though his voice is too artificial, while the scenery and the staging showed skill, forethought, and artistic feeling. I passed my delicious box of candy round the party, and one of the ladies, understanding that it was a gift to her, took it away, rather to my inward disappointment.

Tuesday, June 20

WENT to the Claytons' for dinner at seven-thirty at Stafford Terrace, Kensington West. Among the guests was an Irish friend of Chief Justice Cockburn who had been at Geneva with him, but he said nothing of that famous international case. Much interesting conversation, some of it on American women, who received no little praise, which I was glad to hear for they are so often misjudged as a class on account of the few conspicuous *nouveaux riches*.

Wednesday, June 21
BREAKFASTED again with Lord Coleridge, who presented me with some of his printed speeches, among them his argument in the Saurin *vs.* Starr case — 1869 — a case of alleged petty persecution in a convent which excited great public interest, and his still greater argument in the Tichborne Claims suits. He had thoughtfully put his autograph in each. Prayers as usual. He spoke of the India questions. He said that there was very little interest in Parliament in them. That was one of the subjects on which the members seemed bribed, they had so many relatives in the India service or private interests there of various kinds. Of course Lord Coleridge did not mean direct bribery, but that sort of insidious self-interest that prevents a free discussion from the point of view of the good of the natives.

In the cab going to the court he spoke again of Cockburn at the *Alabama* trial at Geneva and of how he lost the influence that his unusual knowledge of languages and law should have given him. He told me the story, which I have related before, of Caleb Cushing; how Cushing, one of the counsel for the United States, a linguist perhaps quite as good as Cockburn himself, asked in what language — German, French, Italian, or English — the court would prefer to be addressed, and how Cockburn leaned forward and said, in almost angry tones, "In Choctaw, in Choctaw."

Coleridge spoke of Admiral Farragut and his intrepidity. There were numerous other topics, one relating to whitebait; how at first one always had to go to Greenwich until it suddenly occurred to some one that they could carry the whitebait to London as well as carry themselves to the old town down the river. He told me some story about briefless barristers which I forget, and something about old dogs and that we must not believe all that is told us about them, and then of trees, their planting, and development, and some story about Sir Roundell Palmer, now Lord Selborne.

To-day all the judges wore red gowns. Lord Cockburn, while listening, was working his jaw. He was not chewing anything, but just moving it back and forth. The Solicitor-General who was arguing spoke of the United States District Courts and the admiralty jurisdiction as being "Federal." Lord Cockburn interrupted and asked him what he meant by the District Court and the Federal courts of the United States. I believe there were only two judges out of the fourteen — Lord Coleridge and Sir Robert Phillimore — who seemed to know anything about the distinction between them and the State courts. Sir Robert leaned forward and gave a very clear and perfectly accurate account of this difference.

Here were some twelve of the most eminent judges of England who seemed to know nothing about the Federal courts and their powers, and I venture to say that not one of them would have hesitated to have given an opinion that the Southern States had a constitutional right to secede; and yet the establishment of Federal courts which have jurisdiction between States, may declare a State law unconstitutional and void, and which have a right to enforce their decrees through the

Executive, should have great weight in considering the right of secession. Apparently these judges were not aware of anything but State courts and probably were equally ignorant of other provisions of the Constitution, as that Congress may pass laws to guarantee republican form of government in the various States, that the Constitution is the highest law of the country, and that Congress has supreme authority where the Constitution has given it a right to act.

Left in the early afternoon and went to Mrs. Fowler's "at home" from four-thirty to six. Mrs. Fowler is a very interesting invalid, drawing about her many literary, musical, and theatrical people of the best sort. There was much brilliant and interesting conversation on books, authors, the stage, music, and politics. It was almost like a French salon without the delicacy and refinement of French wit.

Dined with Mr. Ferguson. There were present a recent graduate of Caius (pronounced Keyes) College, Oxford, and a captain belonging to the British service in India. Having these engagements I had to refuse an invitation to go for a pleasant coaching party to Oxford and back given me by Mr. Sands, the American yachtsman whom I had met.

Thursday, June 22

A VERY kind letter from Mr. Ferguson to bring my classmates Wigglesworth and Sanger to dine with him in the House of Commons. They, however, were away and I had already accepted an invitation to dine with Lanyon at the Reform Club. Lunched at the Reform Club, where the service is so wonderfully good and the cooking excellent and where one who has been chosen an honorary member is made to feel so much at home and not *de trop* as when I first went there as a mere visitor. Made various calls in the afternoon. After a pleasant dinner with Lanyon at the club, during which he offered to do many things for me, he took me to the Alhambra Theatre. The performance was of a very dull sort with a great deal of ballet and not much of any plot, and the music rather second-rate. In the intervals we talked over American politics, over the question of the responsibility of Ministers to the House of Commons, and whether it would be well to extend that system to the House of Representatives in Congress in the United States, to the extent at least that members of the President's Cabinet might sit in the House, speak and be interrogated; whether it would not make Congress a more responsible body and their debates more interesting and bring the Administration's view to bear more directly upon legislation, as well as to secure information through this direct questioning. On the other hand, there was the fear that Congress might get too much power over the Executive. Again, however, was the argument that the Executive would have a splendid opportunity to present its views to the public, such as it does not have in its formal reports to Congress which are read in that body only by title. (President Wilson has since revived the early custom of reading his most important messages to the Congress assembled, with great effect.)

Friday, June 23

DINNER at Mr. Smalley's. There were present Mr. Brownson, Dr. Priestley, and Mr. Henry Tuke Parker. Brownson is the son of the celebrated Roman Catholic philosopher of America, who died last spring (1875). The son is preparing to publish his father's writings and life. Smalley told us he got the prophecy of Hayes's nomination from Mr. Washburne, our Minister in Paris. This was very fair-minded of Smalley, who might have got great credit to himself for his astuteness in predicting the event.

After this dinner I attended a large ball at Welles's rooms at the invitation of Mrs. Pollock. Welles's is one of the most fashionable halls for large London parties. The dancing was confined to the centre of the room, which was roped off with handsome crimson cord stretched on substantial stands. The mothers and matrons sit about the outer edge of the hall and every young lady is attached to one of these; so that after a turn at dancing, perhaps followed by a short promenade, one always takes the young lady back to her matron. This has one enormous advantage over our American system of no individual matrons at all; none but two or three to preside in general. Here a man is never obliged to sit out a long time with the same young lady, as frequently happens in American society. As a consequence, in England the men are much more ready to dance with young ladies who are not especially popular, and it does not exaggerate the attention to the favorites and inattention to the "wall-flowers," which our system inevitably does.

I found a very charming partner in a Miss Heatly, who danced much better than most English girls. I went home at three-thirty, when the ball had begun to thin out. The light was so bright in the streets that one could read a newspaper easily. I was also invited to a Caledonian costume ball at a later date, but had to give that up on account of other previous engagements.

Saturday, June 24

AT Pembroke Lodge in the afternoon for tea. Warm, mild, rare day in June. At dinner were two Miss Ogilvys, daughters, I believe, of the seventh Earl of Airlie, and if so, then Lady Henrietta and Lady Maud, and their aunt Lady Maria Ogilvy; the Honorable George William Russell, Lady Agatha, and Professor Richard Owen, professor in the Royal College of Surgeons and now the Superintendent of the Natural History Department of the British Museum, living near by in Richmond. (Later he was knighted for his great work in developing the Natural History Department.) Rollo Russell was away. Professor Owen said Newton was not an accident any more than Plato or Aristotle. We discussed Descartes and a good deal of philosophy in general.

I had received an invitation from the Prime Minister, Disraeli, to meet His Royal Highness the Prince of Wales at ten-thirty this evening. I had arranged with a cabman to take me to a train at Richmond that would get me to London for this reception, but the wretch never turned up and when the time for his appearance had passed, it was too late to catch that or any other train that would get me from Richmond to London in time. So I missed this interesting reception by a mere accident. I ought to have offered the coachman double fare to insure his coming. It was good Lord Tenterden who had secured this invitation for me, telling me that it was readily granted by Disraeli, who knew of my father and had heard of my being in England.

Sunday, June 25

SPENT the night at Pembroke Lodge and went with the family to church at eleven-fifteen, walking through the park and seeing the deer, and again we had the old-fashioned beadle in his party-colored gown. We had an informal lunch, but without Lord Russell, who had not come downstairs. After lunch we walked about the grounds and Lady Russell repeated some lines by Bryant which had been a great comfort to her son, Viscount Amberley, in his last illness. She wanted me to let Bryant know of this and promised to write the lines out. I told her I knew Bryant personally and he was a great friend of my grandfather, who gave such high praise in his literary criticism of Bryant's "Thanatopsis" that there has always been a pleasant feeling between the families and a long correspondence.

Walking up the steep path I gave my arm to Lady Russell, who is just a little past sixty, and though seemingly very well, is troubled in going uphill. The Right Honorable Sir Stafford Northcote and his daughter, Lord Romilly and his daughter, and Lord Plunket came in the afternoon. A little lawn tennis was played on the old bowling green, so lovely and velvety and shut in by high, flowering shrubs. Northcote, the eighth baronet, born in 1818, had high honors at Oxford, has received no end of big appointments and responsibilities, and is now Chancellor of the Exchequer and in Disraeli's Cabinet. He was on the Joint High Commission at Washington that drew up the treaty referring the *Alabama* difficulties to arbitration. He is said to have shown great conciliatory powers. He is a thorough gentleman, but seems rather mild in his manners and opinions for a hard fighter in the House of Commons. (He became a few weeks later the leader of the House of Commons when Disraeli was elevated to the House of Lords. In 1885 Northcote was made Earl of Iddesleigh.)

Lord Romilly lately succeeded his father, the celebrated Baron Romilly, Solicitor-General, Attorney-General, Master of the Rolls, and long a leading member of the House of Commons.

Had afternoon tea at which Lady Edith Quin, daughter of the third Earl of Dunraven, turned up. She was somewhat my senior and had that charm for a young man that a slightly older woman so often has. There were more men present than ladies, a rather unusual state of affairs for an afternoon tea in the suburbs.

Lady Russell spoke about natural manners — that is, manners prompted by a good heart that come naturally to one who has been used to meeting cultivated people. She admitted that a good heart alone would not always bring good manners, for want of experience, but she had a dislike to the outward veneer without a good heart behind it, as the imitation was sure to show sooner or later and would always lack spontaneity and freedom. Lord Russell, who appeared at the afternoon tea, discoursed on Sir Walter Scott and his personal reminiscences of him and how Scott had ruined the last part of his life by spending so much money on Abbotsford and getting in heart-breaking debt.

Monday, June 26
THE day of the Duke of Argyll's reception. Opened my eyes on another beautiful June day at Pembroke Lodge. Soon after breakfast Lady Russell went off and I returned to London. She forgot to write out the lines of Bryant. (But later she sent them to me. I forwarded them to Bryant with a note and he sent back a pleasant letter, which I mailed to the Countess.) Went with Mr. and Mrs. Ernest Longfellow and their cousin Miss Mary Longfellow, of Portland, Maine, to the Oxford and Cambridge cricket match at Lords. I had played

cricket at St. Paul's School, where I was captain of both the school and my club eleven, so I watched the play with a critical interest and was delighted to be at Lords, the scene of so many wonderful matches. There were many drags and handsome carriages, fashionable dresses, and elaborate luncheons, with much beauty among the women and fine figures and faces among the men. This is one of the great social events of the London season. Parts of the match were quite brilliant, with some long hitting, but there were periods of blocking and nothing going on. There were long intervals for lunch and afternoon tea.

Dined at the Reform Club and after dinner went to Argyll Lodge, where I met the Duke and Duchess, Gladstone, and others. Gladstone talked on Greece and asked me many questions. He wanted to know about the inhabitants, whether they were being well educated, becoming industrious, etc., and asked me about the bookshops in particular. I told him that I went into all the bookshops there were in Athens and the books seemed mostly intended for travelers — books in German, English, and French. There were, of course, Greek newspapers, but I did not see any Greeks in the bookshops nor did they seem to be intended for Greeks, though, of course, some of the Greeks dress in European costume and read modern languages, so that some few natives might have visited these bookshops without my knowing it. I told him the short, deep-plaited white skirt of the men, with short jacket, and white leggings, was still much worn in Athens, but the European, in the sense of French and English, costumes were coming rapidly into use.

I could not tell him about the modern methods of education or how far the Government was establishing free schools, except that I saw no large public school buildings such as we have in the United States, and, therefore, I gathered that they could not have adopted any extensive system of state or municipal education, though I knew there was some education at public expense I had heard of, but that was of the lower primary grades. I told him I had heard that there was very little, if any, artistic talent among the school children at Athens. I said, too, that the inhabitants were not industrious, were great talkers, fumbling strings of beads, not as a religious ceremony, but as a help to conversation; that they were inclined to be idle, and the peasants, even in the neighborhood of Athens, used very old-fashioned methods of agriculture. On the whole, my observation of modern conditions had been only too superficial and I felt like a college student who was called up unprepared and was trying to make the most of what little knowledge he had to cover his deficiencies.

Gladstone spoke of Bonamy Price and of his ability and earnestness. Lord and Lady Selborne were there and spoke very kindly to me. There were also Lord Walter Campbell and his wife, the Marquis of Lorne, and several of the daughters of the Duke, but Princess Louise was absent. I met there a Lady Palmer who was particularly agreeable. I think she must have been the wife of Sir Archdale Palmer, Bart., and if so, she is a daughter of Earl Ferrers. It was one of those very pleasant receptions where natural good manners, such as Lady Russell spoke of, prevailed, and I quite forgot that I was with such distinguished people in the ease and naturalness of all the conversation, excepting perhaps when I was being cross-questioned by Gladstone.

RT.-HON. WILLIAM E. GLADSTONE

Tuesday, June 27

BREAKFASTED at the Oxford and Cambridge Club with Mountague Bernard, the celebrated English international lawyer, one of the High Joint Commissioners to the United States and signer of the Treaty of Washington; also assistant counsel for the English in the *Alabama* arbitration at Geneva and till recently a professor of international law at Oxford. I was very glad to meet him, especially as my father thought so highly of him. We had no profound conversation; my fault, I suppose, as I should have drawn him out, but it takes some little cleverness and experience to draw a man out on his specialty without its being too patent an effort. I could not have asked him to give a lecture on international law.

(I did not then know that he had written a letter on the Trent Affair after the news of the capture of Mason and Slidell had become known in London. Had I been aware of this letter I might have asked him the grounds for his opinion, which was that, while the taking was in accord with old English law, England had abandoned those principles long ago. She had, however, as a matter of fact, officially refused to abandon her old claims only two or three years before the capture of these gentlemen.)

He was very kind in offering to aid me in various ways and talked pleasantly of his regret at my father's not being appointed Minister to Great Britain and of the value of his notes to Wheaton's "International Law." From so great an authority this was a high compliment, indeed. (A recent high compliment has been paid these notes in that the Carnegie Endowment, in getting up a new edition of Wheaton's "International Law," is to use Dana's notes as the foundation and starting-point for the new work, which is to deal with events since Dana's notes were written.)

Drove to Windsor on a coach and four from London with the Longfellows, back to Twickenham by rail, and then we rowed in a small boat on the Thames downstream to Richmond; a remarkably pleasant excursion. A waterman rowed the boat back, for a shilling or two. From Richmond returned by train to London. I had declined a dinner with Lord Coleridge this evening for fear of being late in getting back, having already made arrangements for this trip. Lord Coleridge, in a letter on my arrival in London, explained that he was in mourning for his father and therefore could not entertain me as he would have liked to do, but with the numerous breakfasts and his second invitation to dinner he could hardly have done more excepting to allow me to meet a greater number of distinguished people among his friends at a larger dinner. In the evening went to hear Albani in "Faust." The audience was cold and some people were going out during the prayer scene and destroying the artistic effect.

Wednesday, June 28

BREAKFASTED with the Longfellows. Called on Edward Dicey, who was at home; on the Argylls, who were out; Lord Coleridge, out; Sir John Kennaway, out; Mrs. Rowcliffe, out; and Mrs. Pollock, who was at home. Dicey was unfailingly interesting. The call was short.

Dined at the Russell Gurneys' and took in Mrs. Gurney and sat at her right. I had to decline a musicale at the Reverend H. R. Haweis's for this same evening. The dinner was a large one, some twenty or more people being present, many of them quite distinguished. As the dinner went on I heard some one farther down on the opposite side of the table talking very loud and monopolizing much of the conversation. The tone of voice instantly recalled to my mind an imitative story that my father told of Professor Bonamy Price at the Union Club in Boston. The dinner had been given for Price. My father was presiding. Price sat at his right and just beyond him, President Eliot. Professor Price shouted out that he did not believe in a constitution which never could be amended and did not see how the people of the United States could endure it. Then my father and President Eliot each tried to explain to him that it was possible to amend the Constitution, but to their first few suggestions he repeated his words, "Of course your constitution cannot be amended," in a raucous voice. Then when it began to dawn on him what they were saying, he replied, "What! What! Do you mean to say that you can amend your Constitution? Why, any constitution that can be amended is no constitution at all. It is not different from a law if it can be amended." Then my father and President Eliot took him gently in hand and began to explain that while it could be amended, it took much more time, formality, and consideration than an amendment to a law, and eventually it had to be adopted by three quarters of the States to be valid.

My father's imitation of the voice; of the persistent, loud assertion, and the wild defense, coming as it did in a flash, made me exclaim to myself, "I believe that is Bonamy Price!" though I had not the slightest idea that he was going to be at this dinner, and I asked Mrs. Gurney if it were he and she said it was.

At the end of the dinner, when it was time for the ladies to retire, Mrs. Gurney made several attempts to rise, but Price was talking so loud and persistently that she had to wait long for an opportunity without interrupting, when suddenly Price turned to her for confirmation of something he had just been stating. She then answered him quite slowly and rose at the end of her remark which just gave her the chance. It seemed so strange that Professor Price, who is a Professor of Political Economy at Oxford, should not have known that the Constitution of the United States was amendable and have had some faint impression as to how an amendment could be brought about. He, however, is a dear man when you come to know him better, as I found from a little talk. It is largely a matter of habit with him, a sort of thinking aloud — very much aloud. After the ladies had gone, the conversation turned on the subject of the row at Constantinople — a German by the name of Mr. Weiser, a boy's tutor, a protest to the German Government, a girl at the Deaconess's School, a scene in Smyrna, a boy recognizing the tutor in a mosque, etc.

After dinner I went by invitation of Baroness Burdett-Coutts to a reading at her house by Henry Irving. He read "Macbeth." In some respects his reading seemed more perfect than his acting on account of his dropping some of his stage mannerisms which are not always suitable to the part and so often spoil the illusion which good acting ought to produce. A large and fashionable gathering in a great house; recognized many friends. The Baroness appeared at her best and gave me a very cordial greeting.

Thursday, June 29

LUNCHED with young Gurney, nephew of Russell Gurney, at the Devonshire Club. He was on the committee of investigation of spiritualistic phenomena. He told me that almost every single case that they had investigated could easily be explained as tricks, for Anderson, the celebrated prestidigitator, whose widow has been giving them help, when living could do the same things with one single exception, and that exceptional case after all seemed to be only a trick just one step more difficult than the others. This latter was this. A woman was sewed up in a bag which was sealed with sealing wax and stamped by the private seals of some of the audience. She was then put behind a curtain in a hotel where there could be no trapdoors or other such arrangements, and the committee remained all the while in the same room. She then appeared outside of the bag, with the seals unbroken when the curtain was removed. Henry Irving, the actor, came into the club during lunch, but we did not talk with him, receiving only a bow.

I went down to the city with Mr. Gurney to see some of the great London banking and financial offices. Called on the Spencers, who were out, and Lady Coleridge, who was at home.

I had to decline an invitation for this evening with Sir Robert and Lady Phillimore for dinner, having previously accepted an invitation to dine with Sir Henry Thompson, F.R.C.S., the celebrated surgeon and Professor of Clinical Surgery in University College Hospital. He is about fifty-six years of age and has a charming, cordial manner. He is generally admitted to be the leading surgeon in Great Britain, yet he is not narrowly confined in his resources to his profession, but is a collector of rare china, an astronomer, an artist in painting and etching, some of his works being hung in the Royal Academy and at the Paris Salon, and in his own profession has made discoveries and dared new kinds of operation. He is also much interested in dinners as a fine art, in both the selection of food and company. He told me that the number should not be over Horace's rule of nine, the number of the Muses, and he usually had eight, for with more than eight he thought general conversation was impossible and it is general conversation that lightens up a dinner. Eight requires a broad table with two at each end to have the host and hostess opposite. He had eight courses also. He is the author of several works on his subject and on some outside matters. He said he was glad to see me, first on my account and second on my father's, a very flattering way of putting it. (He was later made a baronet for his distinguished services.)

There I met Sir Robert Collier, the "Right Honorable," formerly Solicitor-General and Attorney-General, and now a judge of the Court of Common Pleas, member of the Privy Council, and author of various books on law. He told me that he thought Dana's notes on "Wheaton" the best source of international law and spoke of the Winslow case, saying that he believed England was wrong in her attitude. This is the case of a man who had committed forgery in the United States and had fled to Great Britain. Earl Derby, now Foreign Secretary, refused to give him up unless the American Government would give an undertaking that he and other fugitives would not be tried for any offense other than the one for which their extradition was asked. The United States declined to make any stipulations and assurances not provided for in the treaty which now governs the situation. (Later in the same year the British receded from this position and surrendered the fugitives, the American Administration indicating that they were not disposed to try extradited offenders for any crime other than that which had caused their surrender.) Sir Robert Collier is fond of painting and we talked of sketching, how to produce atmosphere, and the effect of distance. He went to India with the Prince of Wales on his recent trip. We talked on the iron trade question. He said that the emigrants were "not starved out on the White Star Line," as stated in some of the newspapers.

On the way home I called at Sir Robert Phillimore's to meet the guests after his dinner, which I had been unable to attend. Canon Liddon and Lady Phillimore were there and very kind. They were quite jolly, threatening to keep me as a hostage until my father was brought over as Minister to England.

Friday, June 30

BREAKFASTED with Sir John and Lady Kennaway at nine-thirty and a number of guests, about ten in all. It was a very heavy breakfast, as is usually the case in England, where but few have adopted the French menu for this meal. They had a variety of meats and eggs, beside coffee, toast, rolls, and marmalade, the guests for the most part waiting on each other. All left promptly, right after breakfast, according to the usual custom. It is this custom that enables breakfasts and lunches to be given without breaking up a large part of the day.

I sat next to Lady Kennaway and she divulged several plans which she and her husband were proposing for me to join in with them. However, I was not able to accept on account of leaving so soon for the Continent. I have been receiving many very kind letters so warm-hearted that I feel I have made real friends with many of these good people and I have come to have a strong affection for them. Earl Spencer has just written me that he has been out of town on business most of the time since my last return to London, with an invitation to luncheon which I cannot accept on account of having made arrangements to go to Henley, and the letter ends up with saying, "Lady Spencer and I will be truly unhappy to have altogether missed you."

Among other interesting men I met was Mr. James Bryce, professor of civil law at Oxford and author of "The Holy Roman Empire." (Later he wrote "The American Commonwealth," was ambassador to the United States, and is now Lord Bryce, a man of great distinction and high honors, who is still doing much useful work at the age of eighty-two and whose mind is as keen and memory as sure as it was years ago. When ambassador at Washington, he and his wife invited Mrs. Dana and myself on several occasions to lunch, dinner, or afternoon tea.) Another distinguished person was Mr. Lyon Playfair, a well-known scientist, a member of Parliament and recently Postmaster-General in Gladstone's cabinet. (He was made K.C.B. in 1883 and raised to the peerage in 1892 under the title of Lord Playfair of St. Andrew's. He died in 1898.)

Many have called at my small lodgings, as Sir John Kennaway, Sir William Vernon Harcourt, the great Gladstone, Sir Henry Thompson, and several others. Kennaway was afraid I was not comfortable and thought I ought to have larger rooms and a separate parlor, but I told him, while I might afford it, I was so much out of my rooms and had the privilege of so many clubs that I hardly needed this extra room and did not like to put the unnecessary expense on my father who had a large family, and that I was very happy as I was, with all my kind friends and overflowing English hospitality, and he said he respected my attitude. I have one good-sized room with writing-table, book-shelves, comfortable chairs, etc.

After the Kennaway breakfast went to Henley to see the boat-races with the Longfellow party. It was a most lively scene with the Chiltern Hills for a background. The surface of the river was almost invisible from the number of boats and punts of various kinds which were pushed to the banks when the various races came off, leaving just room for the racing crews, and as soon as one heat or race was over, the surface seemed to be covered again.

It is a short course of one and five sixteenths miles, rowed upstream, equal to nearly two miles on still water. I saw there Goldie, the celebrated Cambridge stroke, and also Tinné, the captain and largest man of the four-oar that defeated the Harvard four in 1869. Though an Oxford man he was wearing the Cambridge University light blue boating coat, probably one he had borrowed from a friend. It was a bright, sunny day and the people were dressed in gay colors. The races occupied a long time, as there were several and most of them rowed in heats. We only saw the crews distinctly toward the end of each race; the course was just short enough to make the contest pretty much of a spurt all the way and the men seemed to be badly used up in all the races that were close. This tends to prove what I have always contended, that a short race of two miles or so, in which the crews can spurt nearly all the way, is more exhausting and more likely to be injurious to the men than a four-mile one where the crews must settle down to long, steady work, where skill and perfection of rhythm rowed at a slower stroke count for more than mere spurting.

On the whole the rowing was excellent. People took their luncheons on the banks or in the boats. I got Mr. William Bradford, who had been so kind to me at Cambridge lately, to join us.

I was to dine this evening with Mr. Lewis Loyd, 20 Hyde Park Gardens, and had looked up the trains and found the one I should have to take in order to get back and dress in time for the dinner. I left before the races were over and before the Longfellows were to return. At the station I found great confusion. The train started late and we were so held up by extra trains on the way that I did not arrive in the London station till very nearly dinner-time, which was nominally seven-forty-five, that is actually eight. I did not have the Loyds' address with me so that I could not send a message, and all I could do was to fee the cabman to drive at full speed to my lodgings, dress as quickly as I could, and hurry to the dinner, finishing putting on my collar and tying my cravat in the hansom. When I arrived the party had just sat down, but I learned to my regret that they had waited some twenty-five minutes for me, and there were a number of very distinguished guests. I felt much chagrined and sorry too for my hostess. Among the guests was the Right Honorable George John Shaw-Lefevre. He has been very prominent as a member of Parliament, is credited with carrying in the House of Commons the vote for the arbitration of the *Alabama* claims, was Secretary of the Board of Trade under Bright. (He has since, in 1906, been made Lord Eversley for his distinguished services.) There were about twenty persons present. I begged them to let me in with the *plat qui marche*, but they insisted upon bringing me some of the first courses. Shaw-Lefevre was very interesting, the most so of any of the guests.

He has a pleasant, bright, clear-cut, sincere, and earnest manner. I wished I had the opportunity to know him better. He is one of the sort I should have liked to make an intimate friend of. His father was Speaker of the House of Commons and was one of the guests whom my father met at Lord Cranworth's in 1856. There were many others whose names I did not get, but who all seemed *au courant* with the large affairs of the kingdom. I had met Mr. Loyd at the Fortescues' dinner, and it was so kind of him to ask me when he was under no obligation that I felt doubly sorry for my lateness. Of course I explained the situation and tried to carry it off as cheerfully as possible, after expressing my regrets, saying that I had no idea that the crowds returning from Henley would be so great as to delay the trains. Mrs. Loyd was most courteous and kindly, but I was sure that she was a good deal upset or at least had reason to be. The conversation, however, became so interesting that I think before the evening was over my lateness had been forgotten.

Saturday, July 1
WENT for a week-end visit at Cranleigh, near Guilford, to the E. L. Rowcliffes. The other guests were Mrs. Julius Pollock and her daughter Lilian, Mr., Mrs., and Miss Greg, Mr. Harrison, a member of one of the largest firms of solicitors in London, and Mrs. Edward Rowcliffe. It was a delightful, warm, calm evening, in most beautiful surroundings, fine large gardens with roses and many fragrant and brilliant flowers most tastefully arranged, delicious strawberries and various other kinds of fruit, with wandering paths through arbors, and everything that one could imagine to make the place attractive and that care and taste could devise. Dinner

was at half-past seven. In the evening the ladies sang and played the piano.

Sunday, July 2
To church, walking there and back with most of the household.

Monday, July 3
THEY showed me a fishing pond which was just being emptied. To-day was another beautiful day and we all had lunch out of doors and took a drive in the afternoon. We had views of what seemed almost wild country, with no houses in sight and yet such a short distance from London.

Tuesday, July 4
DROVE eight miles to breakfast with Mr. Harrison at seven-forty-five. We saw the assizes with the trumpeters going on before the judge to the Guilford court-house, the sheriffs, marshals, and other officials, all in full uniform, making a great ceremony, the like of which we never see in the United States. Arrived in London at half-past ten and left in a couple of hours for my second trip on the Continent, stopping at Canterbury Cathedral on the way.

Wednesday, July 5
MADE a ten-weeks' trip on the Continent, chiefly in France, Brussels, Germany, Switzerland, and the north of Italy. On the field of Waterloo I had a strange mixture of feeling, a certain sympathy for Bonaparte and a wish that he had conquered, and, on the other hand, a satisfaction that it was the British who won. At Berlin I noticed the hours of meals at the chief hotel to be

early coffee and rolls on waking, cold meat and beer at eleven, dinner at four, and tea or supper from seven to ten. At Potsdam one of the most striking things was the palace, which had such small, convenient, and homelike rooms. The Emperor, William I, apparently preferred this to more grandeur.

Wednesday, July 26
VISITED the Reichstag. The coat-room was very small. There was a buffet. Each member is furnished with a seat with his name on the back of the chair and a desk with inkstand and drawer in front. Moltke's seat was on the right front, the Prime Minister on a dais, and the members when speaking did so from a rostrum. I saw Bismarck's seat. The Prime Minister has a private room for rest, conferences, and work. There is no library or writing-room for members as in the English Parliament. They sit in a semi-circle.

Went to the American Embassy and saw Bancroft Davis. He kindly expressed his regret that father was not his colleague in England. At Munich, staying at the same hotel with myself and friends, were the Crown Prince and Princess of Prussia. I saw them coming out of their carriage after a rain, not at the front door, but at a side one. A carpet was laid, but not close to the carriage, so that the Princess had to step on muddy pavement part of the way. The Crown Prince (Frederick) came after her, but did not, like Sir Walter Raleigh, lay his cloak on the ground for her benefit.

Monday, August 14
HAD a narrow escape. From the top of the Fourca Pass we walked to the Rhone Glacier. On the way we met an English clergyman and his friend, a Mr. Salter, who

was an experienced Alpine climber and supplied with ice-axe and hobnailed shoes. He persuaded us to take a short cut to the glacier. We had stout walking-staffs with sharp points, but smooth shoes. Some other walkers joined us. The descent became steeper and steeper, first over a grass slope and then by an almost perpendicular wall of stone and marl. Some of our companions became frightened and returned. Later, as we kept on it was so steep that we could not see the men below us and hardly the men above. Occasionally stones would roll down, but by holding our staffs above our heads we protected them from any severe blow. How in the world we got through without falling and losing our lives, I do not know. We had no rope to tie us together. Our English friend, an expert climber, after it was all over said "it was the nastiest bit of grass slope, loose rocks, and gravel" that he had ever done.

Monday, August 21
AFTER some training on long walks and in glacier work we tried the ascent of Mont Blanc. As the trip showed some French characteristics it may be worth narrating. We started for the Grands Mulets, my classmate, Mr. George Wigglesworth, myself, and a young Englishman. The weather was fine and we had two experienced guides and two porters. We started in the early forenoon, going through the woods the first part of the way, the porters carrying ladders and planks, and the guides ice-axes and a rope. As we were walking along at a moderate pace we heard a rushing and hallooing behind us and in a few moments a party of three Frenchmen with guides and porters passed us running on the double-quick. Their guide said they, too, were going

up Mont Blanc. Not long afterwards we overtook this same party drenched with perspiration, mopping their brows, wholly out of breath and resting.

As we got on the glacier we were roped together. We had to descend a crevasse and mount again on the other side with steps cut in the ice on both sides. We saw the Grands Mulets in the distance. It was a house on a rock projecting out of the glacier and was kept by a very jolly, good-natured Frenchman. We had dinner in the early evening and sang, waking the echoes. As the sun went down it became cold and we all went to bed early so as to awake and be fresh for our start to the top at morning twilight. All the hard glacial part of the climb up Mont Blanc was to the Grands Mulets. After that it is one steady climb, more or less difficult according to the condition and amount of snow. Just at present the snow is hard and the ascent said to be easy.

During the night I dreamed we were attacked by brigands and in a moment was awakened by sounds of distant calling, answered by the firing of a gun, and saw lights flashed on the window panes. We went out into the night air and found our guides and porters starting to the assistance of the Frenchmen. These Frenchmen were brought in, carried like sacks of meal, by guides and porters and placed on the ground. We woke up again at three o'clock, the hour of starting, and found lightning quite constant toward Geneva, but heard no thunder. There were occasional rains with hail, so we delayed our starting. At six o'clock we saw the wind blowing on the top from the south — "le vent du Midi," as the guides call it — and the snow flying, though at that moment the sky was clear. Soon afterwards the clouds gathered and it did not look very hopeful for our reaching the top.

We talked with our Frenchmen, who said they had taken no previous exercise to prepare themselves for the ascent, but had come straight from the sidewalks of Paris. They apparently expected to reach the top in record time in one magnificent charge with the help of frequent nips of brandy. One of these men was quite ill.

We were impatient to go on, but the guides said we were sure to have a storm and that it would be dangerous. As they were to receive far more compensation if they went to the top than if we turned back from the Grands Mulets, we believed their advice was sincere. With deep disappointment we started back in the forenoon and just as we left the glacier, there came clouds, rain, and fog thick about us.

Wednesday, August 23
WALKED from Chamonix to Geneva, a distance of fifty miles, which we did in about fourteen hours including resting and meals, and though rather footsore, came through in good condition.

Saturday, August 26
LUNCHED with the d'Hermignys, an old French Protestant family who have many friends among the nobility of France, Italy, and England. One of the Rothschilds was present.

Sunday, September 3
BACK again in England on the way home to America. Heard Canon Liddon at Westminster Abbey. Most of my English friends were out of town.

Monday, September 4
IN the afternoon went down for a three-days' visit to my friend Charles Harrison, the celebrated solicitor

whom I met at Rowcliffe's in the spring and to whom Lord Coleridge had introduced me. He lived in an old house at Guilford, built in 1520, with many rare books, Spanish and other curiosities, and uncommon old china about.

Tuesday, September 5
MR. LUSHINGTON, son of the Reform Bill, came to lunch and spoke in high praise of my father's notes to Wheaton's "International Law." How thoughtful and kind these Englishmen are! There was also a Mr. Roy of the United Service Institute. Harrison took us on an excursion to Hampton Court in the afternoon and we saw the usual sights and some not open to the public. In the evening we went to a musicale, where were Mrs. Lane Fox, a Mr. Scott, a young Austrian prince, and two Miss Osbornes, and others.

Wednesday, September 6
AFTER a delightful visit went early to town to pack and prepare for the voyage home.

Thursday, September 7
RECEIVED a telegram from Lady Russell inviting me to Pembroke Lodge and down I went in the afternoon. Lord and Lady Russell welcomed me with great kindness and cordiality. I told Lady Russell about my father's defense of the fugitive slaves and those who were indicted for trying to free them, all done *con amore*. An arithmetical puzzle was given out, which we worked on and solved. That led Russell to tell the story of Pitt's remembering all the accounts in the most exact detail on one verbal hearing and his ability to explain and interest Parliament in them.

Lord Russell said he took a great liking to Lafayette, and told a story of his saving the life of Prince Jules de Polignac, Minister of Foreign Affairs under Charles X, who was imprisoned during the Revolution of July, 1830. The Prince feared murder and got in touch with Lord Russell, who spoke to Lafayette, then head of the Guards. Lafayette made an appointment and at the exact moment turned up at Lord Russell's hotel, the St. Maurice, and said, "It must not be; it shall not be."

Lord Russell spoke in great praise of Charles Francis Adams again and his services to the United States in England during the Civil War. He thinks that the Republicans will elect the President of the United States. He was very much stirred up by the Turkish atrocities,[1] and said to his grandson as he was going to bed, "You will never fight for the Turks." I again renewed my wish at the Wishing Tree and then parted from these my most cordial and dear friends with rather a heavy heart.

One afternoon I went to see the London Rowing Club at their boathouse at Putney. I had a letter from Smalley to Gulston, the captain, but he was out, and some other members took me about, showed me all their boats, and allowed me to make careful measurements of their oars, sliding seats, and rigging, and remembered the Harvard four-oar crew that came over to row against Oxford in 1869 — J. S. Fay, F. O. Lyman, W. H. Simmons, and Alden P. Loring, stroke, and also A. Burnham, the cockswain, and the substitutes, Rice and Bass, and they wanted especially to be remembered to Lyman after I told them he was engaged

---

[1] Those committed against the Bulgarians, which so aroused Gladstone. Disraeli's Government had refused to join the European concert which might have prevented these.

to be married to one of my sisters. They expressed the opinion that if the race had been rowed a few days before, Harvard would have won, as the Oxford crew was a little overworked and had to be taken off to the seashore for a rest. They also thought that Harvard lost considerably by steering under an arch with a back current in order to avoid the possibility of a foul. There are many "ifs" and "ands" in a close boat-race to salve the feelings of the beaten side.

Before leaving for America it may not be amiss to say the ladies wore bustles for both day and evening dresses. Their day dresses were always high at the neck. A quite common costume was to have a waist that has the effect of a cuirass — I do not know the proper name for it — made of some heavy, often dark material, with sleeves of a thinner substance and lighter color. There was usually a sort of overskirt, sometimes longer in the front and sometimes longer behind, but usually caught up at the sides. The evening dress was of rich silks with a round low neck. I won't attempt any further descriptions of the very varying ladies' dresses.

I have already described the men's country clothing except that I may add they never put on gloves in mild weather when not driving or riding. Some few men wore knickerbockers and long woolen stockings. In the city the men always wore tall silk hats, long black frock coats coming about to the knee, and dark trousers with some inconspicuous stripe. They almost invariably had on thick kid or dogskin gloves, the most fashionable color being a reddish brown. In the evening the men always wore dress suits, the coat being of the clawhammer style, and black vests with white ties. Gloves they did not wear excepting at dances.

Saturday, September 9

SAILED on the *Scythia*, the largest steamer on the trans-Atlantic service from Liverpool to New York. Near the end of the voyage I talked with a steerage passenger who was a barkeeper in New York. He also had some interest in the iron business. He said he found more drunkenness in Liverpool and Dublin than in New York, especially among the women. He talked much of New York politics. He had got one individual Republican elected in a Democratic district in New York City by printing three thousand "Democratic" ballots with the candidates for Congress and others of the regular party and the name of the Republican he wanted chosen, put in toward the end of the list in place of the Democratic candidate. The trick worked. (These were the days before the Australian official ballot. The party committees usually attended to printing the ballots with the names of their candidates on them and to the distribution of these ballots at the polls, but there was no law against any one's printing and distributing ballots, so "bogus" ones, as in this case, were often given out at the polls, misleading the voters by false headlines.) For this service he was appointed a policeman, a full patrolman with $1100 a year, and said he felt secure in his office on account of his political influence. For example, he said he was caught off his beat at one time and was only reprimanded instead of being dismissed. He hoped to get still more out of politics. He said that if you can only get a friend elected, you are sure of an office with no danger of removal while your friend is in power. He agreed that it was a bad system and a cause of corruption in both parties, but he said this would never be reformed during the lifetime of either of us. (In seven years the United States Civil

Service Reform Act was passed, followed in two years by those of New York and Massachusetts.)

With this conversation I was recalled to thoughts of my country and its sore need of important reforms (in which I afterwards took part), such as the introduction of the Australian ballot law and civil service reform measures, and after a most delightful and I hope instructive and educational trip I am to settle down again to the completion of my law studies at Harvard and to begin my work in a profession which may be made as dry as dust or one of the most stimulating, broadening, and useful to the community, according as it is taken by those who enter it.

EPILOGUE

THE precedence which is so strict in France is not in England kept up in the ordinary dinners excepting for a few of the most distinguished guests. The rules are often cast to the winds for the sake of better arrangement of people at table, to bring out good conversation, and for myself, with no precedence at all beyond my college degree, they have not infrequently given me the place of honor just as a bit of kind hospitality to a stranger.

The aristocracy hold a very high position. The best of them feel their responsibility toward their tenants, giving a great deal of time and thought, as may be seen from this journal, for their welfare, take an interest in all the details of the families, and in return are treated with respect and deference. There is undoubtedly a glamour connected with persons of title in Great Britain greater than in France, Italy, or Germany, but the great changes that have come since the World War of 1914–18, the enormous succession levies and the very high super-taxes for large incomes, will very likely alter the whole situation and indeed has already done so to a considerable degree. Many of the nobility have had to give up part of their big estates, and it was their wealth that undoubtedly gave them their position and the ability to exercise hospitality on a large scale and to keep up great houses. Perhaps we shall never again see the nobility as they were in 1875–76.

As to the situation in the seventies, Mrs. Humphry Ward in her "Writer's Recollections," speaking of her uncle, Matthew Arnold, said: "He never denied — none but the foolish ever do deny — the immense opportunities and advantages of an aristocratic class wherever it exists. He was quite conscious — none but those without imagination can fail to be conscious — of the glamour of long descent and great affairs." And yet that did not prevent Matthew Arnold's having sympathy for the less privileged classes, and in a poem to Arthur Hugh Clough he said:

> "If thoughts, not idle, which before me flow,
> The armies of the homeless and unfed —
> If these are yours, if this is what you are,
> Then I am yours, and what you feel I share."

In contrast to Matthew Arnold's view of the aristocracy, which Mrs. Ward shared, is that brought out in "The Education of Henry Adams." He says he "met in England a thousand people, great and small; jostled against every one from royal princes to gin-shop loafers; attended endless official functions and private parties; visited every part of the United Kingdom ... he knew the societies of one or two country houses and acquired habits of ... Sunday afternoon calls; but all this gave him nothing to do and was life wasted." And again, "of his daily life he had only to reckon so many breakfasts, so many dinners, so many receptions, balls, theatres, and country parties, so many cards to be left, so many Americans to be escorted; all counting for nothing in sum, because ... it was mere routine, a single, continued, unbroken act which led to nothing and nowhere except Portland Place and the grave."

For myself, I took a position somewhat between the two. Without generalizing too much, I know that those I met were the most delightful, well-bred, courteous, true-hearted, generous people, by and large, that I have ever come in contact with. They were well informed, some of them brilliant and delightful talkers. I made many sincere friendships and their acquaintance enlarged my view of life and its possibilities and was to me at once an education and an inspiration. I shall never forget these good people. I did not meet the fast set or the few *nouveaux riches* of the aristocracy, and I may have been particularly fortunate in the groups that I met. Then, too, they were human beings after all, and to picture the scene to one's self as an American I sometimes thought what the situation would be did we in the United States issue patents of nobility. Had we done so, General Grant would have been Duke of Richmond, with sub-title of Marquis of Vicksburg and Earl Donelson; General Sherman would have been, let us say, the Marquis of Atlanta; Chief Justice Marshall would have been made an earl, and Horace Gray and Oliver Wendell Holmes, Jr., Massachusetts representatives on the United States Supreme Court, would have been made barons or at least baronets. If Roundell Palmer, who conducted the losing side of the *Alabama* arbitration at Geneva, Switzerland, was made a baron with title of Lord Selborne, surely William M. Evarts, the chief counsel for the American or winning side, would have been made the Viscount or the Earl of Windsor, Vermont, and so on.

But to come back to my experience, it was the human side of these delightful people that interested and instructed me, and I never shall forget their hospitality. Let me give a little example in addition to those already related. I received a letter from Mr. Mark J. Stuart, an eminent member of the House of Commons, to whom I had no letter of introduction and whom I had not even met, saying that he had heard from our mutual friend, Mr. Robert Ferguson, M.P., that I was in London, only to remain a few days longer, and would I lunch with him at his house the next Saturday, saying that when in the United States he had spent a pleasant afternoon with my father. That Saturday was engaged and a day or two afterwards I left for the Continent.

Perhaps I made a mistake in not staying on in London longer to see more of old friends and make new ones, but I felt, whether rightly or wrongly, that for my education and for increasing my interest in history I ought to visit the important parts of western Europe, which I had not seen, before returning to America in September, a thing I had to do in order to complete my studies at the law school.

Among the various changes and chances in our human life it has been my misfortune not to have kept up friendships with any but a few of my English acquaintances. It was not their fault as is clearly shown by their quick response whenever they were given a chance to show us hospitality. It was delightful to find how they welcomed my sons and friends, and when in England in 1920 not only did I see or hear from all those then living of my old friends, but what showed the traditions of hospitality most remarkably was to see how the second generation carried it on. I received kind notes from several of them and made some weekend visits and had other invitations I could not accept. President Hayes offered me, through William M. Evarts, the Secretary of State, the position of Chief Secretary of Legation at either Paris or London as I might choose, a year after my return to America. Had I accepted the offer and chosen London, I should have had the best opportunity possible for seeing again my old friends, but the diplomatic service was not then a career. A change of administration, even with no change of party, meant a change of all diplomatic officers. It was not till some years later, in 1883, that Mr. Henry White began his long and honorable diplomatic career, and even that was broken by a gap of four years during Cleveland's second administration.

Any good I might do for Uncle Sam on account of my knowledge of London ways would have been only temporary. Therefore, on the advice of my father and of Mr. Longfellow, who was about to be my father-in-law, I declined the offer.

Notwithstanding the regret I have in not seeing them again, the memories of those golden days of friendships abroad have remained in the stronghold of my heart and have been an inspiration in all the work for public good I have ever taken a hand in.

What is the explanation of the wonderful English hospitality? The hospitality is not vague and general, expressing itself to one and all, but is confined to those who are properly introduced or well known. Beside the wealth, the great estates, the large establishments, the hunting, fishing, cricket grounds, lawn tennis and the stables, which make it easy to entertain guests, is the fact that the country life without guests would in many cases be lonely. But, in addition, the English people seem educated to entertain, and I believe that education comes from the universities of Oxford and Cambridge. Whether by design or accident, the students do not breakfast in hall, but in their own rooms, and as they do not chum together in the English universities, they naturally fall into the habit of asking friends in; so a student — or one who like myself was staying in college — receives a card, or a short note, or just a verbal invitation to breakfast at eight-forty-five or nine o'clock at some one's room in such and such a college, to meet, let us say, the president of the Oxford Union, or the captain of a boat club, a celebrated cricket player, or a high honor man.

The scouts bring in from the buttery breakfasts of one, two, or three courses, usually one, and place them on trestles composed of tongs, shovel, and poker in front of the fire, where it may keep warm till the guests arrive. Indeed, it is rather an exception for a man to breakfast alone. Freshmen even are invited to breakfast with upper classmen. Besides the breakfasts in each other's rooms there is another custom which has induced hospitality among the educated English, and that is of the wines or desserts after dinner. The dinner in hall is rather meagre and this meagreness is made up by delicacies and wines served in the college rooms, to which they invite friends.

In America our students either dine in large halls at the same table with the same men for substantially the whole of the year, or form small and exclusive clubs where they take all meals with the same group day after day, and there is no easy hospitality or interchange of companionship at meals as in England.

With all the other inducements to hospitality in Great Britain I think the greatest factor is this university education in comradeship and conviviality.

Hospitality is not confined to the B.A.'s and M.A.'s of Oxford and Cambridge. It is a human instinct, as testify the earliest literatures sacred and profane. Chaucer, before modern Oxford could have blossomed out, has his hospitable Franklyn, the "newe" St. Julian. Shakespeare was not at the universities nor was the banished Duke in "As You Like It," but how sweet the greeting to Orlando, "Sit down and feed and welcome to our table," though the young hero had just tried to seize the food by force, and Orlando replies:

> "Speak you so gently? Pardon me I pray you
> . . . .
> If ever you have looked on better days;
> . . . .
> Let gentleness my strong enforcement be:
> In the which hope, I blush, and hide my sword."

And then the Duke replies:

> "True is it that we have seen better days,
> And have with holy bell been knoll'd to church,
> And sat at good men's feasts, and wiped our eyes
> Of drops that sacred pity hath engender'd:
> And therefore sit you down in gentleness,
> And take upon command what help we have,
> That to your wanting may be minister'd."

And then you remember how Orlando would partake of nothing till he had hospitably fetched his old companion Adam to the feast.

Yes, hospitality is almost universal, but is it ever so pervading, so easy, so cultivated and trained as among those who have spent their golden youth at the universities of old England?

THE END

INDEX

INDEX

Abbott, Mrs., mother of Lord Tenterden, 157, 160.
Acropolis of Athens, by moonlight, 210–14.
Acting, French, 159, 177, 179.
Adams, Charles Francis, 37; as a fisherman, 111; as Minister to England in the Civil War, 126, 358.
Adams, F. Ottiwell, 157, 160.
Adams, Henry, his views of the English aristocracy, 363.
Ægean, the, 220–22.
Ætna, Mt., 203.
Agassiz, Louis, 184.
Agricultural Holdings Bill, in Parliament, 11, 12, 17, 32.
Alabama Claims, and Lord Tenterden, 18, 132, 138; and Lord Cockburn, 132–34, 323, 331, 332; and Sir Stafford Northcote, 337; and Shaw-Lefevre, 350.
Albani, 300, 302, 342.
Alexandra, Princess, of Wales, 33.
Alexandria to Cairo, the journey, 223.
All Saints' Day at Paris, 170.
Althorp House, visit to, 69–81.
Amberley, Lord, 37, 40; death, 220, 329.
American conditions misunderstood by Professor Danna, 249, 250.
American politics, 299, 334, 360, 361.
Americans in Paris, 183.
Amory, Jonathan, 302.
Ancient history, value of, 226.
Andrew, John F., 25.
Appleton, Nathan, 9.
Appleton, "Uncle Tom," 5, 6.
Arab, an athletic, 227; as host, 235, 236.
Arabic language, the, 225.
Arbuthnot, Mr., 20.
Archbishop of Paris, the, 192.
Argyll, Duke of, visit to his castle, 103–20; reception of, 338, 339.
Argyll, Duchess of, 103, 111, 112, 120, 328.
Argyll, Lord Archibald, 109, 112.
Argyll, Lady Elizabeth, 105, 106.
Aristocracy, the English, 362–64. *See* Nobility.
Arnold, Edwin, 317.
Arnold, Matthew, son of, 268; on the English classes, 362, 363.
Arnold, Richard P., 273, 276.

Ashburton, Lady, 113, 114.
Ashbury, Mr., 237.
Ashley, Lady Edith, 112, 115.
Ashmolean Museum, the, 280.
Assembly, the French, Monsieur Laugel's views on, 179; a meeting of, 185–91.
Assemblies, after-dinner, 21.
Athens, the romance of, 204, 205; the Theatre of Dionysus, 205, 206; Christmas services at, 206; a funeral at, 207; costumes in, 208; the Acropolis by moonlight, 210–14; Royal Ball at, 214–16.
Austin, Alfred, 87.

Bailey, Mr., of "Lee Abbey," 136.
Balfour, A.J., 290.
Ball, Royal, at Athens, 214–16.
Balliol College, 264, 265.
Balliol eight wine, the, 280–82.
Balls, matrons at, 335.
Baring, Mary Florence, 114.
Barnard, C. Inman, 226, 232.
Batiste, Monsieur E., organist, 182.
Bedrashen, 229.
Beecher, Henry Ward, 22, 23.
Behera, the, steamer, 220–23.
Belknap, W. W., 245.
Benjamin, Judah P., 322, 323, 326.
Benvenue, 100, 101.
Berlin, 352, 353.
Bernard, Mountague, 341.
Bernhardt, Sarah, 192.
Binney, Horace, Jr., 311.
Birmingham, 65–68.
Bismarck, Otto v., 161.
Blackmore, R. D., his "Lorna Doone," 139.
Bluntschli, 322.
Bodleian Library, the, 277, 278.
Brackett, Walter, American sportsman and painter, 110.
Bradford, William, 284, 285, 350.
"Britannia," as name for England, 59.
Brohan, Madame, French actress, 191.
Brougham, Lord, 51.
Brownson, Mr., 334.
Bruce, Lord Charles, 6, 32, 43, 70–76.
Bruce, Lady Charles, 71.
Bryant, W. C., 337, 338.
Bryce, James, 348.

372 INDEX

Buckstone, benefit of, 306, 307.
Buffet, Monsieur, French Premier, 189, 190.
Burdett-Coutts, Baroness, 314–16, 344.
Burke, Edmund, 54.
Burnett, Waldo, 271.
Burrows, Professor, of All Souls, 263, 267, 268.
Burrows, Mrs., 263, 267.
Burrows, Miss, 263.
Burrows, F. R., 263, 265, 266, 270, 271.

Cabmen, London, 301, 308.
Cairo, from Alexandria to, the journey, 223; soldiers' boys' school at, 225; Volunteer Corps at, 225.
Calvo y Capdevila, Cárlos, 198.
Cambridge (England), 283–93.
Campbell, Lord Colin, 4, 5, 49, 50, 114.
Cardwell, Lord, 50, 51, 53.
Cardwell, Lady, 50, 52.
Cargin, I., French violinist, 182.
Carlton Club, the, 37.
Cavendish, Lord Edward, 40, 105, 108–12.
Cavendish, Lady Edward, 40, 105.
Cavendish, Lord Frederick, 28; appearance and manner, 4; his public services, 11; takes Dana to the House of Commons, 11, 13; Dana at dinner of, 40.
Cavendish, Lady Frederick, dinners of, 4; 19, 28, 40; appearance, 11; Dana calls on, 42.
Chabrol, Vicomte de, 184, 196, 197.
Chapin, Horace D., 42.
Chapuy, Madame, actress, 181.
Chatsworth, country seat of Duke of Devonshire, 57.
Chaucer, Geoffrey, 367.
Chitty, Mr., 304.
Christmas services in Russian church at Athens, 206.
Claytons', the, 330.
Clifden, Lady, 6, 7, 71, 77–81.
Clifden, Viscount, 77.
Clubs, English, 13, 18, 19, 36, 37, 46, 333.
Cockburn, Lord, and the Alabama Claims, 132–34, 323, 331; and the Strathclyde case, 321–23; and "Wheaton," 322; and Bluntschli, 322; and American courts, 332.
Coffee houses, 93.
Coleridge, Lord, 10, 309; visited by Dana, 121–34; on Lord Cockburn, 132–34, 323, 331; Dana dines with, 310; his views on the House of Lords, 311; and the Speaker of the House of Commons, 311, 312; on the Duke of Wellington and dueling, 312; and Goethe's name, 313; as a classical scholar, 313, 314; breakfast with, 317; as Chief Justice, 318, 319; other breakfasts with, 320, 331; morning prayers by, 320; and vivisection, 320; further invitations of, 342.
Coleridge, Lady, 121, 127.
Coleridge, Bernard, 127, 130, 131, 321.
Coleridge, Edward, 124, 127.
Coleridge, Mrs. Edward, 124, 127.
Coleridge, Sir John Taylor, 131, 310.
Coleridge, Mildred, 124.
Coleridge, Stephen, 127.
Coleridge, Miss, sister of Lord Coleridge, 131.
Collier, Sir Robert, 346, 347.
Colossal statue, Egyptian, 229.
Colosseum, the, 240.
"Columbia," as name for United States, 59.
Comédie Française. See Théâtre Français.
Commons, the Speaker of the House of, 311, 312.
Commune, the, 179, 180.
Concrete cottages, 95.
Constantine, Basilica of, 240.
Constitution of the United States, Dana explains, 44, 45, 54; on amending, 343, 344.
Convicts, discharged, employment of, 92, 93.
Convocation, 273, 274.
Cornice Road, the, 200, 201.
Cornish, Rev. George Kestell, poem by, 129.
Cosmopolitan Club, the, 46, 329.
County judges, 72, 73.
Courts, American, and English judges, 332, 333.
Cowen, Mr., 326.
Cowley Fathers, the, 269, 270.
Cranleigh, seat of the Rowcliffes, 351.
Cricket, 338, 339.
Croisette, actress, 159.
Cross, Mr., 217.
Cunard Line, the, 26, 27.
Cushing, Caleb, 133, 331.

Dalkeith, Lord, 44.
Dalton, Colonel, 241.
Dana, Charles A., 174.
Dana, Edmund, 49.
Dana, Francis, 49, 54.
Dana, Paul, 174.
Dana, Richard Henry, his "Two Years Before the Mast," 30, 48; rejection

INDEX 373

by Senate Committee as Minister to Great Britain, 245, 246, 310, 314, 329, 341; his notes to Wheaton's International Law, 247, 248, 322, 341, 346, 357; author questioned concerning, in English railway carriage, 255; as a *raconteur*, 329.

Dana, Richard Henry (son of Richard Henry), urged to stay in England, 45; mentioned in Dundee "Advertiser," 94; his plan for raising sunken ship, 116, 117; elected member of the Reform Club, 328; offered post as Chief Secretary of Legation at Paris or London, 365, 366.

Dana family, the, 250, 251.
Danna, Professor, 247-51.
Danna, Mrs., 251.
D'Arcy, Rev. G. B., 208.
Davis, Bancroft, 353.
De Bornier, Henri, 177.
Deer-hunting, 139.
Deldevez, Monsieur E., 182.
Derby, Lord, 231.
Derby race, the, 294-99.
Devonshire Club, the, 36, 44.
Dexter, Arthur, 246.
D'Hermignys', the, 356.
Dicey, Edward, 174, 329, 342.
Dicey, Mrs. Edward, 174, 196.
Dickinson, G. Lowes, his "A Modern Symposium," 16.
Dinners, in England, 21, 150; precedence at, 362.
Disraeli, Benjamin D., neutral in our Civil War, 10; in the House, 12; appearance, 15; his humor, 46, 47; incidents concerning his veracity, 60-62; speech of, 66; and the Suez Canal, 231; and the Speaker of the House, 312; gives invitation to meet Prince of Wales, 336.
Domestic system, the English, 75.
Donkey-boy who spoke English, 228.
Donkeys on shipboard, 221.
"Don Juan," 194.
Dorr, Mrs., 241.
Drummond, Henry, 323.
"Duc Job," play by Laya, 193.
Dueling, 312.
Duff, Mr. and Mrs. Gordon, 25, 26.
Dundee, reform school at, 90, 91; linen works at, 91, 92; library in Albert Institute at, 92; convict system at, 92, 93; coffee houses at, 93; flower show at, 96.
Dyer, Louis, 264, 267, 271-76.

Ebre, the, steamer, 237.

Edinburgh, picturesqueness of, 83.
Egypt, 223-36.
Egyptian women, 229.
Egyptians, the, 224.
Eleusis, Bay of, 217.
Ellen's Isle, 100, 102.
Elliot, Admiral, 37.
Elliot, Sir Charles Gilbert, 37.
Elliot, Lady Harriet Emily, 37-39.
England, feeling in, toward America, 125-27.
English dress, 359.
English hospitality, 151, 152, 364-66; the source of, 366-68.
English judges, their ignorance in regard to American courts, 332, 333.
English music, 309.
English politics, ladies in, 319.
English pronunciation, 25, 112, 119.
English voices, 77.
English words and expressions, 72, 77.
Episcopal Church of America at Rome, 244, 245.
Errol, 96.
Eton College, 302-05.
Eversley, Lord. *See* Shaw-Lefevre.
Exeter, cathedral, 135.
Exmoor, 139.

Favart, Mademoiselle, actress, 177.
Febvre, French actor, 177.
Felton, Tom, 56.
Ferguson, Robert, 2, 17, 43, 365; Dana lunches with, 3; Dana at Reform Club with, 36.
Ferguson, Mr., 333.
Fishing, 140-43.
Fishmongers' Hall, dinner at, 330.
Fortescue, Lady Camilla, 310.
Fortescue, Dudley, 306, 309, 310.
Fouret, René, 162, 163.
Fowler, Mrs., 333.
Franceschi, Signor, singer, 252.
Franco-Prussian War, 174.
French, the, character of, 171.
French Academy, the, opening of, 167, 168; prizes awarded before, 170; a meeting of, 176, 177.
French court, a, 255.
French National Library, the, 252-54.
French politics, 171, 172.
French senate, composition of, 162.

Gambetta, speech by, 188, 189.
Garrick Club, the, 18, 19.
Geneva, 356.
George, King of Greece, 208, 214-17.
Ghost story, a, 123.
Gibbons, Professor, 286.

Girton, 285.
Gizeh, 228, 229.
Glaciers, 353–56.
Gladstone, W. E., rather Southern in his feelings during our Civil War, 10; sincere in his thoughts, 15; change in feeling toward, 16; his assumption of being morally right, 16, 17; Dana at family party at house of, 21–23; drew information from others, 24; his voice and manner of speaking, 24; his appearance, 25; his pronunciation, 25; in the House, 31; at dinner and theatre party, 40, 41; autograph letter of, 49; removes to Harley Street, 308; questions Dana on Grecian conditions, 339, 340; calls at Dana's lodgings, 348.
Gladstone, Mrs. W. E., 23, 24, 40.
Gladstone, William H., 22, 40.
Gladstone, Miss, 274.
Glasgow, 121.
Glazebrook, jumper, 280.
Glenthorne, seat of Mr. Halliday, 139.
Goldie, Miss, 84, 87.
Goodwin, Professor W. W., 206.
Got, French actor, 191, 193.
Grain, unloading, 199, 200.
Grant, President, 209, 246.
Greece, landing at Piræus, 204; Athens, 204, 205; contrast between the extent and the influence of, 218; was unable in antiquity to form a united country, 219; Gladstone questions Dana on, 339, 340.
Greek funeral, a, 207.
Greeks, the, character of, 203, 220.
Greenwood, Frederick, editor of "Pall Mall Gazette," 231.
"Greville Papers," the, 51.
Gurney, Professor, 300, 301, 305, 315.
Gurney, Mrs., 315.
Gurney, Mrs. Russell, 326; dinner with, 342–44.
Gurney, Mr., nephew of Russell Gurney, 344, 345.
Guy's Cave, 63.

Haggard, Rev. C., 237.
Hall, Major, officer in the Confederate Army, 225.
Halliday, Mr., 139.
Hamilton, Lord George, quoted on Mrs. Hamilton, 24; in politics, 44.
Hammond, Miss (afterwards Mrs. Dr. William Appleton), 201, 202.
Haoverman, Baron, 197, 238.
Harcourt, Sir William Vernon, 48; Dana goes to House at invitation of, 28; Dana dines with, 31; his career, 31; and the Agricultural Holdings Bill, 32; dinner to Dana given by, 44–46; on the veracity of Disraeli, 60, 61; his standing, 175; character of, 175, 176; calls at Dana's lodgings, 348.
Harrison, Charles, 351, 352, 356.
Hartington, Marquis of, 57; speech of, 66.
Harvard and Oxford, race of 1869, 267, 358, 359.
Harvard Dining-Hall Association, 89.
Haweis, Rev. Hugh Reginald, 305, 325.
Healey, Mr., 183, 184, 192.
Hearse, scene with, 239, 240.
Heathcote, Sir William, visited by Dana, 146–50; at Mentone, 201; picture of, 263.
Heathcote, Lady, 147, 201.
Heathcote, Rev. Mr., 148, 149.
Heath's Court, 131.
Heatly, Miss, 335.
Henley, boat-races at, 349.
Herzegovinians, the, 203.
Highlands of Scotland, the, 100–02.
Hoffmann, Baroness, 241.
Honey, George, actor, 41.
Honiton, 121.
Horsfall, Mr., 256, 294, 302.
Hospitality. See English.
Hottin, Monsieur, singer, 182.
Houghton, Lord (Richard Monckton Milnes), 314–17.
Hughes, Tom, 19.
Hursley Park, visited by Dana, 146–50.

Ilfracombe, 135, 145.
Inchture, 94.
Inner Temple, the, 36.
Institute of France, the, 167–70.
Insurance, marine, 29.
Intemperance in English society, 51, 52.
Inverary, 103.
Inverary Castle, visit to, 103–20.
Inversnaid, 102.
Ireland, condition of, 7.
Irving, Henry, as Joseph Surface, 307; his manner, 314, 330; reading by, 344.
Italian Parliament, the, 242, 243.
Italians, the, 248, 249; taxes of, 176.

James, Henry, 196.
Japanese, an English opinion of, 160, 161; about their civilization, 160, 161.
Johnston, Sir Harry, has "Gay Dombeys," 13.
Jonassain, Mademoiselle, actress, 177.
Jones, Dr., 17, 43.

INDEX

Jonson, Ben, 74, 75.
Jupp, of Magdalen, 270.

Keble chapel, 277, 279, 280.
Keble College dormitory, 257, 258.
Kenilworth, 63.
Kennaway, Sir John, 13; invitations from, 2, 5, 64; dinner with, 19; at Carlton Club with, 37; breakfast with, 347; calls on Dana, 348.
Kennaway, Lady, 20, 43, 347.
Kew Gardens, 53.
Kinnaird, Lord, 49; visited by Dana, 88–96; his philanthropies, 90–93; a useful member of the House of Lords, 97; his family, 98; his collection at the Priory, 99.
Kinnaird, Lady, 88, 96.
Kinnaird, Arthur, 2, 49.
Knox, Mr., 181.

Lanyon, Charles, 324–26, 333, 334.
Laugel, Monsieur, 174–76, 179, 180, 196.
Law, one attitude toward, 300.
Laya, Madame, 164, 166, 181, 182, 254.
Laya, Mademoiselle, 164, 165, 173.
Laya, Monsieur, 164, 165, 173, 178, 191, 197.
Laya, Jean Louis, 193.
Layas', the, 169, 171, 174, 180, 193, 251, 252.
Leaf, Herbert, 283, 284.
"Lee Abbey," 136.
Leemouth, 144.
Lehmann, R. C., 289.
"Leyces Ter" Hospital, Warwick, 65.
Library, at Althorp House, 73–75; at Milan, 74.
Lincoln's Inn, 6.
Littlejohn, Bishop, 244.
Lloyd, Mr., of the Priory at Warwick, 64.
Loch Achray, 100.
Loch Katrine, 100–02.
Loch Lomond, 102.
Lockhart, grandnephew of Walter Scott, 265.
Lombard, Howard, 276.
London, first visit to, 1–62; return to, 256; revisited, 294–352.
London post-office, efficiency of, 60.
London Rowing Club, 358.
Londonderry, Lord, 7.
Lords, the House of, Lord Coleridge's views on, 311.
Lords, a cricket match at, 338, 339.
Lorne, Marquis of, 105–19.
Louise, Princess, 104–19.
"Louisiana Lowlands," 281, 289.
Lowell, James Russell, 106.

Loyd, Lewis, 350, 351.
Loyd, Mrs , 350, 351.
Lushington, Judge, 324, 325, 357.
Lynmouth, 135–45.
Lynton, 136.
Lyttelton, Alfred, 5.
Lyttelton, Lord, 268.
Lyttelton, Lady, 40.

Macbeth, site of his castle, 95.
Mackarness, Alethea, 127.
Mackarness, John Fielder, Bishop of Oxford, 127, 131.
Mackarness, the Misses, daughters of the Bishop of Oxford, 131.
Mackintosh, Mr., son of Sir James, 8, 9.
Mackintosh, Mrs. Robert, 5, 19.
MacMahon, Madame General, 182.
Magdalen College, 270, 271.
Mann, James Bradford, 290, 291.
Marmier, Xavier, at home, 154, 155, 191; on the street, 156, 195; courtesies of, to Dana, 157, 164–68, 170, 181, 184, 194, 195; presents his books to Dana, 159, 178, 195.
Marseilles, 199, 200.
Marsh, George P., American Minister at Rome, 239, 244–47.
Marsh, Mrs. G. P., 243, 244.
Marshall, Professor A., 285.
Mass, at St. Roch, 170; at St. Eustache, 182.
Mayne, his "Ancient Law," 44, 86.
McMillan, Mr., 272.
Mellor, Francis H., 284, 286.
Mentone, 201.
Messina, 202.
Milan, Library at, 74.
Mildmay, Archdeacon, 147, 149.
Millais, Sir John E., 44, 56.
Milnes, Richard Monckton. See Houghton, Lord.
Mitchell, Cambridge oarsman, 287.
Mitrahenny, 229.
Mohl, Madame, 155–59, 195, 196.
Mohl, Monsieur, 155, 156.
Monaco, 201, 202.
Moncur Castle, 98.
Mont Blanc, climbing, 354–56.
Monte Carlo, 201, 202.
Montucci, Monsieur, 169.
Moody and Sankey, views on, 59.
Morality, of different nations, 163, 164.
Moss, Edward, 268, 271.
Munich, 353.
Mylne, Bishop, 276, 277, 279.

Naples, 237–39.
Napoleon, Prince, 172.

"Nasty," English use of, 20.
Neapolitan nobility, the, 238.
Neilson, Miss, 307.
Nile, the, 223.
Nobility, English, method of addressing, 97; lack of scientific and historical knowledge among, 97, 98; differing views of, 362–64.
North Devonshire, 136–45.
Northampton, 68.
Northcote, Sir Stafford, 337.

Ogilvy, Angus, 94, 95.
Ogilvy, Mr., 90, 96.
Olga, Queen of Greece, 215, 216.
Opera at Paris, 160, 169, 194.
Opéra Comique, 181.
Orange, 199.
Ottery St. Mary, 131.
Owen, Professor Richard, 336.
Oxford, arrival at, 257; appearance of students, 257; river barges, 258; rowing, 259–61, 272, 275; the Union, 260–63; glimpses of life at, 263–80; the Cowley Fathers, 269, 270; the Balliol eight wine, 280–82; examinations, 282; the charm of, 283.

Paget, Sir Augustus, 239, 241, 242.
Paget, Lady, 241, 244, 246.
Paintings, at Althorp House, 81; at Rossie Priory, 89, 99.
Palais de l'Industrie, 181.
Palermo, 202.
Palmer, Sir Roundell. See Lord Selborne.
Palmer, Lady, 340.
Palmer, Professor, of Oxford, 274.
Paris, first visit to, 153–98; second visit to, 251–54.
Paris Salon, 254.
Parker, Charles P., 263, 269, 270.
Parker, Edmund M., 257, 271.
Parker, Henry Tuke, 11.
Parker, Mrs., 19.
Parliament, the English, debates in, 11–13, 17; procedure in, 14, 15, 32, 34, 35; a violent scene in, 28–31.
Parthia, the, 26, 27.
Peabody, Francis, 284, 288.
Peel, Sir Robert, and Disraeli, 61, 62.
Pembroke Lodge, visits to, 34, 37–40, 49–56, 328, 336, 338, 357.
Pen works, in Birmingham, 68.
Penrose, J. P., 289.
Peterboro, cathedral, 82; Bishop of, 245.
Pérusse, Vicomte de, 173, 181, 192.
Pérusse, Vicomtesse de, 166, 173, 181, 192, 197.

Phillimore, Sir Robert, 19, 36, 326, 347; dinner with, 2–4; in the Strathclyde case, 321, 322.
Physicians, French and American, 173.
Piper, William T., 288.
Playfair, Lyon, 348.
Plimsoll, Mr., and the Merchants' Shipping Bill, 28–30, 46–49, 88.
Pollock, Chief Baron, 136, 314.
Pollock, Sir Frederick, 48, 314.
Pollock, Sir J. Frederick, 35.
Pollock, Dr. Julius, 138, 314.
Pollock, Mrs. Julius, 142–44, 305.
Pollock, Sir William Frederick, 35, 36, 48.
Pollock, Lady, 35, 48, 56, 314.
Pollock, Mr. and Mrs., relatives of Sir Frederick, 136.
Portland, Lady, 320.
Potsdam, 353.
Praslin, Duc de, 197.
"Previous question," the, 15.
Price, Bonamy, 340; anecdote about, 343; his manner, 343, 344.
Priory, the, at Warwick, 64.
Proust, Monsieur, singer, 182.
Pyramids, the, 226–29, 232–36.

Quin, Lady Edith, 338.
Quincy, Dr. Henry P., 11.
Quintilian, 313, 314.

Railroads, English and American, 135.
Rawlins, Mr., barrister, 286, 300; in Lincoln's Inn with, 6; dinner with, 13, 14.
Rawlins, Mr., master at Eton, 303.
Read, General, United States Minister to Athens, 207, 209, 210.
Read, Mrs., 209, 210, 220.
Reform Club, the, 36, 328, 333.
Reform school at Dundee, 90, 91.
Reichstag, the, 353.
Reszké, Madame de, 169.
Rhodes, 221.
Rhone Glacier, the, 353, 354.
Ribblesdale, Lady, 54.
Richmond church, 53.
Richmond Park, 39.
Rifle contests at Wimbledon, 33.
Robinson, Douglas, 267, 273.
Robsart, Amy, 63, 65.
Roman law, Lord Young's opinion of, 85, 86.
Rome, 239–46.
Romilly, Lord, 337.
Rosalie, Monsieur, 180.
Rossie Priory, Lord Kinnaird's seat, 88–96; the house, 98; the art collection at, 99.

Rouen, 255.
Rowcliffe, E. L., 145, 305; Queen's Councilor, 138; illness of, 138, 139; a week end with, 351, 352.
Rowcliffe, Mrs., 138, 139, 145, 305; a drive with, 306; dinner with, 324.
Rowe, Mrs., 140.
Rowing, at Oxford, 259–61, 272, 275; at Cambridge, 288, 291.
Royal Art Exhibition, 3, 56.
Royal Titles Bill, the, 299.
Russell, Lord John, career, 34, 39, 40, 50; his manner, 34; conversations with, 34; his views on men and things, 37, 38, 54, 55; anecdote about his overcoat, 43; on William IV, 51; on intemperance in London society in his younger days, 51, 52; and the Trent Affair, 57, 58; on Walter Scott, 338; final visit to, 357, 358.
Russell, Lady, 114; at Pembroke Lodge, 38–40, 54, 328, 329, 357; on the names of England and the United States, 59; and Bryant, 337; on natural manners, 338.
Russell, Lady Agatha, 38, 39, 50.
Russell, Rollo, 38, 49, 50.
Russell, William Henry, 278.
Rutson, Albert, 300.
Ryland Public Library, Manchester, England, 74.

St. Cyr, 169.
St. Eustache, mass in, 182.
St. Philippe, sermon in, 192.
St. Roch, mass at, 170.
Sakkarah, 228.
Salmon fishing, 110.
Salomon, French singer, 169.
Savile Club, the, 13, 14.
Schenck, General C. R., United States Minister to England, 60.
Sclopis, Count, 247–49.
"Scrutin d' arrondissement" and "scrutin de liste," 179, 186–91.
Secession, the right of, 45, 226.
Selborne, Lord, 19, 274; his title, 18; conversations with, 50–53.
Selborne, Lady, 50.
Senate, the French, 179.
Shaftesbury, Earl, 112, 113, 118, 119.
Shakespeare, William, bust of, 19; and Ben Jonson, 74, 75; quoted, 367, 368.
Shaw-Lefevre, George John (Lord Eversley), 350, 351.
Sherman, John, 38.
"Shipping articles," 29.
Shipping Bill, the, Mr. Plimsoll and, 28–30.
Shoe pegs, the manufacture of, 67.
Sicily, 202, 203.
Sid River, the, 129.
Sidgwick, Professor Henry, 290.
Sidmouth, 128.
Silverknowe, Lord Young's cottage, 85.
Simeto, the, steamer, 202.
Smalley, George W., 19; editorial correspondent of the New York "Tribune," 35; conversation with, 36; on American politics, 309; dinner with, 334.
Smalley, Mrs., 19.
Smith, Rev. Samuel F., 26.
Smyth, Piazzi, 228.
Soldiers' boys' school at Cairo, 225.
Spencer, Lord, personal appearance, 6, 7; his career, 7; courtesy of, 10; his dignity and tact, 33; at the theatre, 41; visit to his country house, Althorp House, 69–81; as county judge, 72, 73; and Lady Spencer, 79; invites Dana to luncheon, 348.
Spencer, Lady, attractiveness of, 7, 8; at lawn tennis, 75; and her boudoir, 78, 79; and Lord Spencer, 79; plays at "go bang," 79, 80; death, 79.
Spencer, Herbert, 38.
Spencer House, 6, 8–10, 32, 43.
Sphinx, the, 234.
Spiritualism, 344, 345.
Stanley, Dean, 314–16, 326, 327.
Stanley, Lady Augusta, 326.
Stanton, General, British Consul-General at Cairo, 224–26, 230–32.
Steamships, 26.
Stevenson, Mr. and Mrs., 232.
Stone, General Charles Pomeroy, 224.
Stone, Mrs., 232.
Story, Edith, 175.
Story, Judge Joseph, 175, 232.
Story, Julian, 271.
Story, Waldo, 264.
Story, William Wetmore, 174–76.
Story, Mrs. W. W., 174, 243.
Strada, Mademoiselle, 171.
Strada, Marquis, 171.
Stratford-on-Avon, 64.
Strathclyde case, the, 321–23.
Stromboli, 237.
Stuart, Gertrude, 22.
Stuart, Mark J., 364.
Stuart, William, English Minister to Greece, 207–10.
Stuart, Mrs. William, 209, 210.
Sturgis, Russell, 306–09, 317.
Suez Canal, purchase of shares of, 231.
Sullivan, Rev. Mr., headmaster of Winchester School, 208.

INDEX

Sultan of Turkey, 305, 306.
Sunken ships, plan for raising, 116–18.
Sunset, a Greek, 217, 218.

Table customs in England, 8, 9.
Talbot, Dr. and Mrs., 20, 274, 275.
Taormina, 202, 203.
Taylorian library and gallery, the, 276.
Teas, five o'clock afternoon, 150.
Tennant, Laura, 5.
Tennyson, Alfred, 17.
Tenterden, Lord, 18, 42, 132, 306; visited by Dana, 136–45; second marriage, 138; his views of the death of the Sultan of Turkey, 305; a day with, on the borders of the Thames, 327, 328; secures invitation to meet Prince of Wales, 336.
Tenterden, Lady, 136, 143, 145.
Terry, Ellen, 41.
Terry, Mrs., 243.
Théâtre Français, the, the acting at, 159, 177, 179.
Theatre of Dionysus, Athens, 205, 206.
Thebes, the Grecian, 203.
Thompson, Sir Henry, 345, 348.
Thornton, Mr., 288.
Tichborne, Sir Roger Charles, the "claimant" of his estate, 59.
Tinné, J. C., 267, 349.
Titus, arch of, 240.
Trent Affair, the, 57–59, 132, 341.
Tribout, Mademoiselle, 169.
Trollope, Anthony, 46, 329.
Trollope, Miss, 241.
Trossachs, the, 100–02.
Turin, 247–51.
Turkey, 203.
Turkish atrocities, 358.

University reform, 268.

"Valued" policies, 29, 30.
"*Vanguard*," plan for raising, 116–18.
Vatican decrees, 23.
Vaughan, Dr., 36.
Venus Fly Trap, the, 53.
Versailles, 185.
Vesuvius, 237.
Victor Emmanuel, King of Italy, 321.
Victoria, Lady, 105.
Victoria, Queen, at the Wimbledon Encampment, 33; autograph letter of, 38; and the German language, 38; birthplace, 128; influence on society, 130; title Empress of India, 299.
Vivisection, 320.

Ward, Mrs. Humphry, 276, 362.
Warwick, 63–65.
Warwick Castle, 63.
Warwick, Rev. M., 230.
Washburne, Elihu Benjamin, 174, 335; United States Minister to France, 153; his pronunciation of French, 153, 154.
Washington, George, 37, 56; and the American flag, 76, 77.
Washington, Treaty of, 18, 132.
Waterloo, 352.
Welles's, London hall, 335.
Wellington, Duke of, 128, 312.
Westlake, John, 20, 299.
Westminster Abbey, 10, 11, 48.
Whalley, Mr., 12.
White, Henry, 366.
Wigglesworth, George, 354.
Wilde, Mr. and Mrs., 143.
William IV., 51.
"William Tell," the opera, 169, 170.
Williams, Dr. Charles H., 42.
Wilson, President, 334.
Wilton, Marie, 41.
Wimbledon Encampment, 32, 33.
Winchester, hospital and cathedral, 149, 150.
Winslow case, the, 346.
"Woodside," Lord Tenterden's cottage, 136, 137.
Wurts, Mr., American Secretary of Legation at Rome, 241, 243.
Wyndham, Hugh, 158, 207, 208.
Wyndham, Mrs. Hugh, 158, 164, 207, 208.

Yonge, Charlotte, "The Heir of Redcliffe," 149.
York, cathedral, 82.
Young, Lord, 44, 46; visited by Dana, 84–87; his opinion of Roman law, 85, 88; stories of, 86, 87.

The Riverside Press
CAMBRIDGE . MASSACHUSETTS
U . S . A

www.ingramcontent.com/pod-product-compliance
Lightning Source LLC
Chambersburg PA
CBHW020345170426
43200CB00005B/54